Football and Community in the Global Context

Football clubs across the world continue ... ls, identifications and processes of connectivity v ... notion of 'community'. In recent years, however, ... e focus of renewed interest within popular discour... nd policy makers. It has become something of a 'b... a lament to more certain times and as an appeal to a better fu... ...ued with all the richness associated with human interaction.

'Community' has also been employed increasingly within football, for instrumental reasons concerned with policy and stadium redevelopment, and in broader rhetoric about clubs, their localities and fans.

This book brings together a range of key debates around contemporary understandings of 'community' in world football. Split into four sections, it considers

1. political and theoretical debates around football and its connection with community;
2. different national and ethnic football communities;
3. instrumental uses of football to bridge gaps within and between groups;
4. future directions in the football and community debate.

This book was published as a special issue of *Soccer & Society*.

Dr Adam Brown, Professor Tim Crabbe and **Dr Gavin Mellor** are Directors and founder members of Substance, a UK-based social research company specialising in areas of sport, youth inclusion and community regeneration. www.substance.coop

Football and Community in the Global Context

Studies in theory and practice

Edited by Adam Brown, Tim Crabbe and Gavin Mellor

LONDON AND NEW YORK

First published 2009 by Routledge
2 Park Square, Milton Park, Abingdon, Oxfordshire, OX14 4RN

Simultaneously published in the USA and Canada
by Routledge
711 Third Avenue, New York, NY 10017

First issued in paperback 2014

Routledge is an imprint of the Taylor & Francis Group, an informa business

© 2009 Edited by Adam Brown, Tim Crabbe and Gavin Mellor

Typeset in Minion by Genesis Typesetting Ltd, Laser Quay, Rochester, UK

All rights reserved. No part of this book may be reprinted or reproduced or utilised in any form or by any electronic, mechanical, or other means, now known or hereafter invented, including photocopying and recording, or in any information storage or retrieval system, without permission in writing from the publishers.

British Library Cataloguing in Publication Data
A catalogue record for this book is available from the British Library

ISBN 13: 978-1-138-88352-9 (pbk)
ISBN 13: 978-0-415-44816-1 (hbk)

CONTENTS

Series Editors' Foreword — vii

1 Introduction: football and community – practical and theoretical considerations
   Adam Brown, Tim Crabbe and Gavin Mellor — 1

Politics, theory and practice

2 'The Janus-faced sport': English football, community and the legacy of the 'third way'
   Gavin Mellor — 11

3 Contemporary community theory and football
   Tony Blackshaw — 23

4 'Our club, our rules': fan communities at FC United of Manchester
   Adam Brown — 44

Nations and ethnicities

5 Football, *komyuniti* and the Japanese ideological soccer apparatus
   John Horne and Wolfram Manzenreiter — 57

6 'The nation and its fragments': football and community in India
   Kausik Bandyopadhyay — 75

7 Coming in from the margins: ethnicity, community support and the rebranding of Australian soccer
   James Skinner, Dwight H. Zakus and Allan Edwards — 92

Community and the instrumental use of football

8 Anyone for Football for Peace? The challenges of using sport in the service of co-existence in Israel
   John Sugden — 103

9 *Vamos, Vamos Aceirteros:* soccer and the Latino community in Richmond, California
   Ilann S. Messeri — 114

Postmodern community and future directions

10 Fishing for community: England fans at the 2006 FIFA World Cup
    Tim Crabbe — 126

Index — 137

Series Editors' Foreword

SPORT IN THE GLOBAL SOCIETY was launched in the late nineties. It now has over one hundred volumes. Until recently an odd myopia characterised academia with regard to sport. The global *groves of academe* remained essentially Cartesian in inclination. They favoured a mind/body dichotomy: thus the study of ideas was acceptable; the study of sport was not. All that has now changed. Sport is now incorporated, intelligently, within debate about *inter alia* ideologies, power, stratification, mobility and inequality. The reason is simple. In the modern world sport is everywhere: it is as ubiquitous as war. E.J. Hobsbawm, the Marxist historian, once called it the one of the most significant of the new manifestations of late nineteenth century Europe. Today it is one of the most significant manifestations of the twenty-first century world. Such is its power, politically, culturally, economically, spiritually and aesthetically, that sport beckons the academic more persuasively than ever – to borrow, and refocus, an expression of the radical historian Peter Gay – 'to explore its familiar terrain and to wrest new interpretations from its inexhaustible materials'. As a subject for inquiry, it is replete, as he remarked of history, with profound 'questions unanswered and for that matter questions unasked'.

Sport seduces the teeming 'global village'; it is the new opiate of the masses; it is one of the great modern experiences; its attraction astonishes only the recluse; its appeal spans the globe. Without exaggeration, sport is a mirror in which nations, communities, men and women now see themselves. That reflection is sometimes bright, sometimes dark, sometimes distorted, sometimes magnified. This metaphorical mirror is a source of mass exhilaration and depression, security and insecurity, pride and humiliation, bonding and alienation. Sport, for many, has replaced religion as a source of emotional catharsis and spiritual passion, and for many, since it is among the earliest of memorable childhood experiences, it infiltrates memory, shapes enthusiasms, serves fantasies. To co-opt Gay again: it blends memory and desire.

Sport, in addition, can be a lens through which to scrutinise major themes in the political and social sciences: democracy and despotism and the great associated movements of socialism, fascism, communism and capitalism as well as political cohesion and confrontation, social reform and social stability.

The story of modern sport is the story of the modern world – in microcosm; a modern global tapestry permanently being woven. Furthermore, nationalist and imperialist, philosopher and politician, radical and conservative have all sought in sport a manifestation of national identity, status and superiority.

Finally, for countless millions sport is the personal pursuit of ambition, assertion, well-being and enjoyment.

For all the above reasons, sport demands the attention of the academic. *Sport in the Global Society* is a response.

J.A.Mangan, Boria Majumdar and Mark Dyreson
Series Editors
Sport in the Global Society

Sport in the Global Society

General Editors: J.A. Mangan, Boria Majumdar and Mark Dyreson

Football and Community in the Global Context
Studies in theory and practice

Sport in the Global Society
Series Editors: J.A. Mangan, Boria Majumdar and Mark Dyreson

As Robert Hands in *The Times* recently observed the growth of sports studies in recent years has been considerable. This unique series with over one hundred volumes in the last decade has played its part. Politically, culturally, emotionally and aesthetically, sport is a major force in the modern world. Its impact will grow as the world embraces ever more tightly the contemporary secular trinity: the English language, technology and sport. *Sport in the Global Society* will continue to record sport's phenomenal progress across the world stage.

Other Titles in the Series

Africa, Football and FIFA
Politics, Colonialism and Resistance
Paul Darby

Amateurism in British Sport
'It Matters Not Who Won or Lost'
Edited by Dilwyn Porter and Stephen Wagg

Amateurism in Sport
An Analysis and Defence
Lincoln Allison

America's Game(s)
A Critical Anthropology of Sport
Edited by Benjamin Eastman, Sean Brown and Michael Ralph

American Sports
An Evolutionary Approach
Edited by Alan Klein

A Social History of Indian Football
Striving to Score
Kausik Bandyopadhya and Boria Majumdar

A Social History of Swimming in England, 1800–1918
Splashing in the Serpentine
Christopher Love

A Sport-Loving Society
Victorian and Edwardian Middle-Class England at Play
Edited by J.A. Mangan

Athleticism in the Victorian and Edwardian Public School
The Emergence and Consolidation of an Educational Ideology,
New Edition
J.A. Mangan

Australian Beach Cultures
The History of Sun, Sand and Surf
Douglas Booth

Australian Sport
Antipodean waves of change
Edited by Kristine Toohey and Tracy Taylor

Barbarians, Gentlemen and Players
A Sociological Study of the Development of Rugby Football,
Second Edition
Eric Dunning and Kenneth Sheard

Baseball and Moral Authority in Contemporary Cuba
Edited by Benjamin Eastman

Beijing 2008: Preparing for Glory
The Chinese Challenge in 'the Chinese Century'
Edited by J.A. Mangan and Dong Jinxia

'Blooding' the Martial Male
The Imperial Officer, Field Sports and Big Game Hunting
J.A. Mangan and Callum MacKenzie

Body and Mind
Sport in Europe from the Roman Empire to the Renaissance
John McClelland

British Football and Social Exclusion
Edited by Stephen Wagg

Capoeira
The History of an Afro-Brazilian Martial Art
Matthias Röhrig Assunção

Crafting Patriotism for Global Dominance
America at the Olympics
Mark Dyreson

Cricket
International and Interdisciplinary Perspectives
Edited by Dominic Malcolm and Boria Majumdar

Cricket and England
A Cultural and Social History of Cricket in England between the Wars
Jack Williams

Cricket and Identity in Pakistan and Anglo-Pakistan
Sporting Nations of the Imagination
Edited by Chris Valiotis

Cricket in Colonial India, 1780–1947
Boria Majumdar

Cricketing Cultures in Conflict
Cricketing World Cup 2003
Edited by Boria Majumdar and J.A. Mangan

Cricket, Race and the 2007 World Cup
Edited by Boria Majumdar and Jon Gemmell

Critical Events in Baseball History
Class, Race and Politics
Edited by Benjamin Eastman and John D. Kelly

Disciplining Bodies in the Gymnasium
Memory, Monument, Modernity
Sherry McKay and Patricia Vertinsky

Disreputable Pleasures
Less Virtuous Victorians at Play
Edited by Mike Huggins and J.A. Mangan

Diversity and Division – Race, Ethnicity and Sport in Australia
Edited by Christopher J. Hallinan

Doping in Sport
Global Ethical Issues
Edited by Angela Schneider and Fan Hong

Emigrant Players
Sport and the Irish Diaspora
Edited by Paul Darby and David Hassan

Ethnicity, Sport, Identity
Struggles for Status
Edited by J.A. Mangan and Andrew Ritchie

European Heroes
Myth, Identity, Sport
Edited by Richard Holt, J.A. Mangan and Pierre Lanfranchi

Europe, Sport, World
Shaping Global Societies
Edited by J.A. Mangan

Flat Racing and British Society, 1790–1914
A Social and Economic History
Mike Huggins

Football and Community in the Global Context
Studies in Theory and Practice
Edited by Adam Brown, Tim Crabbe and Gavin Mellor

Football: From England to the World
Edited by Dolores P. Martinez and Projit B. Mukharji

Football, Europe and the Press
Liz Crolley and David Hand

Football Fans Around the World
From Supporters to Fanatics
Edited by Sean Brown

Football: The First Hundred Years
The Untold Story
Adrian Harvey

Footbinding, Feminism and Freedom
The Liberation of Women's Bodies in Modern China
Fan Hong

France and the 1998 World Cup
The National Impact of a World Sporting Event
Edited by Hugh Dauncey and Geoff Hare

Freeing the Female Body
Inspirational Icons
Edited by J.A. Mangan and Fan Hong

Fringe Nations in Soccer
Edited by Kausik Bandyopadhyay, Martha Saavedra and Sabyasachi Malick

From Fair Sex to Feminism
Sport and the Socialization of Women in the Industrial and Post-Industrial Eras
Edited by J.A. Mangan and Roberta J. Park

Gender, Sport, Science
Selected Writings of Roberta J. Park
Edited by J.A. Mangan and Patricia Vertinsky

Global and Local Football
Politics and Europeanization on the Fringes of the EU
Gary Armstrong and Jon P. Mitchell

Globalised Football
Nations and Migration, the City and the Dream
Edited by Nina Clara Tiesler and João Nuno Coelho

Heritage, Sport and Tourism
Sporting Pasts – Tourist Futures
Edited by Sean Gammon and Gregory Ramshaw

Human Rights in Youth Sport
A Critical Review of Children's Rights in Competitive Sports
Paulo David

Italian Fascism and the Female Body
Sport, Submissive Women and Strong Mothers
Gigliola Gori

Japan, Sport and Society
Tradition and Change in a Globalizing World
Edited by Joseph Maguire and Masayoshi Nakayama

Law and Sport in Contemporary Society
Edited by Steven Greenfield and Guy Osborn

Leisure and Recreation in a Victorian Mining Community
The Social Economy of Leisure in North-East England, 1820–1914
Alan Metcalfe

Lost Histories of Indian Cricket
Battles Off the Pitch
Boria Majumdar

Making European Masculinities
Sport, Europe, Gender
Edited by J.A. Mangan

Making Men
Rugby and Masculine Identity
Edited by John Nauright and Timothy J.L. Chandler

Making the Rugby World
Race, Gender, Commerce
Edited by Timothy J.L. Chandler and John Nauright

Militarism, Sport, Europe
War Without Weapons
Edited by J.A. Mangan

Modern Sport: The Global Obsession
Essays in Honour of J.A. Mangan
Edited by Boria Majumdar and Fan Hong

Muscular Christianity and the Colonial and Post-Colonial World
Edited by John J. MacAloon

Native Americans and Sport in North America
Other People's Games
Edited by C. Richard King

Playing on the Periphery
Sport, Identity and Memory
Tara Brabazon

Pleasure, Profit, Proselytism
British Culture and Sport at Home and Abroad 1700–1914
Edited by J.A. Mangan

Rain Stops Play
Cricketing Climates
Andrew Hignell

Reformers, Sport, Modernizers
Middle-Class Revolutionaries
Edited by J.A. Mangan

Representing the Nation
Sport and Spectacle in Post-Revolutionary Mexico
Edited by Claire and Keith Brewster

Rugby's Great Split
Class, Culture and the Origins of Rugby League Football
Tony Collins

Running Cultures
Racing in Time and Space
John Bale

Scoring for Britain
International Football and International Politics, 1900–1939
Peter J. Beck

Serious Sport
J.A. Mangan's Contribution to the History of Sport
Edited by Scott Crawford

Shaping the Superman
Fascist Body as Political Icon – Aryan Fascism
Edited by J.A. Mangan

Sites of Sport
Space, Place and Experience
Edited by John Bale and Patricia Vertinksy

Soccer and Disaster
International Perspectives
Edited by Paul Darby, Martin Jones and Gavin Mellor

Soccer in South Asia
Empire, Nation, Diaspora
Edited by Paul Dimeo and James Mills

Soccer's Missing Men
Schoolteachers and the Spread of Association Football
J.A. Mangan and Colm Hickey

Soccer, Women, Sexual Liberation
Kicking off a New Era
Edited by Fan Hong and J.A. Mangan

Sport: Race, Ethnicity and Indigineity
Building Global Understanding
Edited by Daryl Adair

Sport and American Society
Exceptionalism, Insularity, 'Imperialism'
Edited by Mark Dyreson and J.A. Mangan

Sport and Foreign Policy in a Globalizing World
Edited by Steven J. Jackson and Stephen Haigh

Sport and International Relations
An Emerging Relationship
Edited by Roger Levermore and Adrian Budd

Sport and Memory in North America
Edited by Steven Wieting

Sport, Civil Liberties and Human Rights
Edited by Richard Giulianotti and David McArdle

Sport, Culture and History
Region, Nation and Globe
Edited by Brian Stoddart

Sport in Asian Society
Past and Present
Edited by Fan Hong and J.A. Mangan

Sport in Australasian Society
Past and Present
Edited by J.A. Mangan and John Nauright

Sport in Europe
Politics, Class, Gender
Edited by J.A. Mangan

Sport in Films
Edited by Emma Poulton and Martin Roderick

Sport in Latin American Society
Past and Present
Edited by Lamartine DaCosta and J.A. Mangan

Sport in South Asian Society
Past and Present
Edited by Boria Majumdar and J.A. Mangan

Sport, Media, Culture
Global and Local Dimensions
Edited by Alina Bernstein and Neil Blain

Sport, Nationalism and Orientalism
The Asian Games
Edited by Fan Hong

Sporting Cultures
Hispanic Perspectives on Sport, Text and the Body
Edited by David Wood and P. Louise Johnson

Sporting Nationalisms
Identity, Ethnicity, Immigration and Assimilation
Edited by Mike Cronin and David Mayall

Sport Tourism
Edited by Heather J. Gibson

Superman Supreme
Fascist Body as Political Icon – Global Fascism
Edited by J.A. Mangan

Terrace Heroes
The Life and Times of the 1930s Professional Footballer
Graham Kelly

The Changing Face of the Football Business
Supporters Direct
Edited by Sean Hamil, Jonathan Michie, Christine Oughton and Steven Warby

The Commercialisation of Sport
Edited by Trevor Slack

The Cultural Bond
Sport, Empire, Society
Edited by J.A. Mangan

The First Black Footballer
Arthur Wharton 1865–1930: An Absence of Memory
Phil Vasili

The Flame Relay and the Olympic Movement
John J. MacAloon

The Football Manager
A History
Neil Carter

The Future of Football
Challenges for the Twenty-First Century
Edited by Jon Garland, Dominic Malcolm and Mike Rowe

The Games Ethic and Imperialism
Aspects of the Diffusion of an Ideal
J.A. Mangan

The Global Politics of Sport
The Role of Global Institutions in Sport
Edited by Lincoln Allison

The Lady Footballers
Struggling to Play in Victorian Britain
James F. Lee

The Magic of Indian Cricket
Cricket and Society in India, Revised Edition
Mihir Bose

The Making of New Zealand Cricket
1832–1914
Greg Ryan

The 1940 Tokyo Games: The Missing Olympics
Japan, the Asian Olympics and the Olympic Movement
Sandra Collins

The Nordic World: Sport in Society
Edited by Henrik Meinander and J.A. Mangan

The Politics of South African Cricket
Jon Gemmell

The Race Game
Sport and Politics in South Africa
Douglas Booth

The Tour De France, 1903–2003
A Century of Sporting Structures,
Meanings and Values
*Edited by Hugh Dauncey and
Geoff Hare*

This Great Symbol
Pierre de Coubertin and the Origins of
the Modern Olympic Games
John J. MacAloon

Tribal Identities
Nationalism, Europe, Sport
Edited by J.A. Mangan

Who Owns Football?
The Governance and Management of the
Club Game Worldwide
*Edited by David Hassan and
Sean Hamil*

Women, Sport and Society in Modern China
Holding up More than Half the Sky
Dong Jinxia

Introduction: football and community – practical and theoretical considerations

Adam Brown, Tim Crabbe and Gavin Mellor

Introduction

During the past 15 years, interest in association football across many areas of the world has risen to a new level. This is manifest in the blanket media coverage that seemingly accompanies every aspect of the elite levels of the game, the increased attendances which have been enjoyed in many countries, and the ritualised identifications with football that have come to permeate wider contemporary social formations. Professional football clubs have been regarded as sites for the expression of common identity for much of the game's history, and it could be argued that recent developments in and around football have seen this process emphasized with renewed vigour. Football clubs now, as much as ever, embody many of the collective symbols, identifications and processes of connectivity which have long been associated with the notion of 'community'.

At the same time that 'community' connections and identities are being expressed strongly through football though, the very term 'community' has itself become the focus of renewed interest within popular discourse and amongst academics, politicians and policy makers. It has become something of a 'buzz' word, wheeled out as both a lament to more certain times and as an appeal to a better future: a term which is imbued with all the richness associated with human interaction. Indeed, a 'crisis of community' has emerged in many areas of the developed world in recent years in which policy makers have sought to blame crime and 'anti-social' behaviour, health problems, poor educational standards and a variety of other 'social issues' on the decline of community and civic culture more generally. In this regard, the very notion of 'community' is increasingly open to debate as people reflect on what it is to be a member of a community, and what reciprocal responsibilities come with such formations.

It was in this context that we were interested in building upon our own research for the English Football Foundation[1] – which sought to explore the responsibilities that football clubs have for 'fan', 'neighbourhood' and other types of 'communities'; the impact that new football stadia have on economic and social regeneration; and the role that professional football clubs have in providing or supporting 'community services' such as health, education and community sport development – to consider developments within the global context. Crucially we want to clarify and better understand who 'football's communities' might be, and analyse how these groups of people can be said to constitute distinct and observable community formations.

Before considering the content of individual contributions to this collection, in this introductory essay we aim to set the scene through an analysis of the historiography of writings on football and community and the contribution that mainstream contemporary social theory can make to debates around football and a variety of community formations.

The history of football and community

It is today seen as axiomatic that professional football clubs have deep roots in 'their communities'. Many of today's most successful clubs and particularly the longest established clubs have their origins in 'community organizations' such as churches, social clubs or work's teams. Indeed the vast majority of football clubs emerged from their formative years with names shared with towns, cities or areas of cities, and as such came to fulfil something of a representational role for large numbers of citizens from urban neighbourhoods.

The development of football clubs along these lines has meant that social historians and sociologists of sport, particularly in England, have frequently written about the historical emergence of relationships between football clubs and communities in relation to the social identity-building properties of football spectating. The eminent labour and sports historian Tony Mason, for example, has written that football 'often contributes to an individual's sense of identity with or belonging to a group or collectivity. It can be district, village, town, city or county. It can be class, colour or country.'[2] Similarly, sports historian Richard Holt[3] has written that football clubs are historically one of the principal agents through which collective social identities are created and reinforced. He claims that football clubs are sites of representation through which people (usually men) are taught norms of behaviour, and that football teams and football 'heroes' have historically acted as exemplars of spirit and behaviour for the communities they represent. He suggests that football clubs enable communities to 'know themselves', and in doing so help signify what differentiates one town, city, region, county or nation from another.

To explain why football clubs emerged as sites for community representation, Holt notes that professional football developed in England at a time of rapid urbanization and provided opportunities for expressions of common identity during a period when it was becoming more difficult to feel a sense of belonging to amorphous, ever-expanding towns and cities. In noting that of the 12 teams that formed the first English Football League in 1888 all came from towns with populations over 80,000, except for Accrington and Burnley, Holt states:

> The massive expansion in the scale and size of urban communities in the second half of the nineteenth century created new problems of identity for their inhabitants ... In essence, football clubs provided a new focus for collective urban leisure in industrial towns and cities that were no longer integrated communities gathered around a handful of mines or mills ... These inhabitants of big cities needed a cultural expression of their urbanism which went beyond the immediate ties of kin and locality. A need for rootedness as well as excitement is what seems most evident in the behaviour of football crowds.[4]

Holt is not alone in adopting this essentially functionalist reading of the development of links between football clubs and communities. Following Durkheim, Richard Giulianotti has stated that early football clubs can be understood as creating 'organic solidarity' and 'collective consciousness' within the potentially atomised urban environments that were common by the beginning of the twentieth century.[5] He notes the arguments of those who suggest that modernity destroyed traditional communities through industrialization, urbanization and rapid social/ geographical mobility, and asserts that sports such as football 'may [have] repair[ed] much of this social damage by enhancing the cultural bonding and integration of disparate individuals within modern societies'.[6] However, Giulianotti ultimately rejects this position and suggests that early football clubs actually had strong connections to pre-modern, 'mechanistic' types of bonding. He notes that football clubs were (usually) named after places, and produced 'the kind of affective tie to a specific locality that one finds in more traditional and localist societies'.[7] According to this line of thinking, football clubs developed links with communities because they helped to sustain the close, face-to-face, geographic, affective communities that were under threat during modernity. To put it another way, they helped to preserve a version of Tönnies' pre-modern *Gemeinschaft* emotional community bonds amongst people who otherwise only encountered modern *Gesellschaft* type connections.[8]

The apparent identification of the social and emotional duties that football clubs performed for new urban communities in the late nineteenth and early twentieth centuries means that much contemporary writing on football and community is based on a fairly commonsense notion of which people actually constitute football clubs' communities. By associating the emergence of professional football with the (re)creation of geographical community ties when they were under threat from modernity, many popular and academic writers now adopt the position that football clubs' communities are principally their immediate 'geographical communities' from which they draw the majority of their support. This has led to a situation in which few distinctions have traditionally been drawn between 'geographical' and 'supporter' communities around football clubs, particularly in writings on the pre-1990s game. As sociologists and social historians worked from the assumption that football clubs' emerged functionally to satisfy geographical communities' needs for new or traditional forms of social and emotional bonding, so it followed *ipso facto* that football clubs' supporters must also be their geographical neighbours (or at least it was assumed that supporters lived in relative geographical proximity to their club). Indeed, in some historical work the impression (whether deliberate or not) is given that everybody identified with their local team, regardless of whether they were a regular, attending 'supporter' or not.[9] This means that little historical (or indeed contemporary) work has been conducted on the specific types of communities that football supporters have constituted. It has simply been assumed that supporter communities have been synonymous with geographical communities in the context of football for much of the game's history, and that supporters' relations with football clubs have historically been based on a need to maintain and/or recreate existing geographical, face-to-face social relations.

In more contemporary writings on sport and community, some appreciation of the distinctions between geographical communities and supporter communities has begun to emerge. Andrews' work on community formations around the Australian Football League[10] is rare in the sociology of sport in that it engages in a prolonged discussion of different conceptualizations of community, including comments on community as a geographical locale, community as a social system, community as a sense of identity/belonging, and community as an ideology. However, this study is, to some degree, still locked into a belief that the 'natural' or 'purest' form of community around a sports club is a geographical community. Similar sentiments can be found in the work of Fawbert[11] and others who have studied the globalization of English football, and the subsequent emergence of dispersed or overseas fans of English clubs. Again, in these studies the presumption is often that the natural historical community of a football club is its geographical community, and that relations between geographical communities and football clubs have been disrupted by *recent* social and cultural change, or, more perniciously, the commercialization of the game. Unsurprisingly, this approach to understanding football supporter communities is also very powerful amongst supporters themselves, especially at clubs such as Manchester United that have developed large 'out of town', and even global, followings.[12]

There is much to be drawn from the work of Andrews, Fawbert and others. They are at least cognizant of the fact that relationships between football clubs and communities are not straightforward, and that the very concept of 'community' is contested. However, they are not particularly historically sensitive and, therefore, tend to overestimate the recentness of the disruption of 'traditional' geographical football communities. From at least the 1930s, and almost certainly before, football supporter communities were not drawn exclusively from the immediate neighbourhoods of football clubs.[13] They were made up of people from relatively wide geographical areas and, therefore, can be said to be specific, relatively autonomous communities that were based around *a choice* to engage in a single cultural/sporting interest. The constitution of football supporter communities along these non-geographic lines became even more dramatic in the post-war period.

Certainly in England but also in a number of other heavily industrialized countries, from the late 1950s, a serious bifurcation can be said to have occurred between many football clubs and their local, geographical neighbourhoods that resulted in a number of tensions between neighbourhood and supporter communities (although these groups are clearly not always mutually exclusive). This was the consequence of a series of social changes in post-war England including 'slum-clearance' programmes in major cities; the changing ethnic profile of certain neighbourhoods within cities brought about by immigration from the Indian subcontinent and the Caribbean; the exclusion of new 'ethnic communities' from football because of cultures of racism both within and without the game;[14] football clubs being increasingly regarded as 'nuisances' from the late 1950s because of hooliganism and associated problems; and the growth of 'out of town' supporters at successful football clubs who did not live in the city (or even the region) of the clubs they supported. This final change was underpinned by the increasing availability and ownership of motor cars and televisions, both of which made it easier for people to support teams to which they had no obvious historical, geographical or familial connections.[15] These changes resulted, to a greater or lesser degree, in developments that made communities around football clubs *even more* specific to their particular cultural contexts. There was then little sense in which football communities could be regarded as geographical inevitabilities as some people (although by no means all) increasingly chose 'their clubs' (or rejected them) on grounds *other than* geographical heritage.

The key point to draw from this debate is that the theorization of community around football (and other sports) has largely started from the assumption that professional sports clubs emerged to satisfy a functional need for social bonding for their supporters: a need that was created by industrialization and associated phenomena such as urbanization. However, very little detailed empirical work has been produced in association with this assumption. Few oral history studies, for example, have been conducted on the types of bonding that people created by attending football matches in different historical periods, and few questions have been asked about whether these forms of sociation were approximate to 'traditional', geographical emotional ties.[16] This has resulted in a lack of debate about the various types of community that have developed around football and other sports clubs, and has stopped sociologists of sport from accessing and reflecting on recent developments in community theory.

Re-theorising supporter communities

In his rare analysis of community in the Australian sporting context, Andrews notes that deliberations over the meaning of 'community' have become so complex and divisive in sociology and associated fields that some authors have suggested that we should abandon the concept altogether.[17] We, like Andrews, reject this suggestion and believe it is important that community continues to be wrestled with and argued over. As evidenced above, community is now, more than ever, a central theme in sporting and social policy, and as such demands critical analysis and theorizing. The point is that, whether theorists find the term useful or not, 'community' continues to be an important and defining 'conceptual reality'.

In our own work, we have begun to formulate ideas about the types of community and sociation that operate around English football clubs, and have related these ideas to contemporary theoretical debates about community formation. It is not possible here to outline fully how contemporary football communities can be understood according to every competing theoretical conception, although many are touched upon in later essays. For now though, we will restrict our debate here to outlining how 'symbolic' and 'post-modern' conceptions of community are contributing to a new framework of analysis which will help us to understand different aspects of community in the context of football supporting. We will then illustrate a new analytical framework that underpins our continuing analysis of football and community in a wider range of contexts.

The first theoretical position to be considered is Anthony Cohen's classic conception of 'symbolic community'.[18] Cohen rejects all attempts to reduce communities to spatial categories (or any other forms of reductionism), and instead stresses the role of symbols in defining community boundaries. Borrowing from the work of Turner (who will be considered below), Cohen states that people enact rituals around or through symbols and thereby define their belonging to different community groups. He also notes that symbols are acted upon in relation to other symbols, and that people understand their communities always in relation to other groups.[19] A key point in Cohen's work is that he claims that symbols are not fixed entities that can only be interpreted in set, predetermined ways. Instead, he suggests that they are constantly being reinterpreted and re-negotiated and as such can lead to changes in the constitution of community groups.

Cohen's work is potentially important for understanding historical and contemporary supporter community formations around football clubs. He points us towards understanding football clubs as symbols around which rituals of communality are acted out. He also provides a theory which enables us to see communal symbols (such as football clubs) as contested phenomena which can mean different things to different people in different historical periods. In this regard, Cohen's theory allows us to move beyond geographically-deterministic understandings of football supporter communities which see functional and inevitable relationships emerge between people and sports clubs in set spatial areas. Instead Cohen allows us to identify individual actors' agency in creating their community formations, and their different interpretations of them. For some people, football supporter communities may be (and may have always been) entirely geographical affairs. That is simply the way that they choose to define them. However, even these communities can be read as symbolic or 'performative' as people within them seek to 'display' *their* geography through their football support. For others, football communities may represent an entirely different type of bonding. The key point is that Cohen allows us to see football communities as fluid and always open to change.

The second position to be considered is Victor Turner's work on *communitas* and liminality.[20] Turner's functionalist anthropological work analysed 'those "between" moments such as carnivals, pilgrimages, rites of passage or rituals in which normality is suspended'.[21] Centrally, Turner was interested in the role of these moments in producing 'communitas', or the symbolic renewal of collective identity for particular groups. In asserting that communitas occurs 'between' normal moments, Turner contended that it is a special 'out of time' and anti-structural type of bonding that temporarily obliterates differences between people around specific cultural practices or events (such as football matches). He claimed that this type of bonding is 'liminal' and marginal to 'real' life, although he did note that it can persist for groups in the form of 'normative communitas'.

It is interesting to note that Turner's work has recently been appropriated in the sociology of sport. In Smith and Ingham's recent study of sport and community in Cincinnati, they claim that sports fans in the city display communitas-type bonding in their fandom rituals.[22] This may indeed be the case. In our research with football supporters, we have observed many moments in which the 'out-of-time' social drama of the football match, be it watched 'live' in the stadium or in groups in a public house, produces moments of intense group bonding and feelings of associated community. Within football stadiums, it is undeniable that when goals are scored or other moments of high excitement occur, many 'normal' intra-group rivalries and differences within fan communities are obliterated as a new form of community bonding temporarily emerges.[23]

However, whilst Turner's work is valuable in providing a model of communal bonding that is non-geographic and cultural in focus, his assertion that communitas bonding can only take place in opposition to everyday, real existence is not particularly helpful in explaining some of the types of supporter communities that we have observed during our research. Being a member of a football club's supporter community is not a liminal or marginal experience for some of the supporters with which we have spent time. For them, being a supporter is a key part of their 'real' lives: a regular, *structuring* part of their existence that enables them to feel belonging in the relative disorder of contemporary social formations.

If attention is now turned to more 'post-modern' theses on community, our research has also considered recent theoretical developments that try to explain the 'lust' or desire for community in contemporary society as expressed through football supporting. We have observed and encountered several types of sociation around English football, some of which could be read as solidly 'modern' or even 'pre-modern' in that they are based, to some degree, on 'thick' ties of family, kinship, friendship, neighbourhood and so on. This is potentially remarkable, as according to communitarian thinkers modern societies are exemplified by a lack of community that leads to a need for the recreation of shared bonds. However, in the work of Zygmunt Bauman, even these seemingly traditional forms of community which are created around football can be read in a different way. Following Bauman,[24] it could be argued that even when the existence of football clubs contributes to friendship ties and regular social contact, they are only really producing the 'cloakroom communities' or 'ad hoc communities' that are common to post- or 'liquid' modernity. In a society marked by increasing 'individualization'[25], it could be argued that football supporters are not attempting to hold on to, or recreate, the *Gemeinschaft* type communities which Tönnies described, but rather are creating 'communities without commitment' or 'thin communities' that people can dip into to satisfy their occasional needs for security without taking on the reciprocal obligations that define 'community' in the writings of communitarian thinkers. To put it another way, it could be said that supporting a football club allows supporters to indulge their search or 'lust' for community without ever impacting upon the actual roots of their insecurity. In this regard, our supporter communities can never become 'real communities' in a traditional sense because 'traditional' community bonds are no longer possible (if they ever were). For Bauman, the very idea of community is a fiction.

The key point to take from this way of looking at things is Bauman's cynicism about contemporary notions of community. For him, it is not possible to read football communities as grounding, structuring, deep forms of sociation that bring true meaning to people's lives. They cannot be read as functional in a true sense. For Bauman, 'spectacles' such as football matches have become events around which people temporarily unite as communities, only to go back to their individualized lives at the end of the game. People 'perform' all the aspects of community and commonality around football for the time they are together 'as one', but do not knit themselves into deep reciprocal relationships as a result.

As with our earlier comments on Turner's theory of communitas, Bauman's theories do not fit with all the types of bonding which we have encountered through our research. We have found very deep friendship groups that were initially established through football and have persisted outside of the frameworks of the game. We have also found family units that are almost entirely maintained through the 'spectacle' of football. However, this does not mean that Bauman's work should be dismissed. It is vitally important in sensitizing sociologists to the qualitative differences that exist within different types of community, and in pointing out the temporary nature of much contemporary community bonding.

Another post-modern thesis on community which is pertinent to the themes considered here is Scott Lash's work on 'reflexive communities of taste'.[26] Lash's work (and associated writing, such as that by Maffesoli[27]) is important in that it theorizes the *choices* involved in being part of contemporary communities. 'Reflexive' communities for Lash have four central aspects:

> First one is not born or 'thrown', but 'throws oneself' into them; second, they may be widely stretched over 'abstract' space, and also perhaps over time; third, they consciously pose themselves the problems of their own creation and constant re-invention far more than do traditional communities; fourth, their 'tools' tend to be not material ones but abstract and cultural.[28]

We would actually argue that some of the properties of reflexive communities identified by Lash are not only common to contemporary football supporter communities, but actually may have been more apparent in historical supporter communities than is usually considered to be the case. It is possible, for example, that people exercised more choice in their belonging (or otherwise) to football communities in earlier historical periods than traditional 'football and civic pride' studies have suggested. What is certain is that Lash's work is vital for pointing out a number of key elements of football communities as identified in our research. Football supporters do 'throw themselves' into football communities, and do so with varying degrees of commitment and enthusiasm. Football communities are also generally non-spatial, or at least they are not bound by geography. People come and go from football communities all the time, and their members are continually reflexive about who makes up 'their community' and what this means for how the group is perceived by its own members and others. Finally, the community that coalesces around any football club is doing so not around a reified, solid, immovable, static entity. They are consuming and creating a 'product' which, culturally at least, 'belongs' to them.

New perspectives on football and community in the global context

Many of the theoretical developments considered in this opening analysis have pertinence beyond the realm of football supporters alone as they have developed in relation to a critique of the broader community studies literature. As such, in the course of our own research we have sought to embrace the usefulness of fresh approaches to the task of re-conceptualizing 'community' in the context of football more generally. The principle challenge associated with this project relates to the imperative of giving these theoretical trajectories some relevance in terms of contemporary policy and practice, both domestically and also within a global context.

As such, our consideration of football, belonging and family/kinship is important in that it has helped to develop our understanding of the 'lived' experience of football and 'community' in the classic close, affective, face-to-face understanding of the term. It has also enabled us to explore the 'deep' attachments that people form in football supporter communities, whilst understanding how supporter communities display 'distinctions',[29] and can operate exclusively with specific cultural boundaries.

Beyond this outlook though, our considerations of football and the symbolic community, and football and post-modern theories of community, have enabled better understandings of contemporary supporter connections with football clubs. The notion of the symbolic community can help us to overcome the search for geographical football communities in these increasingly 'placeless' times, whilst post-modern understandings of community can sensitize us to the multiple, 'light' and fluid ways in which people opt in-and-out of their associations with 'like minded souls'.

Through an engagement with urban sociology and its analysis of the fragmentation of urban communities,[30] we have also aimed to bring some conceptual clarity to debates about contemporary football supporter communities, and also to generate greater insight into the issue of how football clubs' stadia, particularly in the ongoing context of redevelopment and relocation, impact upon people living and working in post-modern cities. This is especially important now as more clubs are being drawn into wider city or sub-city regeneration programmes through their facility development strategies. These are vital issues, not least in the context of the communitarian debate about the supposed loss of community, and football's place in recreating 'traditional' community connections.

The strategic and political use of football clubs as key agencies in the delivery of social policies has indeed created new relationships between football clubs and 'communities' of various kinds. Football clubs' communities are today (in a formal sense at least) as likely to be the agency-defined 'communities of disadvantage' or 'social problem communities' that exist in urban centres as they are the broadly defined supporter communities that sports historians and sociologists of sport have traditionally discussed.

It is in this context that we begin this collection with a broader consideration of politics, theory and practice. In the first of three essays Gavin Mellor provides a critique of English football's attempt to reconcile the exclusionary impacts of the Premier League's rabid commercialization with the rhetoric of community, concluding that the football industry has begun to understand social responsibility as being a 'pay off' for the arguably socially 'irresponsible' ways in which it conducts other forms of business. The impossibility of this task is further exposed through Tony Blackshaw's thorough going engagement with the contemporary community studies literature and his ultimate conclusion that 'those intent on re-running community's narrative, digitally re-mastered and free of its more insidious and invidious imperfections – endlessly appropriated, endlessly used to give credence to yet another media persuasion or spectacular manipulation strategy – would be best advised to recognize its limitations'. In the final essay from this section Adam Brown provides an applied illustration of how we might think about football's supporter communities within an alternative response to these contradictions through his insider account of the emergence of FC United of Manchester.

In the next section we turn our attention to the relationship between notions of football and community in the context of considerations of nationality and ethnic identity. More specifically, the focus of this series of essays is upon national contexts which lie outside of football's traditional heartlands in South America, Europe and Africa. In the first of these, John Horne and Wolfram Manzenreiter draw upon their extensive research into the development of professional football in Japan to contrast 'top down' and 'bottom up' approaches to the emergence of football clubs and the new stadia within the context of the broader 'Japanese ideological soccer apparatus'. Kausik Bandyopadhyay then goes on to consider football's role in India as both a marker of nationalist community against British imperialism and latterly as a signifier of the fragmentation of community and identity in the 'new' India. Finally in this section, James Skinner, Dwight Zakus and Allan Edwards consider the marginal position of professional association football in Australia which they relate primarily to the game's historic associations with migrant communities, before considering the processes which are contributing to its movement towards the mainstream of the 'world game', a process which itself marginalizes those traditional communities.

The collection then moves on to consider football's more instrumental role in terms of attempts to 'build' community in the context of local conflict. In a section dealing with the broad themes of young people, identity and community we begin with John Sugden's essay on the history and development of the Football for Peace (F4P) project, a joint University of Brighton and British Council initiative that aims to use values-based football coaching to build bridges between neighbouring Jewish and Arab towns and villages in Israel. This is followed by Ilann Messeri's essay on soccer and the Latino community in Richmond, California. In the context of a broader consideration of youth soccer in the United States, Ilann uses a largely functional analysis to consider the more specific role that the game plays within a particular neighbourhood, focusing in particular on the ways in which it serves the impoverished urban immigrant population but also the wider super-structure through its strengthening of community ties.

From this more hopeful consideration of the communitarian 'uses' of football the book then comes full circle in the final, concluding essay in which Tim Crabbe offers a more contemporary reading of the ephemeral, performative nature of 'community' in the context of the global gathering at the 2006 FIFA World Cup. Focusing specifically on the social formations which emerged amongst England football fans during the tournament, this essay provides a rather more bleak assessment of a temporal, consumerist *desire* for community which does not always carry with it the responsibilities which sit at the heart of the communitarian project.

Notes

1. The Football and its Communities project was carried out by the editors of this book and two other researchers: Tony Blackshaw and Chris Stone at Sheffield Hallam University. We would like to thank Tony and Chris for their contributions which helped to inspire this collection.
2. Mason, *Sport in Britain*, 118.
3. Holt, *Sport and the British*; Holt, 'Heroes of the North'; Holt, 'Football and Regional'.
4. Holt, *Sport and the British*, 167.
5. Giulianotti, *Football*.
6. Ibid., 14.
7. Ibid., 15.
8. Tönnies, *Community and Association*.
9. See Hill, 'Rite of Spring'.
10. Andrews, 'Transformation of "Community". Part One'; Andrews, 'Transformation of "Community". Part Two'.
11. Fawbert, 'Football Fandom'.
12. Brown, 'Manchester is Red?'.
13. Mellor, 'Social and Geographical Make-up', 29–34.
14. Back, Crabbe and Solomos, *Changing Face of Football*.
15. Mellor, 'Genesis of Manchester United', 151–66.
16. For an introduction to this see Mellor, 'Professional Football', 166–72.
17. Andrews, 'Transformation of "Community". Part One', 105.
18. Cohen, *Symbolic Construction of Community*.
19. Delanty, *Community*, 46.
20. Turner, *Ritual Process*.
21. Delanty, *Community*, 44.
22. Smith and Ingham, 'On the Waterfront', 259.
23. See, for example, Crabbe and Brown, 'You're Not Welcome Anymore'.
24. Bauman, *Liquid Modernity*, 199–201.
25. Beck and Beck-Gersheim, *Individualization*
26. Lash, 'Reflexivity and its Doubles'.
27. Maffesoli, *Time of the Tribes*.
28. Lash, 'Reflexivity and its Doubles', 161, quoted in Delanty, *Community*, 139.
29. Bourdieu, *Distinction*.
30. See Harvey, *Condition of Postmodernity*.

References

Andrews, I. 'The Transformation of "Community" in the Australian Football League. Part One: Towards a Conceptual Framework For Community'. *Occasional Papers in Football Studies* 1, no. 2 (1998): 103–14.

———. 'The Transformation of "Community" in the Australian Football League. Part Two: Redrawing 'Community Boundaries in the Post-War AFL'. *Football Studies* 2, no. 2 (1999): 106–24.

Back, L., T. Crabbe, and J. Solomos. *The Changing Face of Football: Racism, Identity and Multiculture in the English Game.* Oxford: Berg, 2001.

Bauman, Z. *Liquid Modernity.* Cambridge: Polity, 2000.
Beck, U., and E. Beck-Gersheim. *Individualization.* London: Sage, 2002.
Bourdieu, P. *Distinction.* London: Routledge, 1984.
Brown, A. 'Manchester is Red? Manchester United, Fan Identity and the "Sport City"'. In *Manchester United: A Thematic Study,* ed. D. Andrews, 175–89. London: Routledge, 2004.
Cohen, A. *The Symbolic Construction of Community.* London: Tavistock, 1985.
Crabbe, T., and A. Brown. 'You're Not Welcome Anymore: The Football Crowd, Class and Social Exclusion'. In *British Football and Social Exclusion,* ed. S. Wagg, 26–46. London: Routledge, 2004.
Delanty, G. *Community.* London: Routledge, 2003.
Durkheim, E. *The Division of Labour.* Houndmills: The Free Press, 1984. First published 1863.
Fawbert, J. 'Football Fandom and the 'Traditional' Club: From 'Cockney Parochialism' to a European Diaspora?'. Paper presented at the European Football: Influence, Change, Development Conference, Preston, UK, September 1–2, 2004.
Giulianotti, R. *Football: A Sociology of the Global Game.* Cambridge: Polity Press, 1999.
Harvey, D. *The Condition of Postmodernity.* Oxford. Blackwell, 1990.
Hill, J. 'Rite of Spring: Cup Finals and Community in the North of England'. In *Sport and Identity in the North of England,* ed. J. Hill and J. Williams, 85–112. Keele: Keele University Press, 1996.
Holt, R. *Sport and the British: A Modern History.* Oxford: Oxford University Press, 1989.
———. 'Heroes of the North: Sport and the Shaping of Regional Identity'. In *Sport and Identity in the North of England,* ed. J. Hill and J. Williams, 137–64. Keele: Keele University Press, 1996.
———. 'Football and Regional Identity in the North of England: The Legend of Jackie Milburn'. In *Football and Regional Identity in Europe,* ed. S. Gerhrmann. New Brunswick, NJ: Transaction Publishers, 1997.
Lash, S. 'Reflexivity and its Doubles, Structures, Aesthetics, Community'. In *Reflexive Modernization: Politics, Tradition and Aesthetics in the Modern Social Order,* ed. U. Beck, A. Giddens, and S. Lash, 110–73. Cambridge, Polity Press, 1994.
Maffesoli, M. *The Time of the Tribes: The Decline of Individualism in Mass Society.* London: Sage, 1996.
Mason, T. *Sport in Britain.* London: Faber & Faber, 1988.
Mellor, G. 'The Social and Geographical Make-up of Football Crowds in the North-West of England, 1946–62: "Super-Clubs", Local Loyalty and Regional Identities'. *The Sports Historian* 19, no. 2 (1999): 25–42.
———. 'The Genesis of Manchester United as a National and International "Super-Club", 1958–68'. *Soccer and Society* 1, no. 2 (2000): 151–66.
———. 'Professional Football and its Supporters in Lancashire, circa 1946–89'. PhD Diss. University of Central Lancashire, 2002.
Smith, J., and A. Ingham. 'On the Waterfront: Retrospectives on the Relationship Between Sport and Communities'. *Sociology of Sport Journal* 20, no. 4 (2003): 252–74.
Tönnies, F. *Community and Association.* London: Routledge, 1974.
Turner, V. *The Ritual Process: Structure and Anti-Structure.* London: Routledge and Kegan Paul, 1969.

POLITICS, THEORY AND PRACTICE

'The Janus-faced sport': English football, community and the legacy of the 'third way'

Gavin Mellor

Introduction

English professional football is becoming an increasingly complex sport to follow and understand. Over the past few years, the game has been subject to almost routine formal and informal inquiries into all areas of its business: investigations which have required its supporters to gain more than a passing understanding of the intricacies of company, employment and finance law. From issues of players' freedom of contract, to debates around 'foreign ownership' of English clubs (and not to mention more prosaic matters like ticket pricing) the game – especially at the top end – has been under sustained attack from those who question the motivations and competencies of the game's governing bodies. These attacks tend to concentrate on one key area of debate: whether football is merely another business or whether it is a *sport* which should be protected from the worst excesses of relatively unregulated free-market business practices.

Commentators who adopt the latter interpretation frequently draw attention to the 'social' and 'community functions' of football clubs to explain why the game is too important to be left to the whims and unregulated practices of the free market.[1] For them, professional football is not simply a form of mass commercial entertainment: it is a deeply embedded community activity which expresses and reinforces the cultural identities of large numbers of people. For these writers the game demands special protection. Indeed, some have gone so far as to assert that English football requires an independent, state-run regulator which will protect the 'community' status of clubs and intervene when governing bodies fail to act in ways which defend the interest of all the game's stakeholders and not just those with economic interests.[2]

Calls for independent regulation of English football have reached arguably unprecedented heights in the past two years following the emergence of a popularly held belief that English football is – at the very least – economically excessive and unsound. From the Lord Stevens inquiry into payments to football agents,[3] to popular newspaper campaigns to reduce ticket prices,[4] there is an increasing sense that the English football authorities are not exercising their regulatory responsibilities around the game in accordance with expected standards. However, calls for independent regulation are by no means new. Since at least the mid-1990s, a small number of academics and commentators have argued consistently that the governance structure of English football was failing to protect the game's status as a community asset. For many of them, the restructuring of the game in the 1990s had seen it embrace, rather too enthusiastically, the neo-liberal economic philosophy of the then Conservative British government,[5] leading to a situation in which the traditional collectivism and community focus of English football had been sacrificed in the pursuit of economic profit. Football was clearly not alone in this regard, and many writers pointed out that this process was occurring across other areas of national culture. As the game is the national sport, however, it was hoped that concern amongst the game's supporters and other stakeholders would be such that the collective, community focus of English football could be defended, if not by the game's governing bodies then by independent regulation.

This debate around the regulation of English football coincided in 1997 with a change of ruling party in British politics for the first time in nearly 20 years. Whilst it had been accepted by critics of the game that the economically liberal and non-interventionist Conservative government was extremely unlikely to intervene in the matters of 'private business', it was hoped that the incoming Labour Party would be more willing to take up their cause. The British Labour Party is, of course, historically a party of the left: a party which believes in the pre-eminence of the state; close economic regulation and the defence of working-class culture and institutions. Whilst Labour had not directly intervened in the business matters of football during previous terms of office, there were certain elements to the party's past which suggested it may be willing to become involved with current concerns. In 1964, the Labour government had created the Sports Council thereby setting out a clear structure for the public funding and governance of British sport for the first time.[6] In 1968, it also commissioned and published the first government report into the national football industry in Britain which commented on, amongst other things, the importance of the game to local and national communities.[7] In more recent decades, at a local level, the Labour Party – under the guise of Calderdale Council – had also been willing to support Halifax Town Football Club with local tax revenue when the club was encountering severe economic difficulties. Its rationale for doing so was based on the *cultural* importance of the club to the local community.[8]

The Labour Party which came to power in Britain in 1997 was very different from its predecessors. It was a 'New Labour' party which, through a long and bitter internal ideological battle in the 1980s and 1990s, had discarded many of its formerly key principles in order to regain power. Before the 1997 election, it openly dismissed, amongst other things, its former commitments to raising personal taxation levels amongst the most wealthy and nationalizing British industries. As such, a gap opened up in terms of the philosophical coherence of the party. If Labour was no longer concerned with redistribution of income and state control of business, what were its organizing principles?

In the early days of the New Labour government, the key phrase which came to represent the party's new philosophy was 'the third way'. The phrase itself was oppositional: it was designed to suggest a reaction against the traditional dichotomy of 'right' and 'left' in British politics. Instead, a 'third way' was proposed which would embrace the best of both traditions and thereby ensure economic freedom and prosperity on the one hand (the old battle ground of the right) and social security, equality and justice on the other (the old preserve of the left). The question for advocates of increased regulation in English football was, what would this mean for their cause? Would New Labour's commitment to economic freedom mean the game would be allowed to continue to pursue profit without consequence, or would the party's new commitment to tackling 'social exclusion' mean that football would be reinterpreted as being primarily a community concern?

This essay reflects on what has happened to English football since the early days of the New Labour government. It seeks primarily to understand present governance arrangements around English football in terms of the legacy of third-way inspired ways of thinking. It does not claim that the British Labour Party mobilized a set of coherent third way policy initiatives post-1997 which shaped the game we know today, and it does not suggest that the present Labour government – now under the stewardship of Gordon Brown – still slavishly adheres to third way principles. Rather, through close analysis of the policies and practices around English football, it seeks to understand how the 'ideological space' created by the third way created a unique period in English football's history where economic relations around the game continue to be relatively unregulated, whilst clubs are increasingly asked to engage with new social obligations. In this sense, it tries to make sense of the seemingly contradictory ways in which English football is currently dealing with the 'problem of community'. As stated at the start of this essay, English football is still currently beset with concerns over its economic and other practices and their effects on the game's stakeholders. However, and as we will see, it is also more keen than ever to asserts its 'socially-minded' credentials and its role in supporting the multiple communities of which it is part.

The third way

In 1998, Anthony Giddens – the most prolific and famous writer on third way thinking – published his first book on the topic.[9] This sought to set out a 'unique' agenda for the New Labour administration and ultimately proved to be hugely influential in shaping understandings of the defining principles of third way politics. Drawing on ideological shifts in the American Democratic Party, the book set out a number of key characteristics of political thinking in the 'new era'. These, it was claimed, would help politics to move beyond old Leftist ideologies (which, it was said, had proved unworkable in the 1970s) and neo-liberal approaches to government (which, Giddens' argued, had produced such devastating social consequences under the Conservative administration in the 1980s). Giddens, and other third way thinkers, now aimed to redefine political debate and specifically the concept of 'social democracy' in order that centre-left governments would gain power and flourish across Europe, the United States and elsewhere.

As writers such as Finlayson have pointed out, the routine use of the term 'third way' in politics and elsewhere actually emerged before it had a clear and definite content.[10] Blair, Giddens and others did not begin to write about the third way until after the phrase had entered into the political and public consciousness. This has led some to claim that third way thinking never really constituted a coherent political project, but rather was a 'post-rationalization' of ideas, approaches and policies with Labour adopted before and after its election in 1997.[11] In short, this type of thinking has led to charges that 'the third way' was empty political rhetoric designed to disguise the lack of coherence at the heart of the New Labour project.

Despite such concerns, much has been written on the third way by its proponents and critics. From these writings we can begin to understand its major components and its sociological underpinnings (such as they are). If we start with the 'High Priest' of third way politics, Tony Blair, we can begin to unravel his understanding of the need for an alternative form of politics that was different from traditional socialism and contemporary neo-liberalism. For Blair, political thinking needed a third way because of the 'sociological' claim that the world in which we lived in the late twentieth century had changed out of all recognition.[12] Just as neo-liberalism was a reaction to the unique conditions of the late 1970s and 1980s, so the third way was cast as a response to changing social and economic relations at the end of the twentieth century. For Blair, Giddens and others the world in the 1990s was too complex, too fluid and too diverse to be managed by a central state. Governments needed new tools and tactics with which to manage. Most importantly, they needed new ways of redeveloping or repairing social cohesion and solidarity as this is viewed as the key challenge for the new era.[13] For Giddens and similar thinkers, hitherto unknown levels of reflexivity or self-awareness had come to mark the social actions of people in late modernity. This means that people had more power to determine their own paths through life than ever before. In this sense, power was said to be everywhere in late modernity and could not be monopolized by an autocratic socialist state. The job of the state was therefore not to dominate or determine the actions of individuals, but to generate circumstances in which people would 'freely' accept that their actions could have positive and negative consequences for others. If people accepted this essential 'truth', they could be encouraged to act in ways which could ensure high levels of social cohesion.

Third way thinkers' understandings of individual freedom extended to their analysis of market relations, and this is where the third way philosophy proved most controversial with leftist thinkers. Giddens, for instance, was unequivocal on this issue. For him, there was simply no alternative to market capitalism as the organizing principle of modern economic relations. Traditional socialist interventions into markets are seen to be out of date and totally unworkable. If people are increasingly reflexive and individualized in the ways in which they approach and understand the modern world, then, according to Giddens, it is inevitable that economic relations should also provide people with personal opportunities to engage in 'free' economic activities and enterprises. To defend this position, Giddens provided a new interpretation of market capitalism as being essentially benign. For him, it was in no way inevitable that capitalism produces inequality and exploitation: 'Markets have, or can have, beneficial outcomes that go beyond productive efficiency.'[14] Giddens claimed that a successful market economy has an important 'hidden curriculum' which is conducive to, rather than undermining of, social cohesion and justice. He told us that market relations are essentially peaceful; that they allow people to make free choices; that they favour attitudes of responsibility 'since participants need to calculate the likely outcomes of what they do'; and that they are potentially liberating.[15]

Giddens was not so naive as to believe that, if left totally unregulated, capitalist relations will always and everywhere produce social justice. The evidence of history certainly suggests otherwise. Indeed, Giddens, Blair and other third way thinkers wrote and spoke directly about the risky and threatening nature of global capitalism as the principal reason why we needed 'a third way'. For Blair, 'what globalisation is doing is bringing in its wake profound economic and social change, economic change rendering all jobs in industry, sometimes even new jobs in new industries, redundant overnight and social change that is a change to culture, to lifestyle, to the family, to established patterns of community life'.[16] But Blair and Giddens saw this economic and social uncertainty as being inevitable and irreversible, and ultimately found no reason to turn away from capitalist market relations. Giddens therefore called for an end to what he termed the 'politics of redemption' where the 'bad guys' of multi-national capitalism are always the enemy and always need eliminating.[17] Giddens accepted that there are economic 'enemies' of the third way project and that some forms of corporate power (particularly tendencies towards monopolization) needed to be checked. However, these were to be tackled through the assertion of third way values, as being 'on the left is indeed primarily a matter of values'.[18]

From Giddens' analysis of market relations, his New Labour followers were left in no doubt that market capitalism was the only way forward. To 'regulate' the worst excesses of the market, he warned the state not to turn to old-fashioned leftist economic interventions. Rather, he said, the state needed to foster a change of values in society through which corporate executives would happily accept their social responsibilities. This was where Giddens turned to address 'civil society' as a key component of the third-way-inspired future. For him and other third way thinkers, one of the principal roles of the future state was to support a strong civil society in which people would have the requisite 'social capital' to lead mutually respectful and rewarding lives. This aim would not be undermined by the competitive impulses of market capitalism because social capital is ultimately defined as a resource which enables people to function within 'trust networks',[19] which, Giddens believed, were central to the smooth running of contemporary capitalist relations. Corporations, he told us, are increasingly caught up in complex webs of interdependence which require cooperation and trust,[20] and they were not alone in this regard. Giddens, Blair and others continually evoked the idea that the central job of government in the third way era would be to promote 'proactive' supply-side policies which would encourage everybody to build social capital and thereby have the tools needed to work in the interests of wider social cohesion. In his first term of office as Prime Minister, Blair frequently evoked the concept of the 'stakeholder' society, in which everybody would enjoy equal rights and responsibilities and nobody would be socially excluded. For Giddens, this was as important for those at the 'top' of society as those at the 'bottom'.[21] Tackling social exclusion would not be just about increasing access to economic resources; it would also be about supporting values of cohesion and mutual obligation which were at the heart of the third way project. The phrase 'stakeholder' society (which Blair borrowed from Will Hutton) has now fallen out of the New Labour lexicon, but the ideas underpinning it are still very much at the forefront of New Labour thinking.

The idea that governments should concentrate on supply side policies was central to third way thinkers' re-interpretations of the role of the welfare state. For New Labour, the welfare state and public policy more generally should not be underpinned by the 'ideological dogma' which beset former Labour administrations. The aim of public policy would not provide people with re-distributed wealth. Rather, it would be there to enable people to take advantage of re-distributed *opportunities*. This required a historical shift in Labour's traditional position on equality. Whilst former Labour governments stressed a policy which can be summed up in the term 'equality of outcome', the New Labour government would be more concerned with 'equality of opportunity', or the provision of resources and values which would enable people to take advantage of what life had to offer. This squarely placed a new emphasis on 'citizens' to take responsibility for the ways in which they lived. The state would guarantee access to opportunities, but if people failed to take these it would not support their ultimately 'anti-social' ways of living.

The lack of 'dogma' in third way thinking around public policy was also expressed in its approach to the actual provision of public services. As Bill Clinton and the New Democrats first claimed, third way thinking was supposed to offer an alternative to the traditional left's attachment to 'big government' and the conservative right's attempts to dismantle the central state.[22] This was expressed most clearly in third way thinking about the balance between the state and the market in the constitution of public policy instruments. For policy advocates such as Geoff Mulgan, the third way meant that there should be no automatic commitment to the public or the private sector in deciding who would provide public services:

> The changing balance between public and private sectors, state and market solutions, cannot be separated from the organisational forms and competences which each brings to bear. It is with these, and with public and private organisations' practical ability to recognise and solve problems in everything from energy to prisons and universities to childcare, that any useful argument has to begin.[23]

In practice, this meant that the long-term 'hollowing out' of the state continued under New Labour. Put more substantively, successive Labour administrations encouraged the extension of 'partnership' working between the state and private/voluntary organizations. This means that the government has come to act as a guarantor of public standards, but is now infrequently a direct provider of public services. This, of course, was made possible by third way understandings of market relations. The market could act to provide public services without any potential conflicts or tensions because, as Giddens told us, if encouraged in the right direction the market has an important 'hidden curriculum' which acts for the public good.

English football clubs: market freedoms and social responsibilities

New Labour's broad adherence to third way thinking was clear in the years after its election in 1997. The party introduced a number of reforms in welfare and other areas of public policy that focused on creating a strong sense of responsibility across society. Rarely, however, did this extend to direct regulation in 'private sector' matters: that was the old socialist way of doing things and did not fit with third way understandings of personal and economic power.

At the time when Labour came to power, and as stated at the beginning of this essay, the football industry in England was coming under something of a sustained attack. For a small but growing number of writers,[24] the game had come to define the very spirit of Conservative neo-liberalism in the 1990s. In the post-Hillsborough context, the football industry, it was claimed, had effectively been 'de-regulated' as 'new directors'[25] moved in to exploit the newfound popularity of the national game. The Premier League was created in 1992, effectively undermining over 100 years of collectivism in English football; new and unprecedented television contracts were signed with satellite broadcasters; and increasing numbers of football clubs were floated on the stock market. In this context, debates raged about the status of the national game and whether it was in need of protection from unregulated markets and the consequences they might bring. Popular and academic writings had traditionally asserted sport's position as a 'community' asset. Football in particular was viewed as a cultural form that expressed community identities and drew on forms of association that were not reducible to producer/consumer relations. For many left-of-centre writers, football clubs were in danger of being financially exploited for the benefit of new directors. This was at the expense of wider psychological feelings of ownership of the game.

As New Labour came to power, many of these debates around English football were well established. Pressure was put on the Labour administration – despite its new non-interventionist credentials – to intervene in the national game and re-establish its community roots. If New Labour was to turn away from neo-liberal forms of economic and social governance, then it would have to respond to the seemingly 'unaccountable' ways in which football clubs were being run. In response to this, the Labour administration established a Football Task Force (FTF) which, amongst other things, would report back on whether the football industry was meeting its 'social obligations'. Through the FTF, some hoped the government would re-establish the belief that football was culturally too important for its economic base to be left to unregulated market relations. At the very least, it was hoped that new governance structures could be found to protect all professional football clubs from the worst excesses of market exploitation.

In 1999, Labour's FTF concluded its proceedings by reporting on 'commercial issues' in the football industry. Uniquely, this report split the task force into two factions: one which advocated an independent regulator for the football industry and one which did not. The New Labour government unsurprisingly supported the latter and went on to advocate an oxymoronic form of 'independent self-regulation' for the football industry under the guise of the Independent Football Commission (IFC).

In the wake of the FTF, the English football industry came to enjoy unprecedented economic freedom. The clubs which made up the Premier League continued to exist outside of broad and historic collective agreements, and this enabled them to operate policies which were primarily, if not solely, in their collective financial interest. The legal basis of this arrangement was tested in 1999 when the Office of Fair Trading (OFT) took the FA Premier League, the BBC and BSkyB to the Restrictive Practices Court. The OFT stated that the sale of television rights by the Premier League to BSkyB and the BBC was collective and exclusive. The claim was made that the Premier League was acting as a cartel and was thus being anti-competitive. The exclusive nature of the deal effectively stopping broadcasters from showing matches in which BSkyB and the BBC were not interested. After a nine-month case, the judge Mr Justice Ferris ruled in favour of the Premier League, but only because he believed the collective TV deal generated wealth which could be redistributed across football. To ease the judge's decision in this matter, the Premier League promised during the court case to redistribute some of its collective wealth to 'grassroots' football. Eventually this led the Premier League, the FA, the government and Sport England to establish the Football Foundation (funded in part by 5% of the BSkyB TV deal): a charitable organization which funds grassroots facilities and community and education interventions around football. This was a classic third way compromise. The Premier League was not directly regulated as a result of the ruling. It did not have to give up on the principle of acting as a cartel. Rather, it was asked to accept its responsibilities to the rest of football and, through the Football Foundation's education and community work, the rest of society.

The compromise which was reached at the conclusion of this court case reflects governance arrangements which still operate around English football. Clubs are largely free to trade in any way they see fit. They do not encounter any special forms of governance or regulation despite persistent claims that sport in general, and football in particular, is culturally too important to be left to whims of market forces. Ironically, the football industry itself is not averse to evoking this idea when it is required. In 1995 UEFA – the governing body for football in Europe – suggested that the football industry should not be subject to laws on the free circulation of workers in the European Union because football is not like other areas of economic activity. Essentially, UEFA claimed a 'cultural' defence for why its member associations should be able to restrict players' contracts. The European Court of Justice ruled against UEFA in this case thereby establishing the principle that the football industry is not, in economic matters at least, different from other sectors of the economy.

The unwillingness of New Labour to regulate the economic governance of English football did not mean the game was able to continue as it did during the neo-liberal years of the previous Conservative administration in Britain. Football clubs were able to trade relatively freely, but increasingly they were expected to engage with other areas of the third way project. In line with Giddens' understanding of the 'hidden curriculum' of market capitalism, football clubs were required increasingly to demonstrate that governance structures around the game operated for the good of football and 'society'. This did not just result in the aforementioned creation of the Football Foundation. It also created the circumstances in which football clubs came increasingly to be asked to engage in work which was previously the preserve of local and national government.

Football clubs in England have a relatively long history of engaging in 'community' based work, especially from the mid-1980s onwards when the national Football in the Community (FiTC) programme was established.[26] At that point, English football was suffering from serious economic problems, and FiTC schemes were established in part as a way of reconnecting professional football clubs with 'their' local communities. When New Labour came to power, however, the community work in which clubs were expected to engage expanded beyond traditional children's coaching schemes and player appearances. Sport in general, and football in particular, was identified by the British government as a potential key deliverer of a range of policy objectives in areas as diverse as health, education, community cohesion, regeneration and crime reduction. The Labour government was not the first administration to believe that the 'power' of football could contribute to these policy areas, but it was the first to make such extensive use of top level professional football clubs in tackling social problems.

To understand why football clubs came to be asked to engage in these areas of policy, we must turn back to the values and objectives of third way thinking. In his second book on the third way, Anthony Giddens explored ideas relating to corporate social responsibility (CSR) as one way in which corporate executives could demonstrate their commitment to social cohesion and civil society more generally.[27] Whilst Giddens rightly notes the cynicism which has frequently accompanied CSR programmes, he claims a commitment from certain corporations to generate a 'new paradigm' for formulating social programmes. Whilst 'philanthropy at arms length' may not have successfully addressed social problems in the past, Giddens claims that a new form of CSR which uses 'social needs as a basis for the development of ideas, technologies and long-term investments' could produce real social change.[28]

It is in this context that we can begin to understand the social interventions in which the football industry came to be involved. From the late 1990s onwards, football clubs, like other corporations, increasingly were expected to indicate their commitment to civil society and social justice by engaging in 'socially responsible' activities. Football clubs, however, came to have a special role to play in this respect which extended beyond other forms of corporate engagement with 'social' agendas. This is because the apparent 'values' of football fitted so perfectly with the third way agenda. In their calls for the consolidation of civil society, many third way thinkers turned to communitarian writers for a way forward. For communitarians, the disintegration of civil society could only be stopped by the re-consolidation of 'communities'.[29] In the communitarian view, a stable sense of individual identity has to be anchored in a community context. Communities provide people with agreed values and beliefs, and shared senses of mutual obligation. If communities could be rebuilt, then a strong civil society would surely follow.

Football clubs (and other sports clubs) came to be seen to have a special role in this communitarian-inspired future as, it was claimed, they possess intrinsic community building properties. In 2000, the Office of the Deputy Prime Minister (ODPM) published its white paper *Our Towns and Cities: The Future – Delivering an Urban Renaissance*.[30] In the paper, it was claimed that sport should be used to tackle social exclusion because it helps to build 'civic pride'.[31] Similarly, the Department for Culture, Media and Sport (DCMS) stated unequivocally that sport could tackle social exclusion because it 'relates to community identity and encourage[s] collective effort'.[32] This type of thinking was certainly not new: a great deal of popular and academic debate has taken place on the community and civic pride building properties of football and other sports clubs. But it did have a new impact within football's governing bodies. In their development strategy for the period 2001–06, the English Football Association wrote of the 'sense of community' that football clubs can create, and of the game's capacity for generating a 'sense of community empowerment amongst those groups who are typically seen as "excluded" from mainstream society'.[33]

In practice, football clubs' engagement with community cohesion and other social agendas has been based around third way 'values' and modes of organization. Through our research with three professional football clubs as part of the Football Foundation funded *Football and its Communities* research project, we identified a typology of areas of work in which the clubs are routinely involved.[34] Many of these are 'supply side' initiatives which are designed to provide people (usually children) with resources to enable them to make 'better choices' as citizens. Such 'asset-based egalitarianism'[35] is expressed through the following types of programmes:

- Health improvement through health education
- Drugs awareness and education

- Study support – educational help for underperforming students
- Social skills, self esteem and life skills
- Sessions and programmes to improve community and family cohesion
- Key employment skills and adult learning
- Anti-discrimination – education and providing opportunities for 'excluded' groups.

These are not the only types of community work in which football clubs are routinely involved, but they do suggest strongly a third way inspired approach to solving 'social problems'. The programmes focus typically on changing people's shared 'values' (thereby helping to create a stronger civil society), and on improving skills which will enable people to enjoy more equal access to work and other opportunities. This is the classic third way approach to tackling 'social exclusion'. If people are provided with better skills and other 'resources', and learn to understand the values of civil society (how to be a 'good citizen'), then they will become more integrated into 'mainstream society'. In short, 'they' (the 'different', the 'deviant') will be helped to overcome barriers which will enable them to be like 'us' (the 'normal').[36]

A large number of community programmes at football clubs in the early years of the twenty-first century also came to focus on using sport to tackle crime and 'anti-social behaviour'. Football clubs frequently came to host football activities aimed at children who are defined by the state as being 'at risk of offending'. These were frequently 'diversionary' (for example, they were hosted at times when certain types of crimes are most often perpetrated), but others tried to use the 'values' of sport (team work, self respect, discipline) to encourage children to become better citizens. These programmes again fitted perfectly with third way thinking. As Giddens points out, third way politicians tended to be 'morally conservative' and criticized those on the left who blamed crime on inequality or poverty.[37] Third way thinkers frequently stressed the importance of personal responsibility in crime (again it is primarily a matter of values), and maintained that tackling crime must be a priority for left-of-centre governments. This is because of the destabilizing effect that crime has on the morals, values and practices of civil society. A 'hard line' on crime is required in order to protect others, and third way thinkers assume that people will accept or even encourage harsh measures against crime in the pursuit of the wider public good. When faced with such issues, Giddens invites us to consider 'how far regulating some sorts of freedoms [will produce] a net increase in freedom for communities as a whole'.[38]

When tackling crime or any other 'social problems', football clubs have tended to build a range of partnerships which again fit well with the aims and objectives of third way thinking. According to the former Department of Social Security key policy document *New Ambitions for Our Country*, the third way was 'about combining public and private provision in a new partnership for the new age'.[39] These partnerships were, according to former Labour Minister for Welfare Reform Frank Field, best encouraged by 'the recreation of a civil society based on a partnership between individuals, organisations and Government'.[40] These partnerships were certainly established by many football clubs. It has become routine for football clubs' community staff to work on various projects in partnership with Primary Care Trusts (PCTs), Drug and Alcohol Action Teams (DAATs), Youth Offending Teams (YOTs), the Connexions Youth Service, Local Education Authorities (LEAs), Local Authority Sport and Recreation teams, Local Authority Disability Partnerships, New Deal for Communities (NDC) agencies, Sure Start, Education Action Zones, Sport Action Zones, individual schools and colleges and many other governmental and non-governmental bodies. These partnerships have been specific to the circumstances in which they have operated. Some have depended on the skills which football clubs have to offer; others have simply borrowed the 'brand' of the football club to engage people in activities. All partnerships are, though, based on an essentially third way belief that many traditional public services are best delivered through local partnerships between the state, commercial and 'third sector' agencies.

Conclusion – squaring impossible circles

The British Labour Party has now been in power for over nine years and, despite a recent change in leadership, continues to pursue a broadly third way inspired agenda (although, of course, the term is no longer used). Since Labour came to power, and since the FTF delivered its final report in 1999, questions have continue to be raised about economic governance of the national game. In 2001, the European Commission launched a new investigation into the exclusive nature of BSkyB Premier League television deal, stating that its selling arrangements were anti-competitive as they eliminated competition between broadcasters and limited the media coverage of matches to the detriment of fans. In 2003, the Premier League accepted an EU ruling that a new system would have to come into place in 2006 where balanced packages of matches would be created and it would not be possible for one broadcaster to buy all the packages. This is a rare example of interference in the economic matters of the English football industry, and it is instructive that it came from European rather than national government.

In general, the economic principles of neo-liberalism have continued unchecked in the English football industry since New Labour came to power. Clubs are not regulated more than they used to be, despite concerns about how current arrangements affect economically disadvantaged supporters (specifically with regard to increased ticket prices and the cost of merchandising) and other issues such as 'foreign' ownerships of clubs and competitiveness within and across Leagues. Changes have, therefore, been confined to other areas of governance, such as increasing the amount of social responsibility which clubs are supposed to demonstrate through community-based initiatives.

The problem with this arrangement is that the football industry has begun to understand social responsibility as being applicable to certain areas of work and not to others. In effect, the socially responsible activities in which clubs are involved through their 'community' activities are seen as a 'pay off' for the arguably socially 'irresponsible' ways in which they conduct other forms of business. This is observable in the ways in which clubs organize and conceive of 'community activities'. Frequently, clubs have community departments (or similar) which initiate programmes and deal with 'the community', whilst other sections of clubs deal with 'customers' or those that can afford to have an economic relationship with the club. This splitting of 'social responsibility' into a separate section of the organization is not confined to football clubs. Increasingly, large corporations have Corporate Social Responsibility or 'Sustainability' departments which deal with specific programmes of work and do not necessarily influence the broad strategy of the business. This makes many industries, including football clubs, appear to be Janus-faced. On the one hand, they are economically liberal organizations which pursue profits sometimes at the expense of 'the public good'. On the other hand, they have social responsibility sections which are designed to address the concerns of civil society.

This is the crucial problem with third way thinking. Whilst Giddens may have believed that capitalist relations are essentially benign and can work for the public good, in practice corporations continue to work in exclusionary and exploitative ways no matter how much the government has encouraged them to embrace third way values. At its worse, third way thinking has seen CSR develop as a form of PR for companies who employ community work as a defence against other more questionable practices. In this sense, the 'social exclusion at the top' which Giddens wrote about has not been tackled by the Labour government. At the very least, there is little evidence in English football that third way thinking has produced more egalitarian policies across the industry.

Notes

1. See, for example, Conn, 'What Money Can't Buy'.
2. Gerry Sutcliffe MP, the present Labour Minister for Sport, held this view before coming to office. See Sutcliffe, 'Independent Regulator'.
3. See Kelso, 'Bung Inquiry'.
4. *The Sun*, Britain's highest circulation national daily newspaper, ran such a campaign during the end of the 2006/07 football season.
5. See, for example, King, *End of the Terraces*, 88–97.
6. See Henry and Bramham, 'Leisure Policy in Britain'.
7. Department of Education and Science, *Report of the Committee on Football*.
8. Russell, *Football and the English*, 222.
9. Giddens, *Third Way*.
10. Finlayson, 'Third Way Theory', 271.
11. Driver and Martell, 'Left, Right and the Third Way', 148.
12. Blair, *Third Way*; Finlayson, Third Way Theory', 271.
13. Giddens, *Beyond Left and Right*.
14. Giddens, *The Third Way and its Critics*, 35.
15. Ibid.
16. In Driver and Martell, 'Left, Right and the Third Way', 150.
17. Giddens, *Third Way and its Critics*, 36.
18. Ibid.
19. Ibid, 78.
20. Ibid, 79.
21. Ibid, 116–20.
22. Driver and Martell, 'Left, Right and the Third Way', 151–2.
23. In ibid., 152.
24. King, *End of the Terraces*; Conn, *Football Business*.
25. King, *End of the Terraces*, 120–47.
26. Russell, *Football and the English*, 221.
27. Giddens, *Third Way and its Critics*, 82.
28. Ibid.
29. See, for example, Etzioni, *Spirit of Community*.
30. Social Exclusion Unit, *Our Towns and Cities*, 126.
31. Ibid., 126.
32. Department for Culture, Media and Sport, *Report to the Social Exclusion Unit*, 5.
33. Football Association, *Football Development Strategy*, 36.
34. Brown, Crabbe and Mellor, *Football and its Communities*.
35. Driver and Martell, 'Left, Right and the Third Way', 152.
36. Powell, 'New Labour', 48.
37. Giddens, *Third Way and its Critics*, 45.
38. Ibid., 49.
39. Department of Social Security, *New Ambitions*, 19.
40. In Powell, 'New Labour', 50.

References

Blair, T. *The Third Way*. London: Fabian Society, 1998.
Brown, A., T. Crabbe, and G. Mellor. *Football and its Communities: Final Report*. London and Manchester: Football Foundation and Manchester Metropolitan University, 2006.
Conn, D. *The Football Business: Fair Game in the '90s*. Edinburgh: Mainstream, 1997.
———. 'What Money Can't Buy'. *Observer Sport Monthly,* 29 July 2007.
Department for Culture, Media and Sport. *Report to the Social Exclusion Unit – Arts and Sports*. London: HMSO, 1999.
Department of Education and Science. *Report of the Committee on Football*. London: HMSO, 1968.
Department of Social Security. *New Ambitions for Our Country: A New Contract for Welfare*. London: HMSO, 1998.
Driver, S., and L. Martell. 'Left, Right and the Third Way'. *Policy and Politics* 28, no. 2 (2000): 147–61.

Etzioni, A. *The Spirit of Community.* London: Fontana Press, 1995.
Finlayson, A. 'Third Way Theory'. *The Political Quarterly* 70, no. 3 (1999): 271–9.
Football Association. *The Football Development Strategy 2001–2006.* London: The Football Association, 2001.
Giddens, A. *Beyond Left and Right: The Future of Radical Politics.* Stanford, CA: Stanford University Press, 1994.
———. *The Third Way: The Renewal of Social Democracy.* Cambridge: Polity Press, 1998.
———. *The Third Way and its Critics.* Cambridge: Polity Press, 2000.
Henry, I., and P. Bramham. 'Leisure Policy in Britain'. In *Leisure Policies in Europe,* ed. P. Bramham, I. Henry, H. Mommaas, and H. van der Poel, 101–28. Wallingford: CAB International, 1993.
Kelso, P. 'Bung Inquiry Names Football's Leading Agents and Managers'. *Guardian,* 16 June 2007.
King, A. *The End of the Terraces: Revised Edition.* London and New York: Leicester University Press, 2002.
Powell, M. 'New Labour and the Third Way in the British Welfare State: a New and Distinctive Approach?'. *Critical Social Policy* 20, no. 1 (2000): 39–60.
Russell, D. *Football, and the English: A Social History of Association Football in England, 1863–1995.* Preston: Carnegie, 1997.
Social Exclusion Unit. *Our Towns and Cities: The Future – Delivering an Urban Renaissance.* London: HMSO, 2000.
Sutcliffe, G. 'Why Football Needs an Independent Regulator'. In *Football in the Digital Age: Whose Game is it Anyway?,* ed. S. Hamil, J. Michie, C. Oughton, and S. Warby, 264–8. Edinburgh: Mainstream, 2000.

POLITICS, THEORY AND PRACTICE

Contemporary community theory and football

Tony Blackshaw

As this edited collection attests, community has become virtually co-extensive with the study of football. You might say that of all the key concepts used to develop some reliable insights into contemporary developments in the game it is the only one that now seems necessary. Indeed today, community exists, unlike class, for example – recently downgraded for reasons including the domestication of football's supporter base and the breakneck appearance of globalization in football studies – only as an eminently serviceable concept for the purposes of critical sociological analysis. It also presents football with the potential of a political mobilizing tool with which to challenge extant inequities in order to give the game a more equitable and inclusive present and future.

Community is undoubtedly one of the frontline feelings of our age. As Bauman points out, it has a warm and friendly sort of air about it; like a balmy summer's day it 'feels good: whatever the word ... may mean, it is good "to have a community", "to be in a community"'.[1] The concept summarily signifies a special way of being together, which seems as if it already has a room in our *doxa* (the knowledge we think with but not about), and not only that, but it is also endowed with an atmosphere all of its own: it stands out among other concepts.[2] In this sense community shares a close affinity with football: if football transcends its status as a sport, community transcends its status as a concept. Community is a concept that has summarily become universal, or so it seems.

Of course community has always been universal in football, in one sense, because any discussion of the game cannot help but be shadowed and cross-cut by the past, where community resides, its status securely sponsored and its fame family-friendly. Indeed, community in football lives off its past. Its narrative is a hymn to the perception of a gentler, more innocent way of life, to days when folk knew their neighbours and stopped on the street to talk to one another. Most football fans know the upbeat story of the golden age of 'the people's game', when working-class communities nestled happily in terraced streets as approximately local cultures of identity and belonging made from the same red brick and mortar as the cathedrals in which they worshiped their local clubs.

Most football fans also have some knowledge of the downbeat version of community, which has no necessary affinity to the past tense. This is the story which, if it too conjures the undeniable 'solidity' of football's 'communities', built on mutual identification and reciprocity, also recognizes that football fans have always sought to express their solidarity in opposition to a supposedly threatening Other; and have always united themselves by vilifying and mocking that Other. In other words, football has always had its own established outlets for prejudice and excessive emotionalism which are located in vicious rivalries that define themselves largely as and by resistance to their bitterest of opponents, blossoming whenever 'we' beat 'them'. Achieving their sensual union through the depredations of their necessary others – a sense of community that is essentially based on and stands for mutual hatred.

Aside the tacit over-simplicity that surrounds such discourses, it is my contention that the way that community is used in football has in recent years become increasingly ubiquitous and tenuous, especially in the way that there is a propensity to either over egg or completely ignore its more insidious features – largely depending on the particular context and the people involved – while appropriating the concept as a signifier of all that is good about the cosy-curl-up-with-your-cocoa side of football. Consequently, the idea of community, both as a theory and an ideology, demands reconceptualization.

At first glance this would seem surprising, since notwithstanding the authenticating trail of its ability to withstand the depredations of time, community is an idea about a collective way of being in the world that unquestionably made its conceptual reputation under the auspices of the 'founding fathers' of sociology. Until now that is, where it seems to exist independently of the academy, like a renegade, forever on the run, always one jump ahead of attempts to identify it with any contemporary conceptual precision. What also makes it so elusive is that there is an edge with community and element of theoretical playing hard to get, which has turned it into a legend of a sort – you might say something like those legends surrounding the great football stars in whose cultural makeup you can see the ghosts of older lives and times – which only furthers its appeal.

Talking tactics

As a result of this conceptual ambiguity, in this essay my intention is to make a fresh contribution to the theory of community with specific reference to football. I make this seemingly prosaic point because the essay is not straight forwardly about football and its communities in the sense dealt with by other essays in this journal. That is it makes no attempt to offer a theory of the relationship between community and football. Rather what it does is problematize the idea of community by asking fundamental questions such as: Is there such a thing as community in the contemporary world? Is community relevant to helping us understand a range of issues related to themes such as identity, collectiveness and belonging in football in a new century? More pointedly, to what extent does the discourse of community ignore those individuals, excluded by the depredations of social class, gender or ethnicity, who can only experience the thrill of being part of a football 'community' by proxy – through the sights and sounds of the internet, television and radio? Is community in football merely a business concept these days? These are essential issues. Not least they raise doubts about the efficacy of community to deal with the inequalities and exclusions that the concept is ostensibly supposed to quell.

My overriding aim here is to develop a theory of community that is made to the measure of the contemporary world of football and which accompanies the purposes of critical analysis better than the current alternatives on offer. In order to go about developing this critique, I unapologetically 'de-centre' football, or in other words, deconstruct the idea that football is a self-contained realm of social and cultural life endowed with its own *causa sui*. My explicit purpose for doing this is two-fold. First, I want to develop a revivified theory of community that is reflective of a world of football that is modern, but which is also modern in different ways than it was in the past. And second, to develop a re-theorization of community with the explicit purpose of offering something by the way of a critique which suggests that to think the unthinkable might just provide us with a more rigorous application of the concept in football studies.

To achieve these aims, the critique developed below is embodied with a dialectic which, to use Tony Giddens'[3] apt expression, is reflective of the double hermeneutic that is the measure of the social world as it is used on the one hand by sociologists and other social scientists in order to 'understand and explain social action' and on the other as it is constituted by everybody else in football, but especially politicians, policy makers and other key 'stakeholders'. Consequently, what follows is divided into two lopsided parts: first, a thorough and critical discussion of the key contemporary theories of community. In this regard, the reader should note that my discussion of orthodox theories of community is deliberately oversimplified. The critique developed here focuses its attention much more closely on recent theorizations, in particular the ideas associated with Anthony Cohen and Benedict Anderson, but especially those of Zygmunt Bauman. And second, a briefer but equally critical empirical examination of the ways in which community is habitually mobilized as a social policy or regeneration tool in professional football in the UK, which focuses specifically on extant ways of dealing with racism in the game.

Contemporary theories of community in football

Isaiah Berlin once said that some things change and some things don't, and that it is important that we distinguish which is which. There is no doubting the fact that the way in which community is understood has changed markedly in recent years. When the concept was theorized in orthodox sociological thought, it was usually defined firstly by breaking it down into the sum of its parts – namely the ideas of geographical propinquity, putative shared identity and common affective union – and secondly by explaining that these constituent parts should only be understood with the proviso that community is also more than these. As Brown, Crabbe and Mellor point out, however, there was (and still is in some cases) a tendency in the sociology of sport literature to centre too much attention on geographical propinquity as being the most 'natural' or 'purest' form of community in football.[4] Perhaps echoing Talcott Parsons' classic structural functionalist assumption that territory is a necessary foundation for the functioning of community: 'a community is that collectivity the members of which share a common territorial area as their base of operations for daily activities'.[5]

Aside this perceptive observation there is another more important reason why we should have reservations about the way in which community was customarily dealt with in orthodox sociology, not least because when it comes to defining the concept these days it may not even be obvious what its constituent parts are anymore. As that most discerning chronicler of the twentieth century 'age of extremes', Eric Hobsbawm, succinctly put it: 'Never was the word "community" used more indiscriminately and emptily than in the decades when communities in the sociological sense became hard to find in real life.'[6] Hobsbawm's crucial observation not only substantiates my argument that when we come to ponder community today there is a certain elusiveness with the idea, but more importantly it also suggests that we cannot hope to deal with the concept in the orthodox sociological sense. However, this metaphysical prognosis is no great help if we are trying to find out something about community's value and meaning in football. Consequently, it is to the Kantian *Ding an sich*, the 'Thing itself', that we must turn if we are going to get to grips with the concept. Indeed, if community is indefinable in the orthodox sociological sense, the only way we can hope to give the concept some clarity is to focus on specific applications and appropriations in the world of football and try to answer and interpret these, and unless this is done the risk is that of conceptual incoherence – a danger, as we will see, exemplified in the work of Anthony Cohen.

The symbolic construction of football's communities

Ostensibly cognisant of the limitations of the orthodox sociological way of defining its key ideas, Cohen points out that it took the genius of Ludwig Wittgenstein to alert philosophy to the efficacy of exploring the ways in which concepts are used in everyday life rather than simply relying on normative definitions.[7] This is the starting point for Cohen's own re-theorization of community, drawn from his empirical research, mainly on the island of Whalsey and the Shetland Isles, which leads him to conclude that boundary marking processes, such as customs, habits and ritual, are vital defining features of community membership because they not only gesture at a shared sense of reality but also shape that reality, even though they are on the face of it merely the imaginary social constructs of both insiders and outsiders. In this respect, Cohen's conception is essentially that of a cultural 'imaginary' of community encapsulated previously in what orthodox sociologists meant when they talked about common affective union.[8] In Cohen's hands, however, the cultural 'imaginary' is something that is also constructed symbolically, and although its 'sense of community' does not necessarily have any spatial significance, putative membership is subject to shared symbolization, shared meanings, and tacit, local knowledge.

However, what Cohen fails to point out is that even if they are empirically informed, concepts have their genesis in the heads of sociologists and other social scientists and can just as well be used to distort social phenomena as they can be said to represent them. Indeed, the problem with Cohen's own account is that it begins with an alternative, applied way of understanding community but ends up 'proving' that theory by referring to *pro tem* events, such as the Notting Hill carnival. In the main this approach crushes atypical anthropological cultures into ready-made mores, cultures and moral ties that make them feel even smaller and tighter, rather than demonstrating that community is still a useful basic concept for interpreting social and cultural life associated with the modern lives of the majority of people.

In spite of this problem there are those who would argue that the usefulness of Cohen's theorization of community for understanding historical and contemporary socio-cultural formations in English football is undiminished, not least because of his argument that 'whether or not its structural boundaries remain intact, the reality of community lies in its members' perception of the vitality of its culture. People [and we might say, football fans] construct community symbolically, making it a resource and repository of meaning, and a referent of their identity.'[9] As Brown, Crabbe and Mellor suggest, Cohen

> points us towards understanding football clubs as symbols around which rituals of communality are acted out. He also provides a theory which enables us to see communal symbols (such as football clubs) as contested phenomena which can mean different things to different people in different historical periods. In this regard, Cohen's theory allows us to move beyond geographically-deterministic understandings of football supporter communities which see functional and inevitable relationships emerge between people and sports clubs in set spatial areas. Instead Cohen allows us to identify individual actors' agency in creating their community formations, and their different interpretations

of them. For some people, football supporter communities may be (and may have always been) entirely geographical affairs. That is simply the way that they choose to define them. However, even these communities can be read as symbolic or 'performative' as people within them seek to 'display' *their* geography through their football support. For others, football communities may represent an entirely different type of bonding. The key point is that Cohen allows us to see football communities as fluid and always open to change.[10]

However, the major obstacle with following Cohen's line of argument is that it would appear that every kind of social relation is potentially and actually a community. As Jenkins points out, one of the key strengths of this theory of community, which is built on a framework that incorporates similarity and difference, is that it 'emphasises that the "belonging" of "community" is symbolically constructed by people in response to, even as a defence against, their categorization by outsiders'.[11] It might have become something of a cliché to suggest that nothing unites football fans like a common enemy, but to paraphrase Jenkins, it is against such a foil that difference is asserted and similarity symbolically constructed in football; it is in the face of the Other that communal identity is necessary. Gregory Bateson's idea of anti-types is useful in this regard because it helps us to recognize that in the realm of football rivalry the other is not merely represented as Other. Rather two opposing sets of supporters polarize and become each other's Other: United as anti-City and City as anti-United. In this way football rivalry can be seen not merely as a clash of opposites, but also as an oppositioning around a clash.

These important insights notwithstanding, another key problem with Cohen's understanding of community – constructed as it is through a theory which puts so much emphasis on inclusion *in spite of* members' ostensible differences – is that it took as its basis Victor Turner's *specific* model of communitas, anti-structure and liminality as it was applied to pilgrimage processes and turned it into a *general* model. There is of course no doubting the efficacy of drawing on Turner's work for understanding the shared rituals associated with the ephemeral social and cultural drama of football spectatorship. However, in adapting a *specific* model which is 'open and specialized' as well as being attuned to 'the immediate realization of release from day-to-day structural necessities and obligatoriness'[12] as a *general* model, Cohen was essentially bringing together what were hitherto separable conventions of the imaginary and the real, the symbolic and the material, the needs of the individual and the collective, as well as similarity and difference, all of which he argued made community real in its consequences in any given context. In doing so he was also surely exaggerating, like Turner, the extent that these opposing conventions can be so easily fused together like an umbrella under which ostensibly anybody, whatever their putative social, cultural, political and economic differences, can potentially shelter.

On the face of it, Cohen's version might appear to be a seductive alternative to classic sociological conceptualizations of community, but it is still in the main an academic rendering of an ideal of community. Indeed, as the history of 'community' relations in football shows, if difference is pivotal to community ways of being in the world, it is always invariably as a response to the incongruity between same and other; that is the *difference* between *our* club and *theirs*. According to Young what always comes with the 'desire' for community is the grounding of two metaphysical essences: on the one hand the metaphysics of *presence* and on the other the logic of *identity*, or what she calls a 'metaphysics that denies difference',[13] which for football means that it is always seems necessary for community to have to define itself by way of frontiers and borders, as Fredric Jameson recently put it, 'by way of a kind of secession: it must always, in other words ... posit an enemy'.[14]

Arguably it is largely due to Cohen that community theorizing has become such a vague and ambiguous activity and it is not unfair to suggest that his contribution to the literature is undoubtedly part of the reason why community has become such an overworked, catch-all concept. We can conclude that what Blackshaw and Crabbe[15] said of that other highly contested concept in sociology, 'deviance', is true of Cohen's arbitrary use of community: it's habitual 'naming' is not really a reflection of some reality; it is rather ideological in that it tends to 'fix' a particular kind of meaning to different and diverse practices and activities and identities, and kinds of belonging, which might otherwise be accompanied by a multitude of other possible meanings and understandings. As Jacques Derrida might have put it, the 'name' community as it is used by the likes of Cohen is so powerful and pervasive that it is its own signature word.[16] And like all other signature words it comes with the promise to consign the present to the future and with it limit the possibilities of choice concerning anything from geographical spaces to social identities, from cultural differences to political exigencies. For example, calling the populace of a poor inner city locality who live in the vicinity of a professional football club a 'community' is not evidence that it *is* a community, but its 'naming' invariably acts as a kind of 'thinking-without-knowing [which] *decides*, precisely, that it is going to know after all in any case. So it *pronounces*, about various matters of which it is ignorant.'[17]

In the end, Cohen's idea of community simply exceeds the possibility of its own representation. Indeed, what he naively calls 'community' is defined not by its ability to transcend the immutability of its orthodox sociological counterpart – in an applied way – but rather by the confirmation of 'community's' immanence, the sense in which its author makes putative assumptions about diverse socio-cultural interaction and institutional orders (and disorders) which are forced to remain within the ontological trajectory of the originary concept itself, but which if he cared to look at through an alternative lens would tell him a good deal more about people's ability to render for themselves imaginative cultural identities and ways of being together somewhere between 'reality' and its 'representation'.

Football's 'imagined communities'

Undoubtedly, the other most influential contemporary use of the notion of community in football studies has been Anderson's idea of the 'imagined community'.[18] Despite any semantic similarities with Cohen's idea that community is to all intents and purposes 'imaginary', Anderson is here engaged with the ideas of nation and nationhood; he is not really talking about community in the way it has been conventionally understood in sociology. As Anderson famously pointed out, the development of print media was the precondition of all modern 'imagined communities' which 'are to be distinguished not by their falseness/genuineness, but by the style in which they are imagined'.[19] With the advent of the appropriate technology it became possible to predicate the nation as a mental construct and the idea of nationhood as a collective state of mind. As he put it, in a much used quotation, 'all communities larger than primordial villages (and perhaps even these) are imagined'[20] – implying that people have to make biased or mythical readings of the past to give the stamp of approval to their values in the present and to enable them to situate and define their collective sense of nationhood.

The idea of the 'imagined community' is something of an oxymoron; that it is a conceptual contradiction in terms because it is difficult to tell what is 'real' and what is not, and what is swinging in the hammock of imaginative supposition strung between the two parts. Unperturbed Anderson suggests the idea of the nation is the ultimate 'imagined community' because it is a cohesive entity that provides its adherents with a common history, a shared culture and apparent sense of purpose. This is perfectly summarized by Bauman, who points out that '[t]he state needed subjects of the state as patriots of the nation, ready to sacrifice their individual lives for the sake of the survival of the nation's "imagined community"; the nation needed its members as subjects of a state empowered to conscript them to the "national cause" and, in case of need, to force them to surrender their lives in the service of the nation's immortality.'[21] In other words, it was only with the emergence of 'imagined communities' that 'the question of nation at the level of creaturely pain and vulnerability and fear of the grave' becomes conceivable.[22]

If as far as Anderson was concerned the nascent nation-state was the first major modernizing attempt to provide collective answers to the questions that previously religions had been capable of making their own,[23] he also purposely developed in his work an understanding of community which did not have its base in social relations, and it is not unreasonable to suggest that he merely 'appropriated the idea ... as a vehicle for explaining the affective loyalties invested in nationalism'.[24] In other words he developed a concept that had close affinities with Hobsbawm and Ranger's idea of the 'invented tradition'.[25] According to Amit, Anderson was not really concerned with the social interaction that compelled ostensibly diverse groups of people to conceive themselves as 'imagined communities', as ready-made nations, but used the concept instead to demonstrate how one particular version of history manages to be tacitly accepted by nation-states and how contemporary circumstances emerged as a result.

However the assumption that Anderson merely used the idea to theorize how the idea could be mobilized by nation-states to predicate the idea of nationhood as a collective state of mind is surely over-simplistic. Still with the publication of the first edition of his book in 1983, it 'wasn't long before imagined communities of one kind or another were popping up almost everywhere'.[26] As Anderson puts it in the preface to the third edition: 'Aside from the advantages of brevity, [the idea of the 'imagined community'] restfully occludes a pair of words from which the vampires of banality have by now sucked almost all the blood'.[27] And so it was the case in football studies where scholars have tended to use the idea in this rather lazy way to suggest that if football supporters believe they are a community – even if it is for only 90 minutes or so – then they are a community.

However, what these kinds of application of Anderson's concept largely fail to recognize is that if football 'communities' are imagined, they are imagined not just because their members will never know most of their fellow-members, but also because the demands and opportunities required by modern living mean that 'imagined communities' are constantly in the process of disembedding and re-embedding, to use Giddens' apt expression. As Sandvoss shows, if football communities are *imagined in structure*, they are also *imagined in content* as football fans claim their individual membership through their putative readings of the values and attributes of the game and their inculcation in its cultural habitus.[28] However, because football fandom today is more transplantable and more transferable, fan communities are increasingly less likely to be bound by propinquity and are more likely to form deterritorialized groupings. As Sandvoss points out, this does not make some football fans 'authentic' and others 'inauthentic': some fans will come, some will stay, and others will go, because today they inhabit a modern consumer culture, and not only that, but they live in a time when it is the liberty of the individual, not the collective, that is the overriding value.[29]

These observations aside, when Anderson said that in the minds of each member of an 'imagined community' lives the image of their communion, which can be conceived as a deep felt mutuality, he was surely onto something else that was useful to scholars of football studies. For they have always pointed out the cathartic, breathtaking intensity of the shared experience of supporting a football club. What he also said about 'imagined communities' being limited by their strictly demarcated, though elastic, boundaries – beyond which lie various threats and uncertainties – suggested something that was obviously pertinent to understanding the dynamics of football rivalry. Sandvoss again demonstrates that this is no longer confined to localities, as football's communities have undergone a transformation from territory to the semiotic space of the 'imagined community'.

The most compelling use of Anderson's understanding of community in the sociology of football literature, however, has featured in the work of Anthony King,[30] who clearly recognizes that in a society which is no longer institutionally enclosed within the framework of the nation-state as it was conceived in early modernity, it was perhaps inevitable that sport, and particularly football, would come to play such a pivotal role in allowing individuals to express their cultural identities through both local and national versions of collective expression. As he puts it:

> the use of the term 'invented tradition' or 'imagined community' to describe ... [football fans] ... should not be interpreted as claiming that they are a specious social group whose political claims can therefore be dismissed. Rather, the notion of invented tradition [or imagined community] highlights the actual process by which this group has come into being. Despite its appeals to a working-class tradition, this group's formation is not primarily determined by objective and prior social facts such a class location but rather the group arises out of the frequent interaction of quite socially diverse individuals at football games. Following these interactions in which these individuals come to recognize each other and form relations with each other, appeals to notions of 'tradition', 'the working class' and 'Manchester' [and we might add community] become the key ways in which a common identity between them is established and the group comes into being. The putatively long-standing traditions to which fans appeal, in fact, refers to the practices of those individuals who are currently present in this group (whatever their social origins and history of support) and the appeal to tradition serves to highlight their shared contemporary experiences and understandings.[31]

What also makes King's analysis all the more convincing is that it provides evidence of an applied sense of Cohen's symbolic construction of community in which both dedicated football fans and less committed consumers of football alike can shelter under the same umbrella.

However, what King perhaps fails to take sufficiently into account is that if the 'imagined communities' surrounding football are sovereign, it is not because they exist at that particular stage in history when freedom is only a rare and much cherished ideal vis-à-vis Anderson's 'imagined communities', they exist because fans *choose* to support their clubs and national teams. In marked contrast to Anderson's nation-state 'imagined communities', football's 'imagined communities' do not make totalizing claims on the individual – nor could they even if they wanted to – and are by contrast never fully guaranteed. Football, as the great Liverpool manager Bill Shankly famously said, 'isn't a matter of life and death, it's more important than that'. But what he failed to point out is that there is a gap between what people actually believe and the way they live, and when all is said and done we all know that football is, after all, only a game. On the face of it this may seem like a rather trite criticism, but implicit to it is the key point that in order to develop a proper understanding of the relationship between community and football we need to do what most other scholars, including Cohen and King, have failed to do, and that it is map out the social conditions which explain *why* community has become the natural noise of football's contingent present.

Zygmunt Bauman: the community that cannot help but be missing

Why community and why now? The starting point of Bauman's theory of community is the paradox that it was only when we were no longer sure of community's existence that it became absolutely necessary to believe in it. In marked contrast to what the current Zeitgeist suggests, community is an achievement of social circumstance that is most secure when it is silent, when it is simply *there*, rooted in daily experience. Community is also absolutist; it makes a total claim on the individual. What is most striking about community is its completeness, the integration of subject and object, individual and society, and to this extent it does not have to justify its existence. As Raymond Williams once observed, community is 'always has been'; it exists – like God – independent of any other ground because its presence is sufficient explanation for its existence.

Drawing on Hegel's famous dictum that 'the owl Minerva begins its flight only with the onset of dusk', Bauman suggests that we embrace community with such aplomb these days precisely because there exists no 'solid' ground under which the conditions of a community could ever be realized.[32] Bauman's key argument is that we need to grasp the basic point that community is incommensurable with the contingency of modern living; and if we were really honest with ourselves we would acknowledge that community ways of being together, in which the identity of the individual cedes to the collective habits of the majority, disappeared with the onset of modernity. His key argument is that we 'imagine' community with philosophy's grey in grey only because we cannot help ourselves 'lusting for community', 'searching for community', 'inventing community',[33] when really we should be talking about the 'end of community', the 'transformation of community' or the 'appropriation of community', instead of fumbling around in the ashes of something that in effect is broken, caput, gone. As he puts it:

> Community can only be numb – or dead. Once it starts to praise its unique valour, wax lyrical about its pristine beauty and stick on nearby fences wordy manifestos calling its members to appreciate its wonders and telling all the others to admire them or shut up – one can be sure that the community is no more ... 'Spoken of' community (more exactly: a community speaking of itself) is a contradiction in terms.[34]

Bauman is suggesting that the key peculiarity about this modern yearning for this dead thing is the one that Raymond Williams would have called unaware alignment turned into active commitment, or in other words, the moving of social relationships to human consciousness.[35] Alignment, like community, is what you are stuck with, while commitment is something that is merely *felt* – as a duty, an obligation, a responsibility or even a desire.

Liquid modern community

Men and women today know that they have to live without the glowing warmth that people born of a community are able to give out to one another, or even the largely 'predictable and therefore manageable' habitus of the 'heavy' and 'solid' hard-ware focused modernity. This is because they inhabit a more 'light' and 'liquid' soft-ware focused modernity which is underpatterned and underdetermined, rhizomatic rather than rooted, its trains of experience busy with unremitting new arrivals and speedy departures, as well as unexpected diversions, derailments and cancellations. As Bauman points out, liquid modernity is not an easy world to live in because it comes with a pervasive feeling of insecurity that is so widespread and overwhelming that people's lives are enveloped by *Unsicherheit*, or in other words, the relentless change, risk, uncertainty, fragmentation and the concomitant absences which mirror the dislocated lives they lead.[36]

To this extent liquid modernity's inhabitants choose to live their lives on the hoof, with social relations experienced as speedy, fleeting and transitory and in effect governed by 'the continuation of disembedding coupled with dis-continuation of re-embedding'.[37] Liquid modern men and women are shape-shifters whose identities lie not within them, so much as in the current form they assume at any particular moment and in their ability to metamorphose, while defying any tacit expectations about gender, age, ethnicity and social class, never mind expectations about community values such as mutual obligation and reciprocity. With liquid modernity, a postulated unity of interests gives way to more specialised *habitats* and associated lifestyles and individuality and men and women become '*operators* who are willing to forego a secure source of fruit for a chance to connect more of the world'.[38] They invest their hopes in 'networks' rather than 'communities', 'hoping that in a network there will always be some mobile phone numbers available for sending and receiving messages of loyalty'.[39] Consequently, individuals going their own way in a world tend to hook up with other individuals with whom they share common interests to form what Bauman, after Maffesoli,[40] calls neo-tribes. In this sense communities today are nothing more than self-defined communities, conceptually formed 'by a multitude of individual acts of *self-identification*.[41] Sucked as it has been into the soft melt of liquid modern identity making, community is but an individualized expression; painted only for individuals, which is also part of its liquid modernity. The truth is that liquid modern community does not deliver any universal cheer; it is imagined only for individual consumption not to alleviate collective shiver.

'Each person is truly alone', somewhat ironically wrote the author of that classic account of community *Gemeinschaft und Gesellschaft* [Community and Society] Ferdinand Tönnies.[42] What Tönnies could never have anticipated, however, is the irrefutability of Bauman's argument that community is by now merely a nourishing antidote to what has become an unquestionably individualized life. It is individualization rather than community which sets the template for men and women's lives and lifestyles. As Bauman points out, 'none of us, or almost none, believes (let alone declares) that they are pursuing their own interests', but that is exactly what a life governed by individualization demands of each and every one of us.[43] Community is merely a conduit for our individualized hopes and fears and it is the fact that men and women know that they are today truly alone that makes it so absorbing. Indeed, if community cannot help but be absent modern men and women nonetheless miss it in their individuality, in the privatized style of independence which they value even more, and which they consider to be the supreme source of their happiness. It is this observation that holds the most important clue to the central meaning of community in liquid modernity.

Liquid moderns only want community the way *they* want community: individually wrapped and ready for individual consumption. Individualized men and women live their lives as if they do not need the support and backing of the world, with its ready made fixtures and fittings, its conventional points of orientation. They are so individualized and independent that they can live their lives anywhere, and wherever they are is potentially home – for the time being at least. They are the point of their own orientation, their own landmarks. They merely need an old-fashioned solution to deal with the intermittent loneliness which comes with being an individual de facto and they find the answer in community.

To reiterate: absence has always worked powerfully on the modern imagination, and it is the paradox that it is in it's very absence that lies the primary reason for our obsession with community. Indeed, its inexhaustible appeal owes much to the idea that it is something long lost that people have decided they do not want to be missing from their lives. But community is especially important to liquid modern men and women not merely because they *covet* the warmth and the comfort of its common denominators, but because they cannot *bear* its never-ending *absence*. This is why they hunt for community, in order to give some *presence* to a life which Milan Kundera would say is unbearably light. This is why the sanctity of the community narrative has become the hymn of the Zeitgeist, its strongly held aesthetic philosophy.

Community is imagined to be something that will transport liquid modern men and women into a place where they believe they won't mind that many of their other future options have been closed off with the fateful 'I commit myself to this community'. The trouble is that liquid modernity is a world 'marked by the dissipation of social bonds, that foundation of solidary action. It is also notable for its resistance to a solidarity that could make social bonds durable – and reliable'.[44] When they have been transported to that place they invariably find that they really do mind, very much; and they can't wait to leave. Indeed, instead of being drawn into the community and embracing the 'responsibility for responsibility' that living one's life in a community brings, the individual is inevitably going to distance him or herself from it. You might say liquid modern men and women hanker for the certitudes of community but they know deep down that they need most of all the latest aids to liquid modern living – both the equipment (most of all their precious mobile phones) and attitude (individualistic and about me, me me) – in reserve to face the present and the future.

In the event, the idea of liquid modern community is a gloss which merely *stands for* deep mutuality and long-standing reciprocal relationships. It is saved from commitments and life-time guarantees by the shadow its own impermanence, which ensures that it remains an admirable way of living, while – like all good consumer durables – redeeming its ostensibly functional qualities. Community has been stripped of its original identity and turned into a commodity for private consumption which makes it a concept made to the measure of the current liquid modern for shaping and training its inhabitants 'as consumers first, and all the rest after'.[45] The upshot of this is that community, in common with other goods on offer in liquid modernity, is likely to self-destruct once it has been consumed, leaving no trace behind it. If it came in a packet, it would have to feature the following consumer warning: as you might expect just one discernable flavour, but no detectable staying power (although quite useful for making its purchasers feel momentarily fulfilled).

Liquid modern community and football

Bauman's theorization of community brings our attention to the disposable nature of contemporary culture, and this is where his ideas have generally been applied to football. As Brown, Crabbe and Mellor point out, 'following Bauman ... it could be argued that even when the existence of football clubs contributes to friendship ties and regular social contact, they are only really producing the "cloakroom communities" or "ad hoc communities" that are common to ... "liquid" modernity'.[46] This is the kind of community that boils over rather than one that simmers – that is its brilliance and its difficulty. According to Bauman these magnesium flare-like ways of relating – usually nothing more than the 90 minutes or so that constitute a cup final win – beg a certain intimacy, but they are not likely to be reciprocated because they are too self-contained. For Bauman, the football crowd is not a community (except symbolically or perhaps unintentionally) but at the very most it is the spectacle of community[47] that knows its own songs – a collective body palpable but nonetheless constructed of individuals, first and foremost, everyone of them.

If the spectacle of football's community is at all real it is constituted by figures of the imagination who simply know the same football narratives. After all football is that realm of popular culture that is most capable of providing the security of a recurring cultural identity, not least because it has the hegemonic power to generate the kind of indelible collective memory experience that is the individual memory of each of its fans. For as that most perceptive of football's interpreters Gordon Burn recently pointed out, drawing on the observations of the American writer Howard Singer, 'the cultural artefacts that carry the memory today are marked not by their privacy, specificity for the individual and implicit insignificance for everyone else, but specifically by their publicness and their claims to significance'[48] – Gazza's tears, Cantona's kung fu kick, Zidane's head butt, and so on. These collective memory experiences might be said to be made and maintained by what Foster identifies as 'predigested forms and programmed effects' and the notion of what he calls, after Adorno, 'fictional feelings' which anybody can experience but no individual can quite possess.[49]

In Bauman's schema such experiences are evidence of the false front of the spectacle of football's community, whose adherents are quick to shed their carnival masks once the partying is over. Bauman suggests that football's brief carnivals of 'targeted solidarity' and 'targeted patriotism' disguise the fact that by and large we treat the 'others' who we encounter on a daily basis as rather 'a vague, diffuse threat', instead of a stream of opportunities for coming together.[50] As Debord might have said, the spectacle is the kind of image that you leave looking forward to a second viewing, but few encounters are likely to invite continued experience as the vitality of the spectacle tends to die in its performance. These are not communities which are intended to outlast the celebrations for which they have been manufactured. Football fans may treasure the sport's collective imagination for its reciprocation of their individual passion for the game, and this is why they return time and again, but the spectacle's potency is likely to fade with too much exposure and its seemingly extraordinary closeness may well crumble at the first sign of ennui – or insufficient victories – and what was once tacit can quickly seem tepid. In liquid modernity, nowhere stays wondrous for very long once you are there, and football is no different from any other aspect of consumer culture.

Dealing with Bauman's detractors

In marked response to Bauman's overly theoretical approach, the idea that the ship of community in football – co-extensive of course with working-class cultural history in football studies – is driven by currents much deeper than individual consciousness runs as a thread through the football literature (for one of the most sophisticated and up-to-date versions see Robson).[51] The central point of Robson's thesis is that football fans differ from the rest of the liquid modern pack in that supporting a football team is a collective experience where it *is* possible to secure for one's cultural identity a degree of continuity over time. Bauman simply misses the point that for most fans being part of football implies an implicit and special pact. For the likes of Robson, it is a permitted space right at the centre of football's togetherness, a separate but still shared silence and concentration. If you are a fan you know when you are in a community because you feel truly at home, truly permitted to be yourself. In this sense, football's community is a profound agreement of cultural identity, companionship and breathing space, one of the most intimate things permissible in a modern public space.

Bauman's response would no doubt be that these allusions to community are but simulated truths in the sense that their artifice is consciously part of their ocular and aural pleasure. There are many currents and cross-currents that run underneath the Zeitgeist, but none of them allude to communal ways of living. His key message is that it is precisely because the era of liquid modernity is 'the time of precarious, insecure and uncertain existence, of fragile and ineffective interhuman bonds' that professional football, with the durability of its city clubs and international teams and its cycles of leagues and competitions, would come to play such an important role for its fans cultural identities.[52] Indeed, there is no doubting the fact that there are many fans whose sense of identity is bound up with football because it is a bonding agent of local and national pride and togetherness like no other. In a world of 'generalised and structurally induced *destabilization* of identity',[53] where else can so many diverse people maintain and celebrate their local and national cultural identities?

What the cultural history approach also tends to overlook is that the problem of looking for 'depth' over 'surface' relations vis-à-vis Robson in order to better understand community in football is ironic since it implies what Amartya Sen calls the centring of a 'solitarist' theory, which tends to discuss football identities as if they are formed by membership of a single group, when the reality is that football fans have always belonged to other 'communities' as well.[54] The other problem with these types of analysis is that they tend to discount too readily the deepening individualization of spectatorship that has accompanied more recent historical changes in professional football in the UK, ignoring the actuality that football is a truly penetrating symbol of popular culture that does not even need direct shared experience, and which speaks between individuals who have apparently little shared social, cultural and economic ground between them.

This leads me to the final criticism of Bauman's theory of community which suggests that what hardly registers in his analysis is the difference between consumers of football and the types of supporter communities discussed by Brown, Crabbe and Mellor in their essay in this issue. There are indeed major variations in degrees of faith and dedication between these two ideal types – one is lightly committed in its performativity, while the other is heavily committed. There is no doubting that for those inclined to light commitment, 'community' has a job on its hands trying to compete with other creedal currency on the market – the shelves are simply overstocked with alternative identities begging for their attention – while for those inclined towards heavy commitment there is one cultural identity that is important in their lives and they are not only fully committed to it but also insistent on politicizing it, for example, the contesting of corporate power at Manchester United by the withdrawal of support and setting up of FC United of Manchester as a community-based club.

However, what Bauman's critics fail to recognize is that he does not refer to this type of collective activity in his discussions of community because following the logic of his critique they do not carry the stamp of a liquid modern community. They should instead be discussed on the basis of what they actually are: collectivities – the kinds of institutions that form 'a bounded area of social order reproduced and recreated by actors who have a sense of membership of that social order'[55] and are constituted by like minded individuals, generous reciprocation and the necessary ups and downs that accompany them.

As that most astute chronicler of the Zeitgeist Adam Phillips recently put it in another context, 'there is something about modern life that generates fantasies of closeness, of intimacy, that are way in excess of human possibility'.[56] We can wrap up this discussion of Bauman by suggesting that what Phillips is describing is something which many people close to football's heart do with community. To reiterate: Bauman's central message is that liquid modern community might come with its own uplifting messages but the shame is that it is simply not convincing. Following Malešević and Haugaard, we can conclude that the movers and shakers behind FC United of Manchester constitute not a community at all but a collectivity *with its own* consciousness (as opposed to an imaginary or imagined community *without* its own consciousness). And we can conclude that, in this regard, Bauman's central message is this: if we are going to use the conception of community, we not only need to use it *critically*, but also *appropriately*, and certainly not in contexts where there are available alternatives (such as the concept of collectivity) better made to the task in hand.

The politics of community policy: or the limits of social capitalism

Yet, even if this guidance seems to make sense, in the present-day political climate it is likely to fall on deaf ears given the ideological domination of community in public and social policy. Left or Right the recipe is repetitive, additive, impressing 'Third Way' adherents with its inexhaustible quality of power and plunder. The basic line is: more community – and more – still more community – still more. The major attraction of 'community' policies is of course that they promise the kinds of social intervention that are 'bottom up', rather than 'top down', and which in the process of delivery are more reflective of the interests of local communities. However, as Bauman points out, social and public policy recast as community policy somewhat more usually rests on a promise of simplification, which

> brought to its logical limit ... means a lot of sameness and a bare minimum of variety. The simplification on offer can only be attained by the separation of differences: by reducing the probability of their meeting and narrowing the extent of communication. This kind of communal unity rests on division, segregation and keeping of distance. These are the virtues figuring most prominently in the advertising leaflets of communitarian shelters.[57]

As Baudrillard might say, communitarian shelters are most effective in depriving their clients of their 'right of revenge' and their capacity to take reprisals. To use an analogy from popular culture, 'all the rage' community initiatives work just like those 'all the rage' comedy television shows such as *Little Britain* and the 'comedy' work of BBC everyman Jonathan Ross, in the sense that by affecting a self-deprecating ironic tone in the delivery of their services they effectively short-circuit our opportunities for criticizing them. As that most acerbic political commentator Peter Preston recently put it:

> Try community charge in poll-tax mode and it's a spoonful of sugar to help the medicine go down. Try care in the community and it's somebody over there calling on poor Mrs Bloggs once a week if she's lucky. Try America's community colleges and we mean comprehensives not city academies. Try community service orders, and the guy over there clearing rubbish could find himself in prison next time.[58]

All of which suggests that community policy, as well as being limited to policing the 'flawed consumers'[59] also tends to exacerbate the conditions it promises to rectify by intensifying the kinds of social and cultural separateness that communitarian's latently dream of, and for which they are hardly ever condemned.

Both Bauman and Preston are perhaps guilty of over egging their pudding by exaggerating the political influence of the communitarian project on UK social policy, which increasingly goes by the name of social capitalism and is the glossy packaged front end of the wannabe street-wise-community-cool the government tries so desperately to trade under. Indeed, social capitalism is most attractive to the government because not merely does it speak the brand confident, popular and stylish, in a 'do-what-the-manual-tells-you' kind of way – stakeholding and capacity building, bridging capital and bonding capital, bottom up and grass roots – but it also gives every appearance of having managed to embrace the ethos of community practice.

However, social capitalism is appealing to politicians first and foremost because it is a social policy intervention 'managed' on market lines. As that most astute observer of the current political scene Ross McKibbin recently put it, Britain is governed by an increasingly narrow political elite, who no matter what their formal political allegiances 'are all the same kind of people who think the same way and know the same things' and who are committed to a 'model of market-managerialism [which] has largely destroyed alternatives, traditional and untraditional' – including the idea of any proper communitarian option.[60] As McKibbin goes on to point out, these politicians might not have conceded, contra Margaret Thatcher, that there is such a thing as '"society", a "we" as well as a "me"', but they nonetheless tacitly adopt the neo-liberalist mantra that ours is a 'highly privatised society increasingly shaped by "social entrepreneurs", charities, do-gooders, people with axes to grind, and our old friend "faith groups": in other words, a society based on the model of a market and restored social hierarchies'. The upshot of this is that so-called 'community policy' often has nothing to do with either a policy or a community in the conventional sense. Indeed, there is frequently not anything remotely 'community' about many so-called initiatives on offer other than what's in their labelling, namely because they do not have the essential conditions or purpose that sustain a 'community'.

Football and its 'black communities'

Football's 'community' is full of such absences. Take, for example, the issue of its relationship with black supporters. Mercifully they no longer have to cope with the sharp ambivalence of 'community' that Caryl Phillips did supporting Leeds United in the 1960s and 1970s, when he came to know what it was like to be under excluding eyes, to be an unwelcome presence meeting a collective gaze of '[t]he same people who would hug you when Leeds scored (which we often did), would also shout "nigger" and "coon" should the opposing team have the temerity to field a player of the darker hue'.[61] Yet, if Phillips' Afro-Caribbean experience of community's more insidious and invidious imperfections is today thankfully a thing of the past, black fans still cut peripheral figures even amongst supporters of clubs in the most 'multicultural' of British cities and towns.

There is no doubt that community-based anti-racism campaigners, such as 'Football Unites Racism Divides' (FURD), which emerged as a response to racial prejudice at Sheffield United,[62] have done a great deal over the last twenty years or so to challenge racism in football. However, on the whole, anti-racist action has hitherto been poor at including football supporters as active participants in anti-racism campaigns through community action. Instead there has been a tendency to develop a technological or managerial strategy for dealing with racism which on the one hand draws on the vocabulary of community through the writing of a variety of media discourses, and on the other stages anti-racist spectacles in the hope that supporters will respond by repudiating discrimination and prejudice based on ethnic difference. The idea being that it is in the very heart of football's community – the stadiums – that the rhetorical effectiveness of media *persuasion* can be effectively combined with the spectacle of *manipulation*, which together will prevail against the irrationalities of racism in the game.

With regard to media persuasion, the National Anti-Racism Week of Action in Football is an example of how football's marketing experts are very capable of design, trapping the 'community's' homely, feel-good features in the themed package-holiday brightness of official football programmes: pop-up communities in rainbow colours – black and white and yellow and brown – which incidentally also feed the voyeurism of those whose job it is to sell the idea of successful 'community integration'. The transforming trick being in the placement of key black characters among the most pleasing attributes of the all-together-now chorus scene, which the photography and its accompanying vocabulary or sales pitch draw on to capture absolutely the sense of community as something fixedly resolute. The point of this kind of photo-montage exercise in 'social inclusion' being to show that community life is not just outside *your* door, but it is also right there in *our* stadium. But the reality is of course more often than not that the community's putative black members will remain just imaginatively constructed walk-on partners wheeled out for the day in what is nothing more than a media-staged appearance.

As part of the research for the 'Football and Its Communities project',[63] I attended the Leeds United versus Blackburn Rovers match during the National Anti-Racism Week of Action on 6 October 2003. True to form the match day programme was themed in the way described above. To its credit, however, Leeds United used the 'voices' of its players to speak up against racism and it also ran two features on Albert Johanneson, the club's black star from the 1960s. One was a report on a project about the player being developed by students at a local high school and the other was an article on the problems of racism he encountered during his time at the club, recalling in particular his negative experiences of Zulu chants from Everton supporters following the release of the film by the same name in 1963, which depicted the siege of Rorke's Drift. Between them these different features helped to focus supporters' attentions on some concrete 'race' issues related to both Leeds United and the city.

However, it was the spectacle of *manipulation* that was foregrounded at Elland Road on that particular Saturday afternoon. Indeed it was the 'star attraction' of that spectacle, 'The Mighty Zulu Nation', a young singing group from South Africa, that specializes in educational activities, performing at community events, schools, universities, where it introduces Zulu culture through dance, song and folklore, which ultimately led to the day becoming nothing less than a staged portrayal of racialized stereotyping, albeit concocted and performed by 'authentic' Zulus. I am not for a minute suggesting that 'The Mighty Zulu Nation' in any way incited the Leeds United and Blackburn Rovers supporters to chant racist abuse, because it didn't. But I think that on that particular day there was a very real sense in which the spectacle of *manipulation* created a kind of manufactured 'exoticism' that operated as a contradictory, or more precisely ambivalent, form of cultural 'imperialism' which ended up 'creating' stereotypes of those who were performing, to the extent that it rendered a distorted reality about what it means to be 'black' and 'African'. I will elaborate.

As I have mentioned already, Debord famously suggested that ours is a society intent on offering us spectacles. However, Nicholas Bourriaud[64] has recently extended Debord's theorem to suggest that the society of the spectacle has been superceded by 'the society of extras, where everyone finds the illusion of an interactive democracy in more or less truncated channels of communication'. At Elland Road these 'channels of communication' were manipulated to predicate the idea of a community as a mental construct in Anderson's sense, assuming that if the crowd could be encouraged to believe it was a community and to act together like a community, even if only for the duration of the match, then it would be a community. In a nutshell, the National Anti-Racism Week of Action activities on that particular Saturday afternoon culminated in the stage management of a community *ex opere operato* ready-made to exist through its own performativity.

The performativity of community in football is of course nothing new and match day always has been a liminal experience which, as Bernice Martin once said of cultural life more generally, is 'pretty carefully programmed as a kind of inversion of workaday role play ... like switching over the TV channel or changing a new script; everyone knows his [sic] part in both channels and both scripts'.[65] The performativity of community in football is a mobilizing force precisely because of the inherent spontaneity of its all-together-now chorus, whose primary goal is to prevent its adversary answering back. Its power is in its communication – an organic performing not a pre-planned cure. However, in this instance the performativity of community was not only stage-managed rather than organic, but it was also shot through with a profound anxiety about political correctness, and at every level, irony. The pre-match events were both entertaining and edifying, particularly the 'raise the flag against racism' which was visually very effective, but from the moment 'The Mighty Zulu Nation' graced the Elland Road pitch during the half time interval the day slipped into stereotypical mode.

The metaphor behind the performance of 'The Mighty Zulu Nation' was the link between the 'local' and 'global' in the fight against racism in football as students from a local school and two Durban schools joined an all-together-now chorus of the world community as one. Yet from the vantage point of the part of the ground where I was sitting the principal absentees from the larger performance were local black people in all their 'Leedsness'. In the absence of the 'real thing', the palette of the imagined community had to brighten its colours and deepen its textures with something staged. In this regard, the spectacle did everything any utopia ought to do, on the surface of things at least: it placed in the collective imagination in an alternative way rethinking the human experience; in this instance the global community. It also evoked a world in which 'The Mighty Zulu Nation's' ancestors lived. And it tried to deliver both of these in the present day of autumnal Leeds, gift wrapped and ready for the crowd's collective consumption.

As Baudrillard might have put it, at Elland Road the spectacle replaced the deluded revolutionary idea of trying to find a utopian community with 'the "fateful" strategy of escaping from the world of ... phenomena into the world of simulation, into an artificial world that was, potentially, virtually perfect'.[66] The major problem with the staged authenticity of this 'perfect crime' was not so much its 'unrealness', more its insignificance in football supporters' day-to-day lives. The spectacle merely performed its acts of manipulation to an audience, and was so artificially constructed that any lasting effect or affiliation was extremely unlikely.

In a nutshell what was performed had no large meaning for football supporters and as a community intervention it had little effect. I doubt whether the spectacle changed any racially segregated hearts and minds of the almost exclusively white crowd as the organizers had hoped. As it was, the lasting memory of attending the match was of a staged portrayal of ethnic stereotyping dedicated to the recycling of exotic otherness – albeit concocted and performed by 'authentic' Zulus. What the supporters got was the spectacle of simulation that was not only culturally blinkered in its struggle for political correctness, but which also, it might be said, perpetuated the very racism it was attempting to alleviate.

As Said famously suggested, a key part of the process of colonization was ensuring that the colonized Others had a distorted representation of themselves.[67] But in this case what the football supporters witnessed was ostensibly 'authentic' representations in a post-colonial world bolstering a process of self-colonization in a deterritorialized global context – which begs the question: should we not be surprised that football supporters have stereotypical assumptions about ethnic minority groups when faced with such a candid exhibition of cliché? As Spivak points out, that 'Othering' is a dialectical process there is no doubt and such events remind us that even when self-representations of 'race' and ethnicity are deemed to be 'authentic', this does not preclude them being component parts of deeply rooted processes which perpetuate racism – albeit in an alternative and less menacing form.[68]

As I have suggested already, the other key problem was that the whole event dealt with things largely outside football fans' day-to-day experiences and as a consequence the moral themes hovering over the issues associated with racism remained merely part of the spectacle itself. Indeed, the evidence for this assertion was on the day plain to see. During the match there was constant barracking of the two black Blackburn Rovers players Andy Cole and Dwight Yorke and the Turkish player Kerimoglu Tugay which, for the organizers, no doubt spoiled the day. The reasons why particular players from opposition clubs are singled out and heckled by football crowds are many and complex. The barracking given to Cole and Yorke was no doubt in part due to their Manchester United history and the Turkish connection with Tugay was undoubtedly related to the deaths of the two Leeds United supporters Christopher Loftus and Kevin Speight, who both died as a result of fatal stab wounds before a UEFA Cup semi-final game against Galatasaray in Istanbul during the 1999–2000 season.

Whilst recognizing that Manchester United are one of Leeds' fiercest rivals and the Turkish issue is obviously sensitive and especially challenging at the club, what the circumstances for these types of incidents suggest to me is that what is required for promoting anti-racism and multi- or trans-cultural community in football is not so much spectacles which are specially choreographed to begin and end on time. Rather we need a process of community development which requires a sophisticated understanding not only of specific cultures but clearly thought out strategies for breathing life into the cross-fertilization which might not have taken place but for ignorance, intolerance or distrust. It is not sufficient simply to provide some exotic fun in order to effect change, and community interventions must have the necessary tools to explain and alter extant relations of power and domination in football.

Conclusions

The foregoing discussion of community and football has revealed not only the limitations of community but also its critique. It has also revealed that notwithstanding the conceptual difficulties and actual problems associated with the continued use of the concept, any discussion, even one as critical as this, is, paradoxically, likely only going to enhance the importance of the term even more. As Bauman points out, today we inhabit a world which perceives that there is something wonderfully seductive about the idea of community; that it has about it an indefinable *flowing* ambience (rather than any definitional *fixity* as such), a feeling of warmth and belonging that attracts like a magnet, to the extent that it is difficult for anybody to think about it without being captivated by its sense of marvel.[69]

To use a football analogy, we can conclude that community today is like a dead George Best which has ascended to a kind of legends hall of eternal fame. But it is also like the living George Best in the sense that no matter what are its good intentions it has descended into a career based on a series of perpetual unsuccessful comebacks. It's as if together these two factors act as guarantors of its popularity, supporting its refusal of a decent burial and ensuring, as Ulrich Beck might say, that it continues to prey on the living in a zombie form, giving it an unlikely kind of permanence in a liquid modern world ostensibly unpredisposed to its vicissitudes.[70] Scholars of ideology might conclude that there is a false consciousness associated with community which is both at the same time something nostalgically remembered and magically recreated, but also something suppressed – a denial of the real.

We can also conclude that we live in an age when community in football cannot be itself – when it has become, to paraphrase Bauman, a poor man's concept forever defiant of 'reality' that will not bend to its shape.[71] Instead, community has metamorphosed into that rare thing, a concept which in the everyday world seemingly has no need to be what it says it is, somewhat ironically doesn't really have to try to be – couldn't be if it wanted. It's as if community merely took on an alternative gloss as a reflection and a response to the absence of its own presence, to its own sense of lack. As Baudrillard might say, it has merely become the simulacrum of itself, which 'feigns' the features of the 'real thing' and in so doing inadvertently reinstates and reconfirms the supremacy of the 'original'.

This is not the same as saying that community in football is fake or bogus, just that it 'renders null and void the opposition between truth and falsity, or between likeness and its distortion'.[72] In the event any attempt to 'prove' that community in football is a sham is likely to be rendered pointless since, as we have seen, everywhere in the game it has all the hallmarks of the 'real thing', present in its brightened look and surface textures, that feel just right, unerringly faithful to the originary concept. To reiterate: the upshot of all this is that community is likely to remain in the foreseeable future the kind of concept whose virtue is taken for granted, and about whose credentials no one is in the least bit interested.

As we saw, Bauman suggests that community came of age in a liquid modern world of *Unsicherheit* (complex combination of uncertainty, insecurity, precariousness) in which economic inequality, social upheaval, collisions of culture, political instability, existential insecurity, environmental disaster, the daily dread of dangers of terrorism, all came to assume new and threatening forms. Given that football is for many people imagined as a tried and tested safe haven from these insecurities and threats, there is no doubt that it will continue to play a pivotal role for individual fans as a key site of the liquid modern ongoing search for identity, for something and somewhere to belong in a world that is constantly changing. For the foreseeable future it is also likely to be increasingly appropriated by politicians, football clubs and community activists as a site for ameliorating these affects on a more civic scale.

However, those intent on re-running community's narrative, digitally re-mastered and free of its more insidious and invidious imperfections – endlessly appropriated, endlessly used to give credence to yet another media persuasion or spectacular manipulation strategy – would be best advised to recognize its limitations. As Wittgenstein used to say, the limits of our language are the limits of our world; and there is evidence enough to suggest that the limits of community in football have begun to contract. What football needs right now are initiatives that deal in the density of the game's collective relationships not in their epic scale, and which allow football's traditional constituencies to assert themselves in their time-honoured loud ways at the same time as allowing entry to those claiming hitherto unimagined rights to space in the game, in the process going some way to helping it find for itself a new kind of dignity.

Notes
1. Bauman, *Community*, 1.
2. Ibid.
3. Giddens, *Constitution of Society*.

4. Brown, Crabbe and Mellor, 'English Professional Football'.
5. Parsons, *The Social System*, 91.
6. Hobsbawm, *Age of Extremes*, 428.
7. Cohen, *Symbolic Construction of Community*.
8. See Bell and Newby, *Community Studies*.
9. Cohen, *Symbolic Construction of Community*, 118.
10. Brown, Crabbe and Mellor, 'English Professional Football', 170.
11. Jenkins, *Social Identity*, 112.
12. Turner, 'Center Out There', 217.
13. Young, 'Ideal of Community', 302.
14. Jameson, 'Pseudo-Couples', http://www.lrb.co.uk/v25/n22/jame02_.html
15. Blackshaw and Crabbe, *New Perspectives*.
16. Derrida, 'Ulysses Gramophone'.
17. Jarvis, 'Thinking-Cum-Knowing', 45.
18. Anderson, *Imagined Communities*.
19. Ibid., 6.
20. Ibid.
21. Bauman, *Liquid Fear*, 37.
22. Clark, 'In a Pomegranate Chandelier', 6.
23. Ibid.
24. Amit, 'Reconceptualizing Community', 6.
25. Hobsbawm and Ranger, *Invention of Tradition*.
26. Amit, 'Reconceptualizing Community', 8.
27. Quoted in Clark, 'In a Pomegranate Chandelier', 6.
28. Sandvoss, *Game of Two Halves*, 92.
29. Bauman, *Postmodernity*.
30. King, 'Outline of a Practical Theory'; 'The Lads'; 'Postmodernity of Football Hooliganism'; 'Football fandom'; 'Abstract and Engaged Critique'.
31. King, 'Abstract and Engaged Critique', 708–9.
32. Bauman, 'Community'.
33. Bauman, *Intimations of Postmodernity*, 134.
34. Bauman, *Community: Seeking Safety*, 11–12.
35. Said, 'American Intellectuals', 336.
36. Bauman, 'A Europe of Strangers', 7.
37. Blackshaw, 'Interview with Zygmunt Bauman', 2.
38. Wellman, Carrington and Hall, 'Networks as Personal Communities', 134.
39. Bauman, *Liquid Fear*, 70.
40. Maffesoli, *Time of the Tribes*.
41. Bauman, *Intimations of Postmodernity*, 136.
42. Tönnies, *Gemeinschaft und Gesellschaft*.
43. Bauman, *Liquid Fear*, 114.
44. Ibid., 21.
45. Bauman, *Identity*, 66.
46. Brown, Crabbe and Mellor, 'English Professional Football', 10.
47. Debord, *Society of the Spectacle*.
48. Burn, 'Waiting For Cloughie'.
49. Foster, 'Yellow Ribbons'.
50. Bauman, *Liquid Fear*, 68.
51. Robson, *No One Likes Us*.
52. Bauman, *Liquid Modernity*, 177.
53. Dunn in Bauman, 'Cultural Variety', 175.
54. Sen, *Identity and Violence*.
55. Malešević and Haugaard, 'Introduction', 2.
56. Phillips, 'Thwarted Closeness', 31.
57. Bauman, *Community: Seeking Safety*, 148.
58. Preston, 'There is No Such Thing'.
59. Bauman, *Work, Consumerism*.
60. McKibbin, 'Destruction of the Public Sphere', 3.

61. Phillips, 'Leeds United', 299.
62. See Back, Crabbe and Solomos, *The Changing Face of Football*, 215–17.
63. The Football and its Communities project was a major three-year research project (2002-2005) for the English Football Foundation that explored the relationship between English professional football clubs and 'communities' of various types, and the ways in which individual football clubs and the English football industry more generally respond to new community development agendas. The final report can be found on the Substance Co-op website: http://www.substance.coop/?q=publications_football_and_its_communities.
64. In Foster, 'Arty Party', http://www.lrb.co.uk/v25/n23/fost01_.html.
65. Martin, *Sociology of Contemporary Cultural Change*, 73.
66. Baudrillard, quoted in Turner, 'The Intelligence of Evil', 12.
67. Said, *Orientalism*.
68. Spivak, 'Can the Subaltern Speak?'.
69. Bauman, *Community: Seeking Safety*.
70. Beck, 'Zombie Categories'.
71. Bauman, *City of Fears*, 5.
72. Bauman, *Liquid Fear*, 45.

References

Amit, V. 'Reconceptualizing Community'. In *Realising Community: Concepts, Social Relationships and Sentiments*, ed. V. Amit, 1–20. London: Routledge, 2002.
Anderson, B. *Imagined Communities: Reflections on the Origin and Spread of Nationalism* 2nd ed. London: Verso, 1991.
Back, L., T. Crabbe and J. Solomos. *The Changing Face of Football: Racism, Identity and Multiculture in the English Game*. Oxford: Berg, 2001.
Bateson, G. *Naven*, 2nd ed. Stanford, CA: Stanford University, 1958.
Baudrillard, J. *The Intelligence of Evil or the Lucidity Pact*. Oxford: Berg, 2005.
Bauman, Z. *Intimations of Postmodernity*. London: Routledge, 1992.
———. *Postmodernity and its Discontents*. Cambridge: Polity Press in association with Blackwell, 1997.
———. *Work, Consumerism and the New Poor*. Buckingham: Open University Press, 1998.
———. *Liquid Modernity*. Cambridge: Polity Press, 2000.
———. *Community: Seeking Safety in an Insecure World*. Cambridge: Polity Press, 2001.
———. 'Cultural Variety or Variety of Cultures?' In *Making Sense of Collectivity*, ed. S. Malešević and M. Haugaard, 167–80. London: Pluto Press, 2002.
———. 'Community'. Paper presented at the *Communities Conference*, Trinity and All Saints College, Leeds, 18 September 2003a.
———. 'A Europe of Strangers'. *European Synthesis* (2003b). http://www.europesynthesis.org.
———. *City of Fears, City of Hopes*. London: Goldsmiths College, 2003c.
———. *Identity: Conversations with Bendetto Vecchi*. Cambridge: Polity Press, 2004.
———. *Liquid Fear*. Cambridge: Polity Press, 2006.
Beck, U. 'Zombie Categories: Interview with Ulrich Beck'. In *Individualization*, ed. U. Beck and E. Beck-Gernsheim, 202–13. London: Sage, 2002.
Bell, C.R., and H. Newby. *Community Studies*. London: Allen & Unwin, 1971.
Blackshaw, T. 'Interview with Zygmunt Bauman'. *Network: Newsletter of the British Sociological Association* 83 (October 2002): 1–3.
Blackshaw, T., and T. Crabbe. *New Perspectives on Sport and 'Deviance': Consumption, Performativity and Social Control*. Abingdon: Routledge, 2004.
Brown, A., T. Crabbe, and G. Mellor. 'English Professional Football and Its Communities'. *International Review for Modern Sociology* 32, no. 2 (2006): 159–79.
Burn, G. 'Waiting For Cloughie'. *The Independent Arts and Books Review*, August 25, 2006.
Clark, T.J. 'In a Pomegranate Chandelier'. *London Review of Books* 28, no. 18 (September 2006). http://www.lrb.co.uk/v28/n18/clar05_.html
Cohen, A.P. *The Symbolic Construction of Community*. London: Tavistock, 1985.
Debord. G. *The Society of the Spectacle*. New York: Zone Books, 1995 (1967).
Derrida, J. 'Ulysses Gramophone: Hear Say Yes in Joyce'. In *A Derrida Reader: Between the Blinds*, ed. P. Kamuf, 569–600. New York: Columbia University Press, 1991.

Foster, H. 'Arty Party'. *London Review of Books* 25, no. 23 (December 2003). http://www.lrb.co.uk/v25/n23/fost01_.html
———. 'Yellow Ribbons'. *London Review of Books* 27, no. 13 (July 2005). http://www.lrb.co.uk/v27/n13/fost01_.html
Giddens, A. *The Constitution of Society*. Cambridge: Polity Press, 1984.
Hobsbawm, E. *Age of Extremes: The Short Twentieth Century 1914–1991*. London: Abacus, 1995.
Hobsbawm, E., and T. Ranger, eds. *The Invention of Tradition*. Cambridge: Cambridge University Press, 1983.
Jameson, F. 'Pseudo-Couples'. *London Review of Books* 25, no. 22 (November 2003). http://www.lrb.co.uk/v25/n22/jame02_.html
Jarvis, S. 'Thinking-Cum-Knowing: a Book Review'. *Radical Philosophy* 117 (2003): 43–5.
Jenkins, R. *Social Identity*. London: Routledge, 1996.
King, A. 'Outline of a Practical Theory of Football Violence'. *Sociology* 19, no. 4 (1995): 635–51.
———. 'The Lads: Masculinity and the New Consumption of Football'. *Sociology* 31, no. 2 (1997a): 329–46.
———. 'The Postmodernity of Football Hooliganism'. *British Journal of Sociology* 48, no. 4 (1997b): 576–93.
———. 'Football Fandom and Post-national Identity in the New Europe'. *British Journal of Sociology* 51, no. 3 (2000): 419–42.
———. 'Abstract and Engaged Critique in Sociology: On Football Hooliganism'. *British Journal of Sociology* 52, no. 4 (2001): 707–12.
Maffesoli, M. *The Time of the Tribes: The Decline of Individualism in Mass Society*. London: Sage, 1996.
Malešević, S., and M. Haugaard. 'Introduction: the Idea of Collectivity'. In *Making Sense of Collectivity*, ed. S. Malešević and M. Haugaard, 1–11. London: Pluto Press, 2002.
Martin, B. *A Sociology of Contemporary Cultural Change*. Oxford: Blackwell, 1981.
McKibbin, R. 'The Destruction of the Public Sphere'. *London Review of Books* 28, no. 1 (January 2006). http://www.lrb.co.uk/v28/n01/mcki01_.html
Parsons, T. *The Social System*. Glencoe: Free Press, 1951.
Phillips, A. 'Thwarted Closeness'. *London Review of Books* 28, no. 2 (January 2006). http://www.lrb.co.uk/v28/n02/phil01_.html
Phillips, C. 'Leeds United, Life and Me'. In *A New World Order*, 298–301. London: Secker and Warburg, 2001.
Preston, P. 'There is No Such Thing as Community'. *Guardian*, July 18, 2005.
Robson, G. *No One Likes Us, We Don't Care: The Myth and Reality of Millwall Fandom*. Oxford: Berg, 2000.
Said, E.W. *Orientalism: Western Conceptions of the Orient*. London: Penguin, 1978.
———. 'American Intellectuals and Middle East Politics'. In E.W. Said, *Power, Politics, and Culture*, ed. Gauri Viswanathan, 323–42. London: Bloomsbury, 2004.
Sandvoss, C. *A Game of Two Halves: Football, Television and Globalization*. London: Routledge, 2003.
Sen, A. *Identity and Violence: the Illusion of Destiny*. London: Allen Lane, 2006.
Spivak, G. 'Can the Subaltern Speak? Speculations on Widow Sacrifice'. *Wedge* 7, no. 8 (Winter/Spring 1985): 120–30.
Tönnies, F. *Gemeinschaft und Gesellschaft* [*Community and Society*]. London: Routledge, 1955 (1887).
Turner, C. 'The Intelligence of Evil: an Introduction'. In *The Intelligence of Evil or the Lucidity Pact*, by J. Baudrillard, 191–230. Oxford: Berg, 2005.
Turner, V. 'The Center Out There: Pilgrim's Goal'. *History of Religions* 12, no. 3 (1973): 191–230.
Wellman, B., P. Carrington, and A. Hall. 'Networks as Personal Communities'. In *Social Structures: A Network Approach*, ed. B. Wellman and S. Berkowitz, 130–84. Cambridge: Cambridge University Press, 1988.
Young, I.M. 'The Ideal of Community and the Politics of Difference'. In *Feminism/Postmodernism*, ed. L.J. Nicholson, 300–23. London: Routledge, 1990.

POLITICS, THEORY AND PRACTICE

'Our club, our rules': fan communities at FC United of Manchester

Adam Brown

Introduction

This essay considers some of the approaches to thinking about 'communities' in football discussed elsewhere in this volume in relation to FC United of Manchester (FCUM). In this essay we will first look at the formation of the club in the changing context of English football and its threat to established communities of Manchester United fans; we will then consider the different community formations amongst the club's fans; and thirdly the political purpose and 'politicized' expressions of community within the club's fan culture.

FC United were formed as part of the rejection by some fans of the take-over of Manchester United by the Glazer family in 2005. Since then the club has been successful in gaining two successive promotions that has lifted them from the North West Counties Division Two to the Unibond Northern Premier League Division One, four promotions from the Football League. They have at times attracted enormous crowds for that level of football, averaging 2,500–3,000 with a high point of over 6,000, in leagues where the average is below 100. However, this progress has not been without its controversies – not least from Manchester United fans opposed to the club – and difficulties, with the club suffering a drop in attendances in 2007/08 and as yet unable to secure a permanent home ground.

'FCUM' – 'Fuck 'em!': formation and threats to established communities

Origins and background

Two key elements of Manchester United's fan culture underlie the formation of FC United which are important to recognize in order to understand the nature of its fan communities. First, is the 'football-political' position adopted by a significant section of Manchester United's Manchester-based match going support over the preceding decade, which sought to oppose the Plc structure of the club and which most notably helped prevent the sale of the club to BSkyB in 1999.[1] This created a lineage and tradition among fans – including the attempts of campaign group Shareholders United to build a collectively owned stake in the club – in which certain principles about football became accepted. This 'common sense' – encapsulated by the cry of 'Not For Sale' – was actively promoted by the Independent Manchester United Supporters Association (IMUSA) and included a belief in football clubs being not-for-profit, owned by their fans (with the Barcelona example routinely cited), and not exclusionary in commercial practices. This itself was fed by the broader development of a constituency promoting fan ownership of football clubs.[2]

Second, this cultural-political position of United fans ran alongside and was underpinned by a resurgence of expressions of a local Mancunian identity among the club's more vocal fans. This sought to contest popular characterizations of Manchester United supporters as 'glory hunters', southern, 'plastic' and lacking in authenticity as fans[3] by affirming their origins in (working-class) Manchester, and re-igniting a rivalry with neighbours Manchester City. This process, at times nostalgic for a pre-Premiership form of football, problematically stressed the importance of 'authentic' notions of football and attacked the 'television-driven', 'commercialized' form of the game.

This linked directly to opposition to the development of the club as a global leisure brand and to successive Plc Chief Executives, Peter Kenyon and David Gill, whose strategy was to 'monetise the fan base' and 'turn fans into customers'.[4] Within this we can see a revitalized, localized cultural 'resistance' becoming a resistance to forces of international capital, the most recent form of which came with the Glazer takeover.[5] This opposition also stood in contrast to the broader direction of the game's development, in particular its symbiotic relationship with media capital and the more recent inward investment of international capital into English football.[6]

Although unique in this context – something which contrasts to previous 'fan movements'[7] – the broad and varied opposition of Manchester United supporters ultimately failed in stopping Glazer's takeover.[8] Thus, whilst both of the forces outlined above fed the opposition to Glazer and later helped shape the characteristics of FC United, the fragility of oppositional fan communities was exposed under the weight of the corporate takeover of the club. These fluctuations and different responses emphasize the fluid, temporary and conflictual nature of football supporter communities and the problematic use of the term. The emergence and persistence of FC United however, which one critic claimed 'won't last until Christmas', also suggests the contrasting sustainability and regenerative resilience of them.

Although the possibility of forming a 'breakaway' club was initially mooted in 1998/99, FC United was first publicly proposed in United fanzine, *Red Issue*, in February 2005. During the Glazer takeover, in May and June, a series of public meetings were held for Manchester United fans which led directly to the founding Extraordinary General Meeting of FCUM on 5 July 2005.

Within these discussions, various references were made to the notion of 'community'. Supporters talked of the need to 'keep the community together' referring to groups of fans who had followed the club home and away over the preceding years, essentially match day communities. People referred to the struggles that had been fought against the Plc and BSkyB and the need to carry that on through FC United, by the more politicized fans who had among themselves developed a sense of collective community during the campaign. There were also claims that the Glazers had taken a club which, despite all the rhetoric and stereotypes maintained a strong fan base in Manchester, away from its 'local communities' and that 'local fans' would be further 'priced out' (a suggestion which perhaps failed to take into account the regenerated and gentrified city).

Two other factors are important to note about this stage of developments. One, that the issue of pricing local fans out sat alongside long-standing complaints about the 'commercialization' of English football, the deterioration of the match-day experience, particularly at Old Trafford, and the antagonism many local fans felt from the 'bag carriers', 'Johnny Come Latelys' or 'new fans' that they felt were displacing them.[9] For these fans the Glazer takeover was a 'tipping point' in a gradual process of alienation from the top flight of the modern game.

Second, the public meetings and pronouncements by fans were dripping in unashamed socialist symbolism. At the meeting at which fans decided to pursue the FC project, in late May 2005, a huge flag hung behind the members of the FCUM Steering committee on stage reading: 'Hasta La Victoria Siempre'.[10] T-shirts to help fund raise for the new project were already on sale, declaring in 1970s style, stencilled type-face around a clenched red fist: 'FC United: Our Club, Our Rules'. This, above all, is the symbolic motto for fans of the club and epitomizes a collective *political* belief in how football should be governed and owned, something which we return to in more detail later.

'FCUM – Judas Scum': fragility and conflict in fan communities

Of course, sentiments such as those above were not shared by all, or even the vast majority of Manchester United fans, local or otherwise, in the light of the Glazer takeover. If the formation of FCUM was the result of an 'atomized football environment' (see below), this atomization was explicit in terms of the division which cut across Manchester United fan communities as the club was formed. The politically symbolic nature of the fans' communities and expressions that we discuss below must also be recognized, as with all communities, as defining 'the other'. In this communities are exclusive as well as inclusive, and it is some of those that have not 'joined' FCUM that demonstrate the limits, fragility and problematic nature of thinking of fan 'communities'.

For all the tangible, long term and deep relationships that may have been formed among groups of FC United supporters that we discuss below, however 'solid' some of the manifestations and protestations of 'community' are, we do also have to recognize that, taking the unity around the Glazer protests as a starting point, the FC collective represents a *choice* and a minority one at that. Faced with the Glazer takeover fans had a number of options with the following polarities:

- Boycotting MUFC and either supporting FCUM or not attending any football versus remaining as before, attending Manchester United matches regularly.
- 'FC loyalists' only attending FC United versus 'Dualists' attending both Old Trafford and Gigg Lane
- Disinterest and hostility to the team being successful which would bolster the Glazer regime versus
- Supporting Manchester United by watching on television and not giving 'one penny' to Glazer

These divisions have rumbled on through the FC fan communities since the club's formation. From the outset – at those meetings held in Manchester's Methodist Hall – the club sought to portray FC United as a 'broad church' to which a broad spectrum of Manchester United fans and local communities would be welcomed. Officials were careful not to be drawn on calling for those still attending Old Trafford to give it up and come over to FC; and many fans worked hard to promote unity across this division.

However, some of those still attending Old Trafford have been particularly antagonistic to FCUM and its supporters. Particularly centred around some of the club's hooligan elements (also some of its most hardcore *local* fans), opposition to FC United was characterized by accusations of 'deserting' Manchester United, of 'disloyalty' and even wild accusations of 'profiteering'. One character, a leading figure in the 'Men in Black' hooligan grouping,[11] even went as far as to hand out leaflets urging supporters to give up FC United – albeit on the one day which saw the club's record attendance of 6,028 on the last day of the 2005/06 season. At one moody FCUM match in Salford in 2006/07, two Manchester United fans ran onto the pitch with a banner reading, 'FCUM – Judas Scum'.

From the very formation of the club there was widespread debate with at times very acrimonious discussions in pubs, between friends and family and on internet message boards. FCUM was for some itself the 'splitting' of a formerly united fan community; whilst for FC fans, the failure of others to uphold the 'no customers, no profits' and 'not for sale' position of the anti-Glazer campaign was itself a betrayal, some describing those that carried on at Old Trafford as 'Vichy reds'.

So as well as FC United's fan communities being understood as based on *gemeinshaft*, face-to-face relationships, themselves a rebirth of community from the atomization of the Glazer takeover; we also have to recognize that these community formations embody both division and unity, inclusion and exclusion, and the personal, cultural, economic and politically motivated choices of individuals which are geared toward collective, political action and community formation. What is certain is that these fluid 'communities' of fans at FC United and Manchester United remain intensely contested.

'Real' and 'liquid' fan communities

'See you at the match': geographical, match-day and face-to-face communities

As we have argued elsewhere in this volume, there are a number of 'common sense' assumptions made about football clubs and the representative role they play for particular geographical communities. Historians such as Holt, Mason and Russell[12] have highlighted the roots of this in the key role football clubs played in creating a sense of common identity for particular geographical areas in the UK in the midst of rapid late nineteenth-century industrialization. Most clubs, through their name, nickname, badge, fan songs and in some cases ground location, to varying degrees still reflect those origins in one way or another.

In some ways the call to 'keep the community together' in the formation of FCUM was an appeal to this notion. It was a concern with the locally-based, match going community of Manchester United fans that are referred to in King and elsewhere.[13] This 'community', which in some ways had been bound tighter during the campaign against Glazer – a process Delanty refers to as 'community as action'[14] – was partly based on notions of what 'authentic' football consumption meant to them and the superiority of consuming it 'live' at the match – the 'you don't know unless you go' philosophy of some fans.

The supporters who 'left' Old Trafford and now follow FC United did not decide to simply gather in pubs to watch Manchester United, although of course many fans do just that, creating communal atmospheres I refer to elsewhere.[15] That would have satisfied the boycott of the Glazer regime and an ability to keep supporting 'United', but instead they decided to form a new club 'in the image that we wanted Manchester United to be'. This was based around their notions of maintaining their match day experience with their friends and families and creating a 'spectacle' around which these communities could continue; as well as propagating a political position about how football clubs should be run. It was in part, a desire to recreate the face-to-face local communities that such geographically based understandings of football communities embody.

Indeed, notions of locality were centrally important to the identity of the club and it has maintained a desire to be locally focused. However, for a club which is based in Manchester, plays its games in Bury and has a fan base that is spread across Greater Manchester (with a handful much farther a field), this is problematic to say the least. The 'nomadic' existence of FC United will continue until it secures its own ground when it will be presented with the issue of creating new connections with long-standing residential local communities.

There have been a number of protracted debates in a variety of contexts (at the match, on internet forums, in pre- and post-match drinking sessions, at members' general meetings, at the Junior Supporters Group) about where FC United should target as its 'home'. Frequently these are very subjective to the individual concerned, but it will present a fascinating process when the club does attempt to lay roots in one particular locality. It will be a relatively unique situation in which a pre-existing fan community that has been, to some extent maintained, to some extent reborn with a new identity, moving into an established area with its own traditions, communities and allegiances. The implications that has for understandings of football clubs representing geographically based communities remains to be seen.

Perhaps more pertinent to FC United's formation is the discussion around Giulianotti's view that football clubs can be understood in terms of providing 'pre-modern' forms of local community bonding:

> According to this line of thinking, football clubs developed links with communities because they helped to sustain the close, face-to-face, geographic, affective communities that were under threat during modernity. To put it another way, they helped to preserve a version of Tönnies' [1974] pre-modern *Gemeinshaft* emotional community bonds amongst people.[16]

As we have seen above, at the very formation of the club, fans talked of the need to 'keep the community together', referring to the shared sense of belonging of match going Manchester United fans and some of those involved in the campaign against Glazer. Faced with the absence, due to refusing to attend Old Trafford, of the only gathering point most fans have – the match – many of those behind FC United felt that they were providing an event, a location, a match day, around which the micro communities of supporters could coalesce. This was about a face-to-face relationship with each other that only attained any sustained meaning around football matches. We have seen how Giulianotti and others talk of an atomized urban environment creating the need for opportunities for people to form collective bonds in the late nineteenth century. For these fans it was the atomized *football* environment of the take-over of Old Trafford that was creating the need for a new club; but in some ways the instrumental nature of the process remains similar.

'This thing of ours': liquid communities?

As outlined elsewhere in this section of this volume, theorists such as Cohen, Delanty and Bauman have contended that it is a mistake to regard communities as uniform, static or singular. For Bauman, although in contemporary society 'community' has been a convenient, warm, catch-all for a 'lament to modern times and as an appeal to a better future',[17] to regard communities as meaning anything substantial is wrong. Bauman goes on to argue that trying to understand communities as solid, meaningful and based on face-to-face relationships of some depth is a mistake, referring to ad hoc or 'cloakroom' communities, temporary in nature, shallow in form. The *choice* that Manchester United fans made to form FC United is perhaps an example of what Bauman would term a 'cloakroom community' in a 'liquid modernity'.

Certainly, observing FC United fans around match days supports the thesis that the club has provided a location for the sustenance of fan communities, the contingency around which they might form. Fans have for instance formed their own, overlapping groupings around travel – with particular groups meeting up in Manchester city centre pubs and travelling on the tram to the ground the club uses for home matches, Gigg Lane in Bury; or travelling together from Prestwich in a minibus now bedecked with the club's name; or on the self-styled 'boogie bus' which some supporters organize for away games.

Occasions such as key away dates in the season's calendar provide opportunities for the reaffirmation of match day communities of fans. FC United's first season threw up an attractive fixture against Blackpool Mechanics to be played at Blackpool FC's ground. Dubbed the club's first 'Euro away' by the 5,000 supporters who made the trip, it cemented many face-to-face relationships of groups still falling and reforming out of the boycott of Old Trafford.[18]

Certain pubs have become the location for the maintenance and creation of both old and new microcosms of fan communities. The Swan and Cemetery on Manchester Road was a favourite FC United pub in the early days and some groups of supporters still gather there loyally. The team's manager routinely took players to The Swan after matches with the deliberate aim of promoting bonding between fans and players and an attempt to contrast it to the isolation of 'celebrity' players at the top of the game. However, this 'closeness' also served to cement the 'local celebrity' of players and, whilst some clearly felt uncomfortable with this new found status, others revelled in it. This reached its apogee at the end of the first season when, as Winners of the North West Counties League Division Two, the team travelled by open top bus the few hundred yards from Gigg Lane to the pub where thousands of fans celebrated in the streets.

However, this pub location was never 'fixed' or challenged as some notions of geographical communities suggest. As fans grew accustomed to the unfamiliar environs of Bury in 2005 and 2006 – which had for many replaced very long standing haunts in Manchester associated with Manchester United match days – new pubs were discovered and there has been a fluidity to the locations for pre- and post-match drinking of different groups of fans. 'The Swan', Waterloo, Pack Horse and Staff Of Life all have vied for the attention of groups of fans and whilst for many it is a case of where it is easiest (or cheapest) to get a drink, for others these pubs are the key to match day rituals of meeting friends, sharing gossip, discussing football and enjoying drunken humour.

Yet even here, divisions are evident between some who refuse to, or can't, watch Manchester United on television, and those that enthusiastically support the team. Furthermore, some fans have been accused of being 'cliques' at away games by deliberately seeking out pubs that have not attracted large numbers of FCUM fans. Again, this is partially pragmatic: less fans means smaller queues, less noise, less attention from authorities, and more chance of establishing a positive relationship with the bar staff and landlord, which could prove invaluable in securing a post match beer. It is also of course part of fans' distinction that King has discussed. This desire of some fans to 'stay under the radar' whilst others 'balloon around' in public (to use local vernacular for excessive displays) reflect different understandings of 'a good match day' which produces different communities of fans that then tend to stick together, particularly around away matches.

These collective expressions and identifications may indeed be very temporary and contingent as Bauman would contend. People who drink together in the same pubs even end up in different parts of the ground during the match. However, it is the very ability to stay together and celebrate as a collective that has been a key attraction for most supporters alienated from the Premier League-era all ticketing which King has described as the 'panoptic isolation of the seat'.[19]

Within the 'home' ground of Bury, a playful rivalry has developed between the Manchester Road End (the first popular area for fans to gather) and the end of the Main Stand nearest to them. The Manchester Road End respond to taunts of 'jesters' (a jibe to 'plastic' fans who wear club merchandise) with chants of 'MRE', to which the Main Stand respond with 'we are the Main Stand, we're louder than you' (a claim to authenticity and the importance of vocally supporting the team). Although this suggests different match day communities forming, however playfully, in practice the space that this rivalry occupies is in part the result of the absence of many opposition fans at this level of football. It is also a 'division' that disintegrates in the instance of unifying celebration or backs-to-the-wall support of the team. Nowhere was this more evident than when a relatively small crowd of 1,800 watched their team crash out of the FA Vase to Quorn FC in December 2006.

Although at the start of the game there had been the usual exchanges between the two stands, by extra time, with FC down to nine men, the disparate communities of friends, families, travel, pubs and stands were unified as a supporter community through unending singing and clapping. Notably, it was also about much more than the moment, much more than an event of bonding that would be soon forgotten as fans returned to their 'mundanity': many reflected that it had been a key watershed for the club and its fans, cementing a collective sense of belonging in the struggle of the match – and a performance of (an imagined) community.

It was a game (albeit a defeat, or perhaps especially because it was a defeat in a season of easy wins) at which fans enthused about how they had felt 'as passionately as I ever did about "big United"', a game which had 'the best atmosphere since the 1980s' and was the 'coming of age' for the newly formed fan communities of FC United. Indeed, the sense of belonging that is evident in internet posts, fanzine articles, interviews and conversations suggests aspects of strong community formations, epitomized by the fans' flag in red, white and black which says simply: 'This Thing Of Ours'.

So, whilst one has to recognize the temporality, fluidity and multiplicity of fan communities, we also have to recognize the unifying, binding, singular, resilient tendencies within fan groups, and in particular the power of football to generate these more lasting senses of unity.

As we argue in the introduction, Bauman's articulation that such spectacles are events around which people temporarily unite as communities, which are *ad hoc*, 'peg' communities, in which they 'do not knit themselves into deep reciprocal relationships as a result'[20] is inadequate in describing some football fan communities. As with our wider research into Football and its Communities, we can see at FC United both the temporary and ad hoc nature of community, but also the forming of deep and lasting bonds between fans, in which their participation at the club – as supporters, branch members, families, volunteers, helpers, propagandists, even manager and players – has been a structuring part of their lives, many of whom will say the experience has 'changed them forever'.

In the first two years of the club's existence, there were at least 300 people regularly volunteering, up to 100 of those regularly on match day. This activity includes: manning the reception and dealing with visiting teams; security; selling draw tickets; writing, editing, designing and selling programmes; selling fan merchandise (at the 'Mega Stall' as opposed to Manchester United's 'Megastore'); running internet sites and fan forums; organizing meetings; raising sponsorship; working on grant applications; the organization of reserve and under-18 teams; drafting club policies and procedures; producing architect's drawings and schemes for a new ground; helping the promotion of the club; and helping with coaching and community work and more. It is a vast input of human resources and for many a huge personal commitment that stretches way beyond match day.

In 2007, the club moved to formalize the volunteering structure so that fans who were working for free for the club received some form of accreditation that might be of use to them in their non-football 'real' work. However, such participation – this deep commitment in very practical ways – does not include both the additional commitment that it has taken from fans to leave their former club and form FC United; the formation of supporter branches and groups which meet outside of match day; the organization of fund-raising events; nor the ongoing, day to day engagement between fans, the emotional commitment supporters give, and the way in which 'real' meaning in their lives is provided through their fandom of FC United.

Even on-line, in internet forums where there is perhaps the greatest possibility to temporarily adopt different characteristics, identities and names, where sociation can be at its most fluid and 'thin', there have developed structuring, deep commitments between fans and between fans and the club. Given the atomization of previous, Manchester United match day fan communities, these 'virtual' forms of association have produced lasting, meaningful friendships and collective identifications in the 'real' world. Crucially, it is the match day that brings the real meaning for fans, the opportunity to do what is being written about, but the internet offers an opportunity to 'extend' the match day long into the week. For some, however, the internet becomes a structuring element in their lives, not only in terms of the amount of time spent on fan forums, but even in the adoption of chat room names in real life. Whilst that is the accepted norm for some supporters, others have disparagingly called those who do this as 'internet mongs'.

Although of course fan communities at FC United do also 'dress for the occasion' and 'return to their ordinary, mundane and different roles',[21] such a level of commitment and structuring of their lives by their decision to support FC United undermines any attempt to dismiss these as lacking in 'grounding, structuring, deep forms of sociation' as in Bauman's cynicism about contemporary communities.

'Our club our rules': symbolic communities and political action

The 'politics' of FC United is not easily thought of in a conventional way, or as suggesting any sort of homogeneous unity among fans. Indeed, the amount of debate is very high, with a recent club poll on ticket prices generating 25 pages of comment within a day. Rather, such statements represent a symbolic summary of one of the central tenets of FC United, that it is supporter owned and democratically run, around which the various debates rage. 'Our club, our rules' was also embodied in the structure and formation of the club, as a supporter-owned, democratic, not-for-profit organization, which was ratified at the EGM in July 2005 and infuses the fan expressions at the club.

Political formations

Fans adopted a legal entity as an Industrial and Provident Society (one of the few mutual forms of ownership possible in English football and still outlawed by the Football League). This enshrined a one-member one-vote governance structure, allowing members to determine the rules of the club as well as policies such as name, badge, shirt design, ticket prices and so on. A 'Manifesto' was adopted and incorporated into the club's rules, which declared:

> FC United of Manchester is a new football club founded by disaffected and disenfranchised Manchester United supporters. Our aim is to create a sustainable club for the long term which is owned and democratically run by its members, which is accessible to all the communities of Manchester and one in which they can participate fully ... a football club which addresses the concerns which many Manchester United fans have had over the last decade or more with how the club and football have developed, culminating in the club's takeover by Malcolm Glazer ... Above all we want to be seen as a good example of how a club can be run in the interests of its members and be of benefit to its local communities. Seven core principles of how the club will operate are set out below, and once agreed by the membership, will be protected by all elected Board members:
>
> (i) The Board will be democratically elected by its members.
> (ii) Decisions taken by the membership will be decided on a one member, one vote basis.
> (iii) The club will develop strong links with the local community and strive to be accessible to all, discriminating against none.
> (iv) The club will endeavour to make admission prices as affordable as possible, to as wide a constituency as possible.
> (v) The club will encourage young, local participation – playing and supporting – whenever possible.
> (vi) The Board will strive wherever possible to avoid outright commercialism.
> (vii) The club will remain a non-profit organisation.[22]

This belief in democracy, mutualism and 'not-for-profit' was a counterpoint to the dominant, corporate, consumer-driven football culture. Yet the *Manifesto* also emphasized issues of accessibility, inclusion (particularly of young people), participation (including volunteering), ownership and responsibility. It placed the club's local context and obligations as a central issue, maintaining a thread about a Mancunian identity which had been a feature of Manchester United fan expressions. All these concerns have been 'buzz words' for New Labour in the last decade, but expressed and executed here very differently indeed.

Songs and stories – the cultural politics of fan expressions

To understand this in the context of FC United, however, also means understanding the individual and collective political project that the club represents and the political-symbolic nature of supporter communities and identities at the club.

As argued elsewhere in this volume, Cohen's notion of symbolic communities seems particularly relevant to understanding football's communities. Certainly at FC United it is important to recognize the individual agency of actors – particularly those who took the decision to completely boycott Manchester United – in actively creating and promoting community formations and their different interpretations of them. Even the extent to which FC United represent communities in the locality of Greater Manchester, is something that is actively promoted and 'performed', emboldened by rituals and match day symbols.

At home games the average 2,500 crowd stands in the Main Stand and Manchester Road End of Bury's 10,000 capacity Gigg Lane. The other two empty sides are adorned with flags and banners proclaiming a huge array of associations. These range from geographical ones such as 'Tameside Reds', 'Bury and Prestwich Branch', 'Monsall, Innit'; to musical associations 'FCUM: Punk Football' (complete with skull and cross bones, a tag promoted by club fanzine and reflecting the 'DIY' and rebellious nature of the club's beginnings) and 'FCUM: Northern Soul'; to personal ones – 'Kev Lewis On Tour' – reflecting the desire for celebrity of some.

These visual representations are enhanced by the adoption of colourful club-related memorabilia, most notably the red, black and white 'bar scarf' that thousands carry to the games. This itself is a symbolic gesture loaded with meaning: some supporters of FC United will have spent the previous decade and a half shunning the 'official' merchandise at Manchester United, not only for their 'distinction' from other fans as King has described,[23] but as a symbol of 'resistance' to the 'commercialization' of Manchester United and football more broadly. Yet, with the twin desires to both resurrect what are perceived as former modes of consumption in football (standing, singing, drinking, ecstatic display) and helping the club by providing funds, supporters have taken enthusiastically to club merchandise. Indeed, even in this, it is not a 'passive' consumption, but one in which fans suggest the merchandise to be produced and at times help design it (the new shirt for the 2007/08 season was voted on in principle by fans, then the design was democratically selected).

Aurally, of course, this performance is enhanced by the songs and singing that are a badge of honour for many FC United fans, some of which we outline below. The manager, Karl Marginson, has described the supporters as adopting a '90/90/90 culture': '90% of the fans singing for 90% of the 90 minutes of the match'[24] and the at times raucous atmosphere is something that is frequently referred to in newspaper and television reports on the club, as well as by opposition fans.

Symbolic nostalgia for a more 'traditional' epoch of football consumption is also evidenced in events such as the hiring of a steam train to take fans to an away game at Ramsbottom – the 'Rammy Rattler' as it became known. In this case, as you looked down the platform from the Victorian railway bridge at the Ramsbottom station toward hundreds of fans disembarking into this Lancashire mill town, through the smoke with bar scarves waving and the cacophony of ancient football rattles, you could be forgiven for needing to check that it was in fact the twenty-first century. Yet the key point about this was that it was not a re-enactment, like the Sealed Knot battle recreations, of a past event, it was not 'fake', but a contemporary event. For many fans it was realizing – through a day long drinking session, chaotic standing conditions behind the goal, match-long singing, and celebrating winning promotion – a mode of supporting football that has been outlawed in much of the higher levels of the English game. Yet, it *was* also deliberately nostalgic and as such performative – something rudely hammered home as fans woke, wearily to the modern world the next day.

Within this process we can see the active pursuit by fans of the 'liminal' moments that Turner describes and which we referred to in the Introduction to this volume. These are the '"between" moments such as carnivals, rites of passage and rituals in which normality is suspended'[25] and the role they play, according to Turner, in the symbolic renewal of collective identity. Days such as the 'Rammy Rattler' may be 'out of time' in more ways than one, but it also produced 'intense group bonding and feelings of associated community'[26] that last far beyond the day itself.

These events are themselves not uncontested. The tendency of some fans to 'go too far', get too drunk (indeed some have bemoaned the 'drinking culture' of FC fans) and even get involved in conflict, for some undermines the 'family' community atmosphere they wish to promote. The boisterous fandom has brought the unwanted attentions of fans of much larger clubs which, on occasion, has resulted in violence. Such was the case when Stoke City fans attacked FC United supporters at their game in Newcastle Under Lyne, only to be met with an equally robust response as well as a police helicopter, possibly for the first time at a 'Step 5' English non-league match. These events, combined with the size of crowd and reputation of some of the fans from their days at Manchester United (whether key figures in United's 'firm' or others' involvement in the at times illegal activities of the anti-Glazer protests) has meant police restrictions. Games have been moved due to safety concerns, some matches have been policed by as many officers as you would normally expect at a Premier League match, and pubs have at times been closed on match day disrupting match day rituals.

Yet even here, some fans have attempted to 'police themselves', chanting against anyone who invades the playing area because of the fines the club (which they own) might receive; holding back others who might be going too far; and recognizing, to some extent at least, a collective responsibility for the club's image. This represents a self-policing in the fan communities, and, whilst the boundaries are drawn very wide indeed, it is one which can exclude on the grounds of acceptable behaviour.

Nowhere are the radical tendencies of FC United more wilfully communicated than through the fans' songs which can confront the very origins of the club, whilst at the same time taking a sideswipe at those who failed to leave Old Trafford:

Glazer wherever you may be
You bought Old Trafford but you can't buy me
I sang 'Not For Sale' and I meant just that
You can't buy me you greedy twat

This is how it feels to be FC
This is how it feels to come home
This is how it feels when you don't sell your ass to a gnome

One 'pub' song (too long for the terraces), borrows from Irish republicanism.[27] This is the only mention of the Manchester Education Committee (which undertook illegal direct action against the takeover[28]) in FC United songs. It also references Glazer's debt, the long-standing opposition to the drift to commercial revolution under former Chief Executive Martin Edwards at United and the '127' years of 'existence' from 1878 to 2005.

Go on home Malcolm Glazer, go on home
Have you got no fucking home of your own
For 127 years, we fought you and your peers

> And we'll fight you for 127 more.
> If you stay Malcolm Glazer you will see
> You will never defeat the MEC
> You can take your fucking debt
> And your Edwards Cheshire set
> And go on home Malcolm Glazer go on home.

There are also reactions to the effects of television on football – especially kick off times being moved from the traditional 3pm Saturday slot – and a rejection of contemporary forms of consumption. However, in others, the division within fan communities is also expressed. This last song also expresses the desire among many FC United supporters to maintain a sense of unity with those that still watch Manchester United – two 'Uniteds' but one 'soul'. So it is particularly through the songs of the fans where the collective expression of cultural politics is perhaps strongest, a symbolic and radical community.

> When FC United go out to play,
> It's 3 o'clock on a Saturday,
> We don't work for Sky Sports anymore[29]

> Won't pay for Glazer
> Or work for Sky
> Still sing 'City's gonna die'
> Two United's but the soul is one
> As the Busby Babes carry on.

Political communities

The desire for a 'return' to a different form of football consumption is a cultural expression of a collective *political* will and desire to affect social change. Delanty has argued that a 'communitarian' understanding of community is essentially conservative and 'reflects a very anti-political view of community'.[30] He seeks to address 'the radical dimension of community as expressed in protest, in the quest for an alterative society or the construction of collective identities in social movements' which seem particularly pertinent to a consideration of supporters communities at FC United.

In this Delanty argues that 'community as dissent or "communities of resistance" are essentially communicative and in this they contrast with the emphasis on the symbolic' as particularly articulated in communitarianism. He says that research on new social movements suggests:

> Community is not a static notion, but is defined in the achieving of it. In this sense, then, community has a cognitive function in imagining and instituting a new kind of society ... this radical impulse has always been present in the idea of community which has often been a quest for a new age. However, what is different about the idea of community implicit in the politics of new social movements is that the search for an alternative society is connected with everyday life and the mobilisation of the resources of the life world ... a culturally radical concept of community comes into play in re-shaping the political field.[31]

This seems particularly relevant to a football club such as FC United which, unlike almost any other in the country, was 'wilfully constructed' around a political belief of how football should be organized, governed, owned and consumed through 'the construction of discourses of meaning'.[32] Its stated ambition of wanting to influence and change the way the game is run may not be at the forefront of everyone's mind at the moments of ecstatic celebration (and there may be as many views on how this is to be achieved), but it runs deeply through the fan culture.

Concluding comment

The formation of FC United of Manchester offers a chance to consider fan communities in unique circumstances. These are also ones which emphasize the fluid, changing, contested nature of community at the same time as the unified, rooted, structuring tendencies we can find in fan communities. The character of the club and its fans is inherently 'political' and oppositional, whilst at the same time providing opportunities for ecstatic consumption and celebration, as well as geographical representation.

The identity of the club and the expressions of its supporters embody symbolic representations and rituals around which FC United fan communities coalesce, but within the politics of football they are highly charged ones. In this, we can move toward an understanding in which different theoretical positions on community can be usefully employed with varying relevance to different aspects.

But the over-riding conclusion has to be that any understanding of community cannot be as a fixed, static, unified or necessarily beneficial entity. The story of FC United has to include an understanding of community as fluid and contested as well as 'real', robust and rooted. In this, it is the overt aim of club, members and fans to use the formation of the club for a political purpose within football that not only binds the many disparate views and approaches within the fan base, but also gives life to its multiplicity. The fascinating question going forward will be whether these binding political principles which have underpinned the creation of FC United and the character of its fan communities can be maintained as the club progresses and meets greater commercial, and footballing, pressures?

Notes

1. Brown and Walsh, *Not for Sale*; although disputed in Bose, *Manchester Disunited*.
2. Football Governance Conference, February 1999, Clore Management Centre, Birkbeck College, University of London. Hamil, Michie and Oughton, *Game of Two Halves*; Conn, *The Football Business*; http://www.supporters-direct.org/; see Hamil *et al. Changing Face of Football*.
3. Brown, '"Manchester IS Red"?'; for a discussion about authenticity in fandom see Crabbe and Brown, '"You're not Welcome Anymore"'.
4. Interviews with Peter Kenyon and David Gill, 2001.
5. For further detail on this and fan resistance to it, see Brown, '"Not For Sale"?'.
6. Haynes and Boyle, *Power Play*; Bose, *Manchester Disunited*; Brown and Walsh, *Not ForSale*; Conn, 'Owners are Treating English Clubs'.
7. Brown, 'United We Stand'; Nash, 'English Football Fan Groups'.
8. Andrews, *Manchester United*; Brown, '"Not For Sale"?'. See also, Bose, *Manchester Disunited*.
9. See King, *End of the Terraces*.
10. 'Hasta la victoria siempre' was the signoff used by Ernesto 'Ché' Guevara in the last letter he wrote to Fidel Castro. It translates as 'Forever, Until Victory' or in other words, 'Keep fighting until victory'.
11. O'Neil, *Red Army General*; O'Neil, *Men in Black*.
12. Holt, *Sport and the British*; Mason, *Sport in Britain*; Russell, *Football and the English*.
13. King, *End of the Terraces*; Brown, '"Manchester IS Red"?'.
14. Delanty, *Community*, 123.
15. Crabbe and Brown, '"You're not Welcome Anymore"'.
16. Brown, Crabbe and Mellor, 'Introduction', this volume, 304.
17. Brown, Crabbe and Mellor, *Football and its Communities*, 160.
18. Crabbe *et al.*, *Football*, 76.
19. King, *End of the Terraces*, 161.
20. Brown, Crabbe and Mellor, 'Introduction', this issue, 308.
21. Bauman, *Liquid Modernity*, 200.
22. FC United of Manchester, 'Manifesto', http://www.fc-utd.co.uk/manifesto.php
23. King, *End of Terraces*, 155.
24. Marginson, speech to FC United of Manchester general meeting, March 2006.

25. Delanty, *Community*, 44.
26. Brown Crabbe and Mellor, 'Introduction', this volume, 307.
27. Adapted from an IRA 'rebel' song 'Go on home British soldiers'.
28. Brown, '"Not For Sale"?'.
29. To the tune of 'Spirit in the Sky'.
30. Delanty, *Community*, 112.
31. Ibid., 124.
32. Ibid., 130.

References

Andrews, D., ed. *Manchester United: A Thematic Study*. London: Routledge, 2004.
Bauman, Z. *Liquid Modernity*. Cambridge: Polity Press, 2000.
Bose, M. *Manchester Disunited: And the Business of Soccer*. London: Arum, 2007.
Brown, A. 'United We Stand: Some Problems with Fan Democracy'. In *Fanatics! Power, Identity and Fandom in Football*, ed. A. Brown, 50–67. London: Routledge, 1998.
———. '"Manchester IS Red"? Manchester United, Fan Identity and the "Sport City"'. In *Manchester United: A Thematic Study*, ed. D. Andrews, 175–90. London: Routledge, 2004.
———. '"Not For Sale"? A destruicao e a reforma das comunidades futebolisticas na aquisicao do Manchester United pelos Glazer'. *Analise Sociale* XLI, 2o Trimestre de 2006, Lisbon: Universidade de Lisboa, 2006.
Brown A., and A. Walsh. *Not For Sale: Manchester United, Murdoch and the Defeat of BSkyB*. Edinburgh: Mainstream, 1999.
Brown, A., T. Crabbe, and G. Mellor. 'Introduction: Football and Community-Practical and Theoretical Considerations'. *Soccer and Society* 9, no. 3 (2008): 303–12.
———. Football and Its Communities. Final report, London: Football Foundation, 2006. http://www.substance.coop/?q=publications_football_and_its_communities.
Conn, D. *The Football Business*. Edinburgh: Mainstream, 1997.
———. 'Owners are Treating English Clubs as Mere Brands to be Consumed'. *Guardian,* February 8, 2008.
Crabbe, T., and A. Brown. '"You're not Welcome Anymore": The Football Crowd, Class and Social Exclusion'. In *British Football and Social Exclusion,* ed. S. Wagg, 26–47. London: Routledge, 2004.
Crabbe, T., A. Brown, G. Mellor, and K. O'Connor. *Football: An All Consuming Passion?* Report for EA Sports. Manchester: Substance, 2006.
Delanty, G. *Community*. London: Routledge, 2003.
Football Governance Conference, Birkbeck College, University of London, February, 1999.
Hamil, S. 'A Whole New Ball Game? Why Football Needs a Regulator'. In *A Game of Two Halves?,* ed. Hamil, S., J. Michie, and C. Oughton, 23–40.
Hamil, S., J. Michie, and C. Oughton, eds. *A Game of Two Halves? The Business of Football*. Edinburgh: Mainstream, 1999.
Hamil, S., J. Michie, C. Oughton, and S. Warby, eds. *The Changing Face of Football: Supporters Direct*. London: Frank Cass, 2001.
Haynes, R., and R. Boyle. *Power Play: Sport, the Media and Popular Culture*. London: Longman, 1999.
Holt, R. *Sport and the British: A Modern History*. Oxford: Oxford University Press, 1989.
King, A. *The End of the Terraces: The Transformation of English Football in the 1990s*. London: Leicester University Press, 1998.
Mason, T. *Sport in Britain*. London: Faber and Faber, 1988.
Nash, R. 'English Football Fan Groups in the 1990s: Class, Representation and Fan Power'. *Soccer and Society* 2, no. 1 (Spring 2001): 39–59.
O'Neil, T. *Red Army General: Leading Britain's Biggest Hooligan Gang*. Manchester: Milo, 2005.
———. *The Men in Black: Inside Manchester United's Football Hooligan Firm*. Manchester: Milo, 2006.
Russell, D. *Football and the English: A Social History of Association Football in England 1863-1995*. Preston: Carnegie Publishing, 1997.

NATIONS AND ETHNICITIES
Football, *komyuniti* and the Japanese ideological soccer apparatus

John Horne and Wolfram Manzenreiter

Introduction: football, *komyuniti* ('community') and Japanese society

The meaning of football in the making and remaking of communities has been the focus of academic as well as political debate – at least as far as the UK is concerned, and to a slightly lesser extent, the countries of continental Europe. For a variety of reasons (identity, class and social change, among others) that are elaborated elsewhere in this volume, football in Europe, over a long historical process that began during the social transformations of the nineteenth century, acquired the characteristics of a representative sport. European football clubs, professional or amateur, came to represent first of all geographical locations, since their roots dated back to times when the entire life world of a community was largely restricted to the territory its members inhabited. Even though technological and cultural change have heavily expanded the frontiers of the life world, while mobility, physical as well as social, individual as well as collective, have largely increased, football clubs have persisted as meaningful sites for ritualized identification with a geographical locality, social groups associated with certain territories, and iconic images deriving from combinations of place, class and style. Today, whilst its supporters need not be restricted to the same geographical area,[3] it remains a club's long-standing association with a locality, a shared history, and a common sense of belonging, that lead policy makers to recognize the potential effectiveness of football for doing the work of community development – either as a tool for community mobilization or community accommodation to wider governmental programmes.[4]

The football-community nexus in Japan differs from the European experience in three major respects. Firstly, football has played no significant role in communal affairs within Japan for most of its hundred-plus year history.[5] In fact, until recently, it could not have because football had never attracted a large follower base either as a spectator sport or as a participant sport before the Japanese Professional Football League (hereafter, J.League) was inaugurated in 1993. Prior to that, Japan's amateur football leagues had been dominated by university clubs or semi-professional teams owned and run by large industrial corporations. Clubs thus usually represented a corporation, or sometimes a brand name, and were meant either to promote the corporate image or to provide their employees with a focus for identification.[6] The company clubs of the likes of Mitsubishi, NTT or Osaka Gas were in need of neither financial nor emotional support generated by a large fan-base and showed no professional interest in raising such support.

A second distinctive feature of Japanese social development, also until quite recently, has been the relative stability of community patterns, which have proven to be far more resistant to the destabilizing effects familiar in modern urban life in Western societies. Even though Japan underwent very similar, albeit slightly delayed, processes of agricultural decline, industrialization and urbanization, collectivist, community, orientations remained powerful cultural norms – even to the extent that they were sometimes employed as self-descriptive (and prescriptive) concepts of Japanese mores and behaviour, as well as for the explanation of Japan's economic miracle in the second half of the twentieth century.[7]

Rather than urbanization, it has been the move toward a technologically sophisticated and service-oriented, post-modern, consumer society that has arguably undermined the social fundamentals of Japanese community patterns. Since the 1980s, towns, cities and rural districts of the northeast, the south and other localities of the Japanese peripheries, that always struggled to keep pace with the rapid industrialization process, have continued to fall further behind the metropolitan areas and industrial zones of Central Honshu (a geographical area stretching essentially from Kanto – Greater Tokyo – in the east to Kansai – Osaka, Kobe and Kyoto – in the west). Gradual industrial decline and steady migration into the overcrowded capital and major cities inflicted severe repercussions on the vitality of regions confronted with a rapidly aging population and a diminishing income tax base. Within this scenario, communities were inevitably threatened by termination. As a result, place, as a focus of communal life, has all but lost its meaning. Individual and familial needs could be satisfied equally outside of the locality. Participation in communal affairs became segmented and selective, dependent on the capacities of the community to respond to the particular interests of specific inhabitant groups.[8] Additionally over the past two decades an increasing number of social anomalies, such as *ijime* (bullying), *enjo kosai* (compensated dating, or school girl prostitution), *oyaji bataki* (youngsters hunting and slapping old men), *parasaito shinguru* ('parasite singles', unmarried adults living with and at the expense of their parents), and *hikikomori* (deliberate withdrawal from social life, most often by young male adults seeking extreme degrees of isolation), have suggested a loss, or at least diminution, of the values and institutions that once integrated the individual into his/her community and regulated his/her life in this collective-oriented society.

As a consequence, the longing for an idealized past as a better alternative to the present has started to ignite debates, fuelled by moral panics, about the future relationship between the public and the private in Japan. Much of Japanese sociologists' and urban planners' contemporary interest in communal life seems to be fuelled by a general discomfort with urban life as the standard mode of living in late-modernity. The nostalgic turn towards the community[9] that once upon a time seemingly gave coherence and continuity to urban life also corresponds with the current dismantling of the social welfare state.

As with the populist discourses on communitarianism and new urbanism in the USA,[10] in Japan, too, there is the tendency to overrate the effects of the idealized community against all threats to the contemporary social order and understate its darker side, as one of the key sites of social control and surveillance, bordering on overt social repression, which was especially the case in early modern and wartime Japan.[11] To fight the flaws of late modern society with the evils of former social formations must certainly be at odds with the changing environment – yet the notion of community, revived or newly constructed, remains at the centre of contemporary debates about town making (*machi-zukuri*) in Japan; and quite a few proponents speak in favour of football as a means with which to do this. This is perhaps less surprising if we turn towards the third big difference between Japan's and Europe's vision of football communities. We will demonstrate in the rest of this essay that throughout its entire, though relatively short, history professional football in Japan has been closely related to predominantly top-down projects of urban regeneration and community development.[12] In this respect we argue that in contemporary Japanese discourses, the organization and institutional practices that promote football and *komyuniti* ('community') are best understood as part of an 'Ideological Soccer Apparatus' (ISA).The rapidly changing and diversifying Japanese society rules out the possibility of formulating a single structural model from which to generalize a typical form of community involvement with football. But we identify a number of key variables responsible for the emergence of distinct patterns of communal football support. In addition, we will show that whilst much of the discourse on football and the Japanese community serves very different interests, it continues to facilitate most of all the proliferation of private consumption, public spending and transnational money flows. Hence, following Althusser's concern with the working of ideology in the maintenance of capitalist class structures, we want to show how the football-community nexus in Japan works as an ISA that inculcates amongst members of a community specific ways of understanding and shaping the relationship between the individual and society.

Some of our earlier work, exploring the seismographic qualities of football in Japanese society, has demonstrated the great importance of common interests and emotional attachment for the formation of a fan culture. Hence we are aware of the socially integrative effects of football for sub-cultural groupings[13] as well as for more part-time members of ephemeral, otherwise dissociated, makeshift communities of the 'event culture'.[14] Yet here we focus our attention on football communities as a group of private and corporate residents sharing a particular local area that roughly corresponds with the geographic boundaries of aggregated support for the local professional team, because of the important role place and territory continue to play for football fandom, even in the most advanced information societies, such as Japan.

Following this introduction the essay is divided into three sections. Firstly we outline the dominant model of football-community relations implicit since the formation of the professional football J.League in 1991. Then we use case studies of J.League club formations to illustrate how football communities have been made by corporate and bureaucratic interventions. After that we identify some alternatives to the 'top-down' formations and explore some of the challenges and alternatives they offer. Finally, in conclusion, we suggest where future research is most needed to explore some of these issues further.

The Corporate Community Model (CCM) of the J.League

The J.League was incorporated as an autonomous, non-profit making, organization in 1991. Aside from footballing prowess the J.League required each club applying to join to be a registered corporation specializing in football, a stipulation designed to force the management of each club, as well as players and coaches, to be fully professional. Since J.League football, unlike semi-professional corporate football and professional baseball, was not to be used simply as a promotional tool, clubs were also requested not to have the names of their owner as the team name. Hence previous amateur side Toyo Industrials turned into professional Sanfrecce Hiroshima, Matsushita Electrics became Gamba Osaka and Mitsubishi Heavy Industries changed into the Urawa Red Diamonds.[15] In the 14 seasons since then the J.League has gone through

Table 1. Professional football clubs in the J.League divisions 1 and 2 in 2006.

J1 Teams	J.League (Phase of joining)	J2 Teams	J.League (Phase of joining)
Kashima Antlers	1991 (1)	Consadole Sapporo	1998 (2)
Urawa Red Diamonds	1991 (1)	Vegalta Sendai	1999 (2)
Omiya Ardija	1999 (2)	Montedio Yamagata	1999 (2)
JEF United Ichihara Chiba	1991 (1)	Mito Hollyhock	2000 (3)
FC Tokyo	1999 (2)	Thespa Kusatsu	2005 (3)
Kawasaki Frontale	1997 (2)	Kashiwa Reysol	1995 (1)
Yokohama F Marinos	1991 (1)	Tokyo Verdy 1969	1991 (1)
Ventforet Kofu	1999 (2)	Yokohama FC	2001 (3)
Albirex Niigata	1999 (2)	Shonan Bellmare	1999 (2)
Shimizu S-Pulse	1991 (1)	Vissel Kobe	1999 (2)
Jubilo Iwata	1994 (1)	Tokushima Vortis	2005 (3)
Nagoya Grampus Eight	1991 (1)	Ehime FC	2006 (3)
Kyoto Purple Sanga	1995 (1)	Sagan Tosu	1999 (2)
Gamba Osaka	1991 (1)		
Cerezo Osaka	1996 (2)		
Sanfrecce Hiroshima	1991 (1)		
Avispa Fukuoka	1996 (2)		
Oita Trinita	1999 (2)		

Source: adapted from *2005 J.League Guide*.

broadly three transformative phases, during which expansion has occurred, league arrangements modified and new clubs allowed to join. Over 30 professional teams have been established, dozens of large stadiums erected, and thousands of players, coaches, match officials and full-time staff have registered with the Japan Football Association (JFA). Table 1 depicts the line-up of the two J.League Divisions (J1 and J2) in 2006. There are 31 full members in the two Divisions, 18 in the top division and 13 in the second rank.[16]

While European social scientists have usually been concerned with the role football has played in the establishment of communal bonds, in the case of Japan the question might be better inverted to ask, what has been the role of communities in the development of professional football? Prior to the J.League, football existed in Japan for several decades yet with rather frustrating results in terms of international comparison. Raising the performance of the national team as well as encouraging popular interest in the game – two central objectives associated with the J.League mission – inevitably required professionalization of players, coaches, club management, sport facility maintenance staff, league administration, marketing, communication and many other institutional aspects of the sport. Since Japanese capital, inter-corporate networks and marketing know-how have been involved in the relatively recent commercialization of sport on a global scale,[17] Japan's football bureaucrats knew that commercialization was key to generating the funds required to help turn a minority sport into a successful and viable market. Capital looking out for new investment opportunities was amply available at the onset of the 1990s when Japan stepped into a crisis of over-accumulation. But building up a loyal customer base, particularly in Japan's well-known fickle consumer markets, required long-term vision, time and a strategic business plan. To bridge the first 10 years of the new football market, a network of investors and stakeholders willing to share the risks of advance financing had to be developed.[18]

Communities were assigned a crucial part in both short-term and long-term perspectives. Having the opportunity to choose from various models of sport financing, the J.League, as the incorporated managing body of the professional football league was named, opted for an amalgam of the North American franchise system and the European sports club system.[19] The J.League copied the art of merchandising meticulously from American Gridiron Football (the NFL). Sony Creative Productions tailored a standardized set of corporate images for the starting line-up of 10 professional football teams that catered for the taste of young female adults, at present Japan's most powerful consumer group that has repeatedly proven its ability to grow entire markets. The closed-club style of the franchise system guaranteed accounting control to the non-profit J.League organization over its member clubs' books as well as over central revenue streams – income from broadcasting rights, merchandising and sponsorship is distributed to all member clubs, after funds necessary to cover operational expenses have been deducted. The cartel-like organization safeguarded the teams, at least during the start-up period, against the sportive and economic dangers of relegation.[20]

The European sports club model, with its characteristic features of a grassroots approach, community service and local roots, has also turned out to be influential in the promotion of football in Japan for three reasons. Firstly, despite the attractions of the 'American model' in many forms of contemporary Japanese popular culture, association football is neither regarded as a mass sport nor as a commercial success in the USA, in the same way that it has been represented in Europe. Hence lessons from the US about launching football were not considered to be productive. Secondly, the driving forces among the advocates and managers of the professionalization initiative came from a generation of ex-footballers who had been socialized into the sport during the 1960s when the German Dettmar Cramer was involved in coaching the Japanese national team. During their occasional visits to football schools in Germany the young Japanese players experienced at first hand the previously unknown quality of training facilities, available for amateur players as well as professionals, and the enthusiastic mass support of the local population. The heart-warming image of 'sports for all'[21] in combination with the organization of top-level sports formed a lasting impression in the minds of the ageing Japanese football bureaucrats. This is very likely a major reason why Germany's sport and football clubs were explicitly picked out as the main role model for Japan's first fully professional football league, despite the multi-faceted problems the European sports club model has faced since the 1960s.[22]

Hence, and thirdly, communities were mobilized as a focal point for club membership and as benevolent sponsors of club activities to secure the success of the J.League. In fact, the J.League demanded from any aspiring member club demonstrable evidence that their 'home town' was willing to support the promotion of football in the region, most clearly by delivering financial guarantees and infrastructure projects such as stadiums and other facilities, if needed by the local clubs, and other more direct forms of capital investment. In exchange, J.League member clubs were required to 'unite with the community, familiarize people with the sport-oriented lifestyle, and contribute to the physical and mental well-being and pleasure of local society', as the official mission statement declares.[23] To facilitate integration and identification, all J.League clubs were asked to forge names combining the geographical place name with a nickname of a particular local flavour. Key words that intimately resonate with the J.League's corporate community model include the technical term of 'home town', where all stakeholders are based, its vernacularised version of *oraga machi* ('our town'), and *chiiki mitchaku*, which means 'regional adherence', or simply having a very close relationship with the home town region. These are core notions to be found in virtually all public statements issued by the J.League concerning its mission. In 1996 when the J.League had lost some of its initial dynamics, it reemphasized its commitment to the public, particularly the inhabitants of home town areas, by the public declaration of the J.Mission, or 'Centennial Plan' (*hyakunen koso*), which refers back to the 100 year history of European sport clubs and forward to the long-term perspective of contemporary football initiatives in Japan.

Another prominent key word is 'trinity' (*sanmi ittai*), referring to the J.League ideal image of 'football in the community', based on the cooperation of civil society (*shimin*, townspeople) with businesses (*kigyo*) and local authority bureaucrats (*gyosei*) from the region. The administration serves as a hub and communication point between the dispersed actors in the region, and it channels public funds into the football community. Broad popular interest in the local team is therefore of crucial importance for the commercial viability of the team. Spectator turnout feeds directly and indirectly into club revenues, since ticket sales are a major source of income and attendance rates are a striking argument for sponsorship activities of the corporate community members. Football clubs also cater to the needs of urban redevelopment programmes since they promise to enhance the quality of life of the local inhabitants in the region by providing 'healthy entertainment' (*kenzen-na goraku*) as well as a source of local pride and communal identification, which the cultural and sporting hierarchy of earlier times largely restricted to the Tokyo conurbation in the East and the area around Osaka in Western Japan. It was clearly desired that these and other intangible benefits of the J.League would play a role in stopping the depopulation of the peripheries, preventing the younger generation from migration into the large cities, and bridging the gap between older residents and newcomers to their neighbourhoods.

According to the J.League community model, football is thus the point of entry into a vibrant community life sustained by actors from the three different fields of business, politics and civil society. While having their own particular interests, needs and potentials, they also provide the three pillars on which the sustainability of football rests. Football should be added as the fourth and distinctive player within the ideal new community, not least because the managing body of the J.League proposed to establish professional football throughout Japan for purposes far beyond the limits of the game. Its stated mission is 'to foster the development of Japan's sporting culture, to assist in the healthy mental and physical growth of Japanese people, and to contribute to international friendship and exchange'. Such statements reveal the operation of the Ideological Soccer Apparatus (ISA); though they do not show whose interests it ultimately serves. The next section, which illustrates the operation of this mission in diverse circumstances, shows how the ISA has been effectively put into practice by different actors during different phases of the development of the J.League.

The making of football communities in Japan: phases 1 and 2

From a macro perspective, the instalment of professional football as an industry has been a remarkable success in an otherwise dark period of Japan's recent economic and social history. As we have noted, the league has expanded from 10 teams in 1993 to 31 competing in two divisions (J1 and J2) in 2006. As with any other market, it has experienced different cycles or phases of development. Between 1993 and 1995 football boomed extraordinarily, attracting more than six million visitors in an average season and generating annual turnover of 10 billion Yen (approximately £50 million) for the J.League. But the hype did not last. During a period of constant and rapid expansion of teams, matches and league divisions, average crowd sizes inevitably declined. In the 1997 season average attendances dropped close to 10,000, down from nearly 20,000 recorded three years earlier. Facing declining spectator numbers and revenues from the turnstile and merchandising sales, most, if not all, clubs were in the red.

In 1999, the first collapse of a football team (Yokohama AS Flugels) alarmed the J.League and compelled them to seek a more reasonable and transparent style of club management from its members. With qualification for the 1998 World Cup in France by the national team, and the 2002 World Cup, to be co-hosted with South Korea, coming closer, football came back into fashion. Since 2001, average attendances for first division (J1) matches have risen again, being close to 19,000 in 2004 and 2005. According to sport market analyst Hirose, professional football created a market volume of 530 billion Yen during its first decade.[24] He also calculated that the J.League itself had contributed only 0.1 per cent of the entire start-up investment: approximately 58 billion yen that were needed for the infrastructure build-up, team development, marketing, and so on, had been solicited from local authorities and communities. Particularly in terms of ownership, the joint efforts of local authorities, citizens and companies from the regions in which the football teams were based introduced a promising new model of sport business which is in marked contrast to traditional Japanese arrangements in professional baseball or contemporary sports business models prevalent in the USA and Europe. But behind these developments lies a tension between the 'top down' and 'bottom up' concepts of community development and its association with football. We will illustrate some of these tensions through the presentation of appropriate case studies.

Community building top down: the corporate approach

A top-down approach dominated attempts to construct football communities during the establishment phase and the first years of operation of the J.League. This period – roughly stretching from 1991 to 1996 – witnessed a rapid period of growth for the league, seeing its gradual expansion from 10 to 14 teams and the confirmation that Japan would jointly host the 2002 World Cup with South Korea. Through this period the home towns of the first generation of professional football teams shared a number of commonalities hinting at the way in which these had apparently been drafted or 'manufactured'. One of the driving forces behind the community building approach was the J.League itself. It acted as a football 'match maker', identifying and associating pockets of football-interest with clubs. From the 10 teams that started the J.League, nine were selected from former company sports teams that continued to benefit from a close relationship with their former host company. Acting now as main sponsor or major share holder of the company stock, their subsidies provided the completely inexperienced football management staff, who were often dispatched form the former Owner companies' middle management, with at least a mid-term guarantee against financial difficulties.

Virtually all of the first phase J.League clubs were founded within the densely populated areas of Japan's main island Honshu. These locations allowed access to the largest spectator and customer bases. Tokyo was deliberately denied home town status because the J.League wanted to avoid a confrontation between representatives of the capital and all other teams. Such a constellation – notably through the Yomiuri media corporation's control of the Tokyo Giants – had tainted power relations, the distribution of market values, revenue streams and spectator support during 50 years of professional baseball. Even when four new teams joined the J.League up to 1995, with the exception of traditional football powerhouse Sanfrecce Hiroshima, all other teams were settled in the Pacific Belt stretching between Osaka in the West and Kashima in the East.

In terms of size, Kashima was something of a surprise package with a population of 45,000 which represented an exception to the rules laid out by the J.League for its prospective member teams in these early years. In order to guarantee capacity crowds on a regular basis, a home town population size of less than 100,000 was not generally regarded as being large enough to fill the required 15,000-seater home stadium. Hence the application of Kashima to be listed among the J.League teams was initially considered to have little chance of success. But Kashima was badly in need of an effective re-imagining strategy. Like so many other towns and villages in the peripheries, Kashima suffered from the late effects of failed land use planning. Located 150 kilometres from Tokyo and close to the Pacific Sea, until the early 1960s Kashima's inhabitants had largely relied on income generated from agriculture and the fishing industry. In the subsequent period of high economic growth the greater Kashima area turned into a specially designated industrial zone, attracting Sumitomo Steel, numerous component suppliers and more than 170 new companies into the area. Within two decades, the population had nearly doubled. Numerous apartment buildings were constructed, a commercial harbour was opened, but in terms of amenities, social services and leisure programmes, the town struggled to cope with the rapid pace of population growth. Under conditions of limited quality and rising real estate prices, Sumitomo Steel, Asahi Glass and others faced difficulties in hiring enough workers, since neither company workers nor the emergent younger generation intended to settle down permanently in Kashima. Being part of the new professional football league offered the potential to make a difference.

Without the support of the industrial giant Sumitomo, which happened to own a company football team playing in a minor regional amateur league, the J.League would undoubtedly have turned down the application. But Sumitomo Steel took the initiative, seeking support among local bureaucrats and business leaders and integrating the surrounding municipalities into its bid campaign. Besides Sumitomo Steel and 40 other companies from the region, five small local authorities became major shareholders of the incorporated Kashima Antlers Football Club. The J.League's main requirement, a roofed stadium with a capacity of 15,000 spectators, or a seat for every third Kashima resident, was largely built at the expense of the government of Ibaraki prefecture that covered 80% of the construction costs, estimated at JPY 10 billion.[25] In addition, public money granted by local authorities was used to renovate the traffic infrastructure. A 20-year-old dream was realized when a branch railway line connecting Kashima to the Tokyo-Northeast track of the high speed Shinkansen or bullet train was opened. Additionally, public money also financed the refashioning of a freight depot into a commuter station, the construction of parking lots, and improvements to sanitary and accommodation facilities.[26]

All these investments were justified by Kashima Antlers' unexpected success on the pitch. In the inaugural season (1993) they won the first stage of the league only to be defeated in the final 'Suntory Championship' playoff against the winner of the second stage, traditional football powerhouse Verdy Kawasaki (now renamed Tokyo Verdy 1969). The team's performances soon sparked interest among local residents. Within a few months the official Antlers fan club increased from just three to more than 3,000 members. They were cheering for a team built around Brazilian talent, including former world footballer of the year, Zico, who went on to manage Japan's national team between the 2002 and 2006 World Cups. Sumitomo Steel not only compensated for the huge deficits due to the high salaries of foreign star players but also helped the Antlers to defray costs coming from the construction of the clubhouse and training grounds. Although reliance on a mother company was out of step with the official J.League community ideology, such subsidies were officially declared as advertising costs, rather than sponsorship expenses that would have attracted much higher taxation.[27]

Thanks to the financial support they received the expected underdog became one of the dominant club sides of the J.League in the 1990s and early 2000s. Victory in the overall championship in 2001 provided the Antlers with their fourth title. The previous season they even accomplished the treble – winning all three domestic competitions. Only Jubilo Iwata, another regular contender for the championship that enjoys the generous support of Yamaha Motors, was able to stop Kashima in 2002. The JFA acknowledged Kashima's leading role in the development of professional football by nominating the city as one of the 10 2002 FIFA World Cup host venues. When the designated World Cup venue was adapted to match with FIFA requirements, the investment of a further 23.6 billion yen in the stadium provided enough seats for almost every citizen in Kashima.

Partly fuelled by these successes the name of Kashima has become famous throughout Japan, a favourite object of study for town planners and local government administrations.

Community building top down: the bureaucratic approach

The success of the J.League tempted numerous communities to emulate the Kashima experiment. The second phase of the J.League expansion however came in the late 1990s when the Japanese economy was badly hit by a series of economic recessions and the Asian financial crisis; what the media dubbed the 'lost decade'. The economy witnessed hardly any growth in productivity, the collapse of real estate markets, a severe financial crisis, rising unemployment, corporate bankruptcies, mounting public debt and stagflation. Since economic growth and future welfare expectations had come to play a crucial role in the collective image of the Japanese (as a kind of economic nationalism), the loss of Japan's competitive edge also brought collective ideas and appreciations about what it meant to be Japanese into question.

Football provided the promise of potential solutions to these problems. First, as a representative sport football provided a metaphor for a new Japan. At international matches rooting for the national team became a new opportunity for showing national pride, particularly since professionalization had also left its mark on the strength of the national team. When Japan qualified for the 1998 World Cup in France, interest in the tournament was more widespread than ever before, producing some of the highest television audience rates in the history of Japanese broadcasting. Second, as an integrative sport, the continuing presence of football in the Japanese regions provided an alternative forum for the search for collective identity, switching from the national to the regional and local levels. Nevertheless the precariousness of these possibilities was revealed as the football industry also experienced sluggish demand, leading to the first – and so far only – closure of a team.

It is revealing of the Ideological Soccer Apparatus that the J.League administrators explained the failure of AS Flugels Yokohama as a lack of interest in the team and unity of supporters, rather than with reference to market effects, sponsorship policies or the economic turndown in Japan that contributed to the decisions of the two main sponsors, airline company ANA and construction company Sato, to withdraw their support. When the forced merger with the other Yokohama-based team (the Marinos) was announced, fans banded together and petitioned the J.League about the dissolution of their club.

Kawabuchi, former chairman of the J.League and now 'captain' of the JFA, remembered in an interview:

> One of them was dressed in a shabby shirt and a tie and he said to me: 'The Flugels is my life. I've taken a day off work to come here today. I'm wearing a suit and tie for the first time ever because I wanted to come here.' That moved me to tears and I thought: 'This is the kind of man we need.' The Flugels case had a powerful impact on me in both a positive and negative way.[28]

Despite this the J.League continued to expand. In 1999, a second professional football division (J2) was launched, increasing the speed of expansion. Jointly hosting the 2002 World Cup played a crucial role in this period since more professional teams were needed in order to raise awareness of the game and the global flagship event, particularly in each of the 10 designated host cities. Almost one in two of the J.League home towns that came into existence during this phase were a potential future World Cup host city. In geographical terms the associated construction driven expansion of the infrastructure contributed to the further spread of football throughout the country, which was also an important step towards the formation of an imagined national football community, a pre-requisite for the World Cup fiesta. Professional football reached Japan's most northerly island Hokkaido for the first time.

In Sapporo Japan's most sophisticated roofed arena was opened. Giant stadiums with seating capacities over 40,000 were also constructed in the hinterland regions of Tohoku in the North East, the back-side of Japan facing the Japan Sea (Niigata), and in the main southern island of

Kyushu (Oita). Three more stadiums of World Cup size were opened in the mega cities of Kanto and Kansai, when Cerezo Osaka, Kobe Vissel and FC Tokyo joined the league. Only three of the new teams – FC Tokyo (Tokyo Gas), Kawasaki Frontale (Fujitsu) and Omiya Ardija (NTT) – were direct descendents of former company sides, but even these could not entirely rely on the goodwill of a major company 'sponsor'. Trust in club management was built more on a new kind of ownership model in which local communities were chiefly involved. Basically in all instances a consortium of some dozen companies and organizations, often including local authorities, constituted the formal owners of the team. The leading role of the bureaucracy and local elites in football community building was another central feature of this period. Two good examples of this development, albeit quite contrasting, are the teams Oita Trinita and Niigata Albirex.

Oita is a small city (by Japanese standards) with a population of about 650,000. It is the capital of the prefecture of the same name, situated on Kyushu Island in the south of Japan. For largely geographical reasons the terrain impeded the development of industry and the integration of the region into larger communication and trade networks. Oita was once famous for being the most depopulated prefecture in Japan.[29] But Oita is also famous for the way football has been used by the local political elites to stem rural depopulation and urban migration. The starting initiative to set up a professional team was proclaimed by Oita governor Hiramatsu Morihiko in front of the local assembly in 1994, making the objective of becoming a World Cup host city most explicit. Since the World Cup was coming to the town, the particularly active prefecture government used the opportunity to channel large amounts of public funds into the expanding communication network of motorways and railway tracks connecting the basically rural city with the busier cities in Kyushu's North West and the main island. In relative terms costs for the Big Eye, Oita's new World Cup stadium, were low. However as local authorities such as Oita were following the lead of the national government, which had built up the largest debt of all the OECD countries, the majority of the funds to cover the construction costs were collected from general obligation bonds issued by Oita Prefecture.

As in the case of Kashima, football was welcomed as a solution to the problems of unbalanced regional development. Since Oita did not have its own Sumitomo, the region neither possessed a semi-professional company team nor the financial support of a potent sponsor company. In comparison, neighbouring Fukuoka had more attractive conditions to offer and hence was able to convince a team (the amateur predecessor of Avispa Fukuoka) from Shizuoka, where other attractive J.League teams such as Shimizu S-Pulse and Jubilo Iwata were based, to move to western Japan. The Oita team, however, had to be built up from scratch, largely using local talent from high school and university teams. In a formal sense support was indeed mandatory for all public employees of the prefectural government since they automatically belonged to a fan club of the team. Public sponsorship for the football club thus could be disguised as buying tickets en bloc for the supporter group. Government employees were also sent as temporary staff workers to run the club office and manage team affairs. A career track bureaucrat from the Ministry of Local Autonomy in Tokyo was officially dispatched as General Manager to help establish Oita Trinity. Without any large corporation available in the home region, the bureaucrats solicited sponsorship fees from numerous small and medium sized companies in the region and even succeeded in recruiting sponsors from the main island.[30] This was basically after Oita's team successfully turned from a local amateur club into a professional team. The football community of Oita took more time to constitute even though the Trinita name had been selected to appeal to the trinity of sponsors from the business world, local administration and citizens in the prefectural region. According to a leaflet from Oita City, 'Oita Trinita have total prefectural support, since not only the prefecture of Oita but also enterprises, companies, and all the inhabitants support it'. Research on the fan communities in the city suggests that grassroots football fan groups in fact did not appreciate this top down promotional role of local elites in running the official supporters club, or the involvement of the bureaucracy in management affairs.[31] However with the new World Cup stadium and the prospect of promotion to J1 ahead, Oita turned out to be one of the best visited J2 teams in 2001 and the following year when it was promoted to J1.

The best supported team in J2 in 2002 and, according to a recent fan survey carried out by the J.League, that with the oldest supporters, hails from the North-East part of Japan, Niigata.[32] The development of professional football there is another example of community formation through football to which we now turn.

No other place in Japan is more closely associated with political corruption than Niigata, an insular industrial city and capital of the prefecture bearing the same name on the coast of the Japan Sea. The Joetsu Shinkansen track, for example, is a relic of the past days of former premier Tanaka Kakuei who had channelled large amounts of public funds in the underdeveloped regions. Despite huge construction projects, Niigata continued to be regarded as a rural, backward (*inaka*) and boring (*tsumaranai*) location, with *koshihikari* rice providing the main source of local pride.[33] Discussions about making a professional team started in Niigata as early as 1994, since the local authorities nurtured the strong desire to host World Cup games if possible. The nomination as a host city corresponded largely with Oita's objectives of urban reimaging. But in contrast to governor Hiramatsu from Oita, Niigata's initial force came from the world of the local business elite. Ikeda Hiromu, head priest of a local shrine who had made his fortune as the owner of a net of prep schools, became first president and also sponsor of the new team. The history of the local club goes back to the Niigata Eleven Soccer Club, founded in the mid-1950s that later advanced to the regional amateur league, and a merger with some more amateur teams from the region. With the support of 30 influential companies in the prefecture and funds provided by around 150 local companies and organizations, 500 million yen were raised to start the move toward full professionalism. Like Oita Trinita, Niigata Albirex joined the J.League as an inaugural member of the newly established J2 division. After three hardly remarkable seasons Niigata's 'Big Swan' World Cup Stadium opened in 2001. Ever since Albirex began playing their home games in the Big Swan arena, the team turned into one of the best-supported teams in the J.League. Regular attendances at home games of more than 35,000 exceed the average for most other J1 and J2 clubs by a long way. In 2002 Albirex faded during the season run-in but in 2003 it captured the league title and gained promotion to J1. Support did not weaken thereafter, in contrast to the familiar pattern of a sudden decline once a newcomer struggles to hold pace with the established J1 teams.

According to Kozu's research team,[34] the club management was extremely successful in raising local support because it placed great emphasis on local culture and local communication. More than in any other locality, Niigata was promoted and received as the team of all the local people, in terms of percentages being closer to the average (age: 36.6 years, male supporters 52.9%) than Oita, for example. But, perhaps more significantly they have invited television documentaries, match reports and popular accounts to emphasize the local roots of football support in Niigata and football's role in community building. But it is an open secret that the fully packed stadiums do not necessarily mean riches for the team. The club has become notorious for giving away free tickets to members of the local population. First, tickets were distributed without a clear strategy. But then the club management began to make effective use of the traditional networks of neighbourhood associations and their communication routes. For example, as soon as the team entered the professional league, Albirex set up a dense network of supporter or 'booster' clubs. Niigata prefecture was divided into more than 40 sections, and each section saw the opening of its own fan club. In many instances, the chairman or directors were usually also board members of other local associations, and these networks were used for spreading the word about Niigata's football team as well as the distribution of free tickets. Similarly, information on match days and ticket availability was passed on through the traditional Japanese communication route of the *kairanban*, an information bulletin that circulates from household to household to inform all residents in an area of important news.[35] Giving tickets away to young children looked like a thinly disguised attempt to lure their paying parents or grand parents into the stadium. But club management reasonably expected to raise awareness of the local team once people from Niigata had actually experienced the impressive atmosphere in the Big Swan stadium.

Despite the traditional and parochial emphasis, the football community in Niigata is not exclusive. It is inclusive because it allows different people from different backgrounds to interact with each other. In general, this aspect is heralded as a distinctive feature by the J.League since it establishes communal bonds solely on the basis of residence. It is not a question of provenance, of the regional ancestry – another traditional variable in community building in Japan, since we have met and talked with numerous Albirex fans within the Niigata region that have moved in only recently. This is a social novelty in Japan that has traditionally employed attributes which were more exclusive. As a social project, and perhaps influenced by these phenomena, Niigata has also found favour with various artistic groups, including the rock band, The Penpals. The popular band remixed their smash hit song 'Believe' to capture the attitude of the Niigata supporters and recorded a live performance with a 30,000-plus background choir, dressed in Albirex team colour orange, expressing their shared belief in, and love for, the team.[36]

Niigata Albirex has now been adopted as a new symbol of the entire prefecture, albeit under very unfortunate circumstances. In October 2003, during Albirex's first year in the J1, an earthquake devastated its home town region. In the aftermath of the Niigata Chuetsu Earthquake, all J.League clubs, players and supporters contributed to disaster relief efforts. Football fans donated generously at every stadium, including a collection of four million yen at a single home game of the Urawa Red Diamonds. But it was the Albirex players and staff members that travelled throughout the region in order to console and entertain displaced families. They gave generously to the victims, contributed to a charity auction organized by the players' association, and played an exhibition match against a 'Dream Team' of past, present and future national team players. In return, fans from the entire Niigata prefecture that has been identified as the new official home town region of the team have kept on flocking to the Big Swan.[37]

The making of football communities in Japan: phase 3

In this section we consider more recent and alternative community-football formations and explore some of the challenges they present for the J.League as it attempts to develop community-based initiatives.

Community building – from the bottom up?

Since the launch of the J2 in 1999, five new clubs have been promoted from the amateur Japan Football League (JFL), and the J1 has expanded from 16 to 18 teams. In 2006 the 13 teams in J2 played each other four times on a home and away basis. Discussions have been held about the possibility of introducing a professional J3, operating in regional divisions. Suzuki Masaru, the J.League chairman, expressed the wish to build up to 100 clubs, or approximately two in each of the 47 prefectures throughout Japan. While the corporate consortium approach is still widely practiced, the Japanese fiscal crisis has forced local authorities to save rather than spend, and the failed attempts to develop clubs from Kagoshima (Volca) and Okinawa (Kariyushi FC) have shown that sustainable alternatives to a reliance on sponsorship income are essential for newcomers. Three of the most recent new entrants – Mito Hollyhock, Yokohama FC and Thespa Kusatsu – illustrate alternative means for the establishment of professional football clubs.

Mito Hollyhock introduced a 'socio membership' system which helped the club to get approval from the J.League. Links with established J.League clubs, including Yokohama Marinos and FC Tokyo that have farmed out young players to Mito as a way of helping them get accustomed to life in the J.League, have kept start-up expenses low, and financial subsidies from Ibaraki prefecture saved the club when it faced its most severe financial problems, to date, in 2004. Yokohama FC emerged as a direct result of the decision to dissolve AS Flugels at the end of the 1998 season. It is therefore the first fan-initiated football club in Japan that also started with a socio-style membership system.[38] With increasing success, sponsorship money came flooding in and reduced the reliance on the socio membership. In recent years however a gap has opened up between club management and the socio members who are demanding more involvement in club affairs than the management has so far been willing to concede.

Thespa Kusatsu was launched in 1997 in the small town of Kusatsu in Gunma prefecture, popular for its *onsen* ('hot spring') with fewer than 10,000 inhabitants. While the small population size itself represents a remarkable breach of (former) J.League regulations, the business model is even more interesting. Until the team was promoted to play in the J2 in 2005, most players were working part time in local shops and hotels, but not for their own income. In the case of Thespa, all sponsor money came from the local economy, which in return received the labour power of the athletes. Thespa management thus used the sponsorship income to pay player salaries and its operational expenses. The town of Kusatsu supported the team by providing free access to the local sport facilities and by subcontracting the management team of the municipal Beltz Hot Spring Centre to the club.[39] Since its promotion Thespa has moved out of tiny Kusatsu, not least because of the J2 requirements on stadium size. The closest appropriate stadium, with a capacity of 15,000, is over two hours ride away by car in Maebashi, the capital city of Gunma prefecture. Hence Thespa Kusatsu has come to represent the towns and cities of Shibukawa, Takasaki and Maebashi, as well as Kusatsu, which is still the home base of Thespa's satellite team. Such an extension of home town area is not a rare incident. In the case of JEF United (which arguably holds the record of garnering least spectator interest in its 14 year existence) the home town area of Ishihara city was officially extended in 2004 to include neighbouring Chiba, capital of the homonymous prefecture, which is now officially part of the team's name and also provided a brand new 18,000 capacity stadium. Kashima Antlers has expanded its home town area since 2005 as well, for the purpose of raising interest among local inhabitants and potential investors. In 1998, Bellmare Hiratsuka relaunched itself with the name Shonan Bellmare, a larger geographical area along the coast of Kanagawa Prefecture, after its main sponsor Fujita withdrew.[40] Municipal mergers caused by administrative reforms have also impacted upon the allocation of clubs. In 2003, the former Shimizu City became a district of the much larger Shizuoka City, the current home town of Shimizu S-Pulse. In the case of Urawa, it was combined with Omiya and Yono to form Saitama City in 2001, which is now home to two J. League teams – the Urawa Reds and Omiya Ardija.

Such transfers, removals and changes of names have sometimes affronted supporters and fans, and sometimes annoyed the local authorities and sponsors waiting for the promised contribution of the football clubs to their social amenities and communities.[41] A study conducted in early 2003 among seven localities of the J.League in Western Japan also revealed that most of the announcements in that region regarding football-community relations had up to then consisted of little more than lip service to the J.League mission statement, largely because of the constrained financial condition of many football teams.[42] It was around this time that the J.League intensified its efforts to promote the ideal of comprehensive communal sports clubs. Clubs were invited to apply for J.League support for programmes aiming at the expansion of their wider sport programme. In 2002 for example Shonan Bellmare established a separate, non-profit sporting organization with a focus on triathlon, beach volleyball and football for under-15-year-old players for the purpose of fostering bonds with the local community and to defray the risks associated with sport entertainment and sport social education.[43] Albirex Niigata presently supports a relay marathon (*ekiden*) running team, a basketball team, cheerleaders and a winter sports club. Urawa Reds became the first J.League club to open a comprehensive centre for community sport. Redsland is managed by the club and has five football pitches, three of which can also be used for baseball, a rugby pitch, eleven tennis courts, a daytime camping area and a farming zone. 'Urawa hope that this composite park will foster sporting activity among the young, encourage lifelong participation in sport and serve as a focal point for community development'.[44] Futsal pitches and other facilities will also be added in due course, and full-scale operation is due to begin in 2007. Through this J.League-sponsored programme, a few teams have turned into multi-sport organizations, although it is difficult to say exactly whether the current phase of expansion will eventually generate mass sport participation.

As the J.League seeks to instil its ideologies and visions for football-community relations at grassroots level in Japan the main efforts have been concentrated on the further promotion of football. J.League membership contracts were changed so that community involvement by all registered clubs and players has become mandatory since 2003. Since then, J.League players, coaches and other club staff have joined in more than 1,000 community activities that included soccer schools, visits to children's and old people's homes, and other forms of social service. For the past seven years annually held 'JOIN Days' have provided special family events, including football training, during the national holiday period at the end of April and beginning of May.[45] Almost literally at grassroots level, the J.League has also launched a campaign to increase the number of grass pitches available in elementary and high schools. 'Mr Pitch', a two-metre tall official mascot – a walking piece of (artificial) grass – has become the 'J.League 100 years vision messenger'. As the icon of the campaign Mr Pitch is a regular visitor to events organized by the J.League and its member clubs.[46]

Conclusions

Can we sustain our argument about the existence of a Japanese ISA? We have identified a number of key variables we consider to be responsible for the emergence of distinct patterns of community-football relations in Japan. In addition, we have shown that whilst much of the discourse on football and the Japanese community serves very different interests, it continues to facilitate most of all the proliferation of private consumption, public spending and transnational money flows. We suggest that talking about community development, and hinting at regeneration and improvement through community mobilization around football, represents one means to create public support and to gain wider acceptance for the J.League mission.

It might be argued that the creation of a commercially viable sports community (and an important component of an ISA) relies upon mediated coverage, and the commercial mass media in Japan has been a prominent ally, patron and sponsor of certain sports.[47] Football in Japan still struggles against the prominence of other sports in the broadcasting networks, most noticeably professional baseball and sumo wrestling. On one weekend in March 2006 for example there was no free-to-air live coverage of the Osaka derby football match between Cerezo and Gamba (the reigning J.League champions) whilst a pre-season friendly between Hanshin Tigers and Tokyo Giants at Koshien Stadium (close to Osaka) was given ball-by-ball commentary on the radio and the Osaka sumo tournament (basho) received live television coverage on NHK. Football in Japan has attracted a loyal fanbase in the past 13 years but media coverage of it is still largely dictated by commercially driven estimates about the audience ratings compared with those for baseball and sumo. In this respect it is through the new media – internet and mobile telephony especially – that networks have been established between clubs, supporters and peripheral visitors. Interactive media in particular enabled the creation of notable cyber fan communities, following football as well as other spheres that the grassroots football community will most likely develop in the immediate future.

Making professional football a viable business in Japan has been a challenge, and for many clubs will continue to be so. As a product, and as a consumer good, however, football has clearly come to stay. As football journalist Keir Radnedge noted in 2005 'Japanese football and the J.League, both through the teams and the individual players, have come of age in European eyes'.[48] In this essay we have argued that the J.League has been successful both in setting up a prospering industry and in shifting the collective Japanese imagination away from the nation to the region and the locality. It is instructive however to view the formation of the J.League in Japan as a distinctive use of football.

If belonging today (i.e. community today) is 'about participation in communication'[49] then the J.League has started something. There appear to be many Japanese people who aspire to belong to the imaginary football family. Despite our emphasis here, on top-down more than on bottom-up developments in football, we think that this is a fair reflection of a Japanese culture of 'friendly authoritarianism'.[50] Hence the creation of football communities is firmly linked to a weak tradition of initiatives from the bottom up, while top down initiatives are widely institutionalized and socially accepted. Like Delanty we also hope to have indicated ways in which the imagined football community can be both constitutive of agency as well as experienced as an imposed institutional structure. This is evidenced by the growing number of players, officials and teams formally registered with the JFA. In 2005 nearly 30,000 11-a-side teams were registered, and there were over 1.2 million players and officials – including 876,702 players and 120,472 futsal players, who enjoy a less formalized way of practicing the game that has proliferated ever since the 2002 World Cup.[51]

The initiatives discussed in this essay reveal how football in Japan is working to give something back to society. We are fully aware of the gaps in our knowledge at this stage and the need to consider in more detail the reality and the image of communities in Japanese football at all levels, particularly below the professional J.League.[52] Hence more investigation is needed into the community relations engaged in by all football clubs to reveal the patterns of clubs' and players' relative attachment to, or detachment from, their local communities. Only in this way can we answer the key question of what benefits grassroots football acquires from commercial success at the top of the game. That is a research question, something for future work.

Notes

1. Castells, *Rise of the Network Society*.
2. Delanty, *Community*.
3. Bale, 'Changing Face of Football'.
4. Cf. Football Task Forc, *Investing in the Community*; Morrow and Hamil, 'Corporate Community Involvement'; DTP, *Active Engagement*.
5. Cf. Horne with Bleakley, 'Development of Football'.
6. Sawano, *Kigyo supotsu*.
7. Although assertions of their historical continuity have dominated public discourse both within and outside of Japan, the prevalence of formal and informal institutions organizing communal life, often at the expense of individuals' desires, was not simply a continuation of traditional practices, as sociological and anthropological studies have shown. The work of Dore, *City Life in Japan*, Fukutake, *Japanese Social Structure*, and Bestor, *Neighbourhood Tokyo*, to name but a few, has provided ample evidence that demonstrates that the so-called characteristic patterns of Japanese social organization were the result of conscious and concerted efforts to adapt traditional small-scale rural settlements and urban neighbourhoods to modern associational forms by finding a balance between expressive solidarity and instrumental association (or in Durkheimian terms, between mechanic and organic solidarity). Modern associations of self-government, such as neighbourhood wards (*chonaikai*) or residents' committees

72   J. Horne and W. Manzenreiter

for organizing local affairs (*jichikai*) were created in response to the general process of urban growth, the particular historical circumstances of the community in question and of Japanese society in general during the twentieth century, and not indicative of the persistence of a deeply rooted cultural archetype; see Bestor *Neighbourhood Tokyo*, 259.
8. Lützeler and Ben-Ari, 'Urban Society'; Robertson, *Native and Newcomer*.
9. Cf. Etzioni, *Spirit of Community*.
10. Harvey, 'New Urbanism'.
11. Cf. Fukutake, *Japanese Social Structure*.
12. Cf. Manzenreiter and Horne, 'Public Policy'.
13. Manzenreiter, 'Fußball und die Krise der Männlichkeit'.
14. Manzenreiter, 'Nihon shakai'.
15. In some cases, the links with the past are quite explicit. The logo of Jubilo Iwata refers, with the words 'Yamaha FC', to the origins of the side as a company team. Similar to the Urawa Reds team, which is owned by the Mitsubishi Motors Football Club, Jubilo Iwata is run by the Yamaha Football Co., Ltd. Both are independent corporations but benefit from the good relations with their former owner company that now acts as a major, but not sole, sponsor.
16. Below the J.League there is the amateur Japan Football League (JFL) where another aspirant clubs – comprising company and university teams, as well as those representing communities from even the most southerly island of Okinawa, as well the main islands of Honshu and Kyushu – compete to earn the right to play-off against the bottom team in J2 and thus gain promotion. Below this level competitive football in Japan is organized into nine District Leagues and on a Prefectural basis (a prefecture is an administrative division, roughly equivalent to a county, and there are 47 in Japan).
17. Manzenreiter and Horne, 'Global Governance', 10.
18. Hirose, 'Making of a Professional Football League'.
19. Ubukata, *J.Riigu no keizaigaku*, 21, 92.
20. The broader background to the establishment of the J.League can be found in Horne, '*Sakka* in Japan'; 'Soccer in Japan'; 'Professional football in Japan'; and Manzenreiter, 'Japan und der Fußball'.
21. Sports for All was the core notion of the Golden Plan, a comprehensive programme to improve the sports infrastructure and to grow sport participation rates by the German government in the 1960s.
22. For example, the J.League enthusiastically describes an over-simplified and idealized image of German sports that ignores the fundamental problems voluntary sport organizations are facing and the efforts of professional clubs to separate their business activities from the social services of amateur sports. 'The German professional football clubs are comprehensive sports clubs where the whole family, from children to the elderly, can enjoy every kind of athletic activity. People of the community enjoy their own sport during the week and turn out as a family to support their professional team on match days. Sports Schule are also found nationwide where practical training is given to future players, coaches, management staff and others in every sport.'. J.League, *2005 J-League sutajiamu*, homepage.)
23. Compare the English references to the J-League Mission at www.j-league.or.jp/eng/mission.
24. Hirose, 'Making of a Professional Football League'.
25. Kubotani, 'Supotsu shinko ni yoru kiban seibi', 50.
26. Koiwai, 'Sakka ni yoru machizukuri', 62ff.
27. Ubukata, *J.Riigu no keizaigaku*, 52ff; 113f.
28. Kinohara, 'J.League Chairman Saburo Kawabuchi'.
29. Arimoto, 'Narrating Football', 68.
30. Kimura, 'Oita Trinita'.
31. Yamashita and Saka, 'Another Kick Off'.
32. J.League, *2005 J-League sutajiamu*.
33. Uchiumi, 'Arubi ga seicho', 121.
34. Kozu *et al.*, *Puro supotsu*.
35. Tsujiya, *Sakka ga yatte kita*, 170.
36. Morisaki, 'Believe'.
37. J.League, *Official Newsletter, January*, 31.
38. Similar in some respects therefore to FC United, the team formed by disgruntled fans following the takeover of Manchester United by Malcolm Glazer in 2005.
39. Tsujiya, *Sakka ga yatte kita*, 97, 124.
40. Kawabata, 'Sekkeizu of tsuita yume', 60.
41. It is noteworthy that Verdy's home town relocation away from Kawasaki to Inari in Tokyo did not face any resistance from fans. Verdy, the former powerhouse of Japanese corporate/amateur football before

the J.League, because of its association with the Yomiuri communications group, and champion of the J.League in its first season (1993) received only a single letter of complaint when it announced its transfer to Tokyo (Kinohara, 'J.League Chairman Saburo Kawabuchi').
42. Manzenreiter, 'Sport zwischen Markt und öffentlicher Dienstleistung'.
43. Kawabata, 'Sekkeizu of tsuita yume'.
44. J.League, *Official Newsletter 33*, 5.
45. J.League, *Official Newsletter 30*, 7.
46. Commencing in 2004, the Japan Football Association (JFA) also supported the setting up of regional sports clubs. Subsidies were offered to regional joint venture projects proposed by prefectural soccer associations, J.League clubs and local governments. Each of the subsidized facilities was to be equipped with a grass soccer pitch, a clubhouse and lighting for night games. Subsidies aimed to cover two-thirds of construction and maintenance costs. The association also trained club managers.
47. Horne, 'Sport and the Mass Media in Japan'.
48. J.League, *Official Newsletter 33*, 6.
49. Delanty, *Community*, 187.
50. Sugimoto, *Introduction to Japanese Society*.
51. Futsal – a form of the five-a-side football game– has been the success story in recent years in terms of participation sport in Japan: http://www.jfa.or.jp/e/news/2006/060417_3.html.
52. One area for future investigation are the relationships between ethnic minority and socially excluded communities and football, such as the fans of J1 team Cerezo Osaka, supported by many of the Korean minority in the south of the city, and the Chosen Shukyu Dan, the leading football team in the Kansai District league, that represents the Korean community in Osaka.

References

Arimoto, T. 'Narrating Football'. *Inter-Asia Cultural Studies* 5, no. 1 (2004): 63–76.
Bale, J. 'The Changing Face of Football: Stadiums and Communities'. In *The Future of Football: Challenges for the Twenty-first Century,* ed. J. Garland, D. Malcolm and M. Rowe, 91–101. London: Frank Cass, 2000.
Bestor, T. *Neighbourhood Tokyo.* Tokyo: Kodansha International, 1989.
Castells, Manuel. *The Rise of the Network Society. The Information Age: Economy, Society and Culture.* Oxford: Blackwell, 1996.
Delanty, G. *Community.* London: Routledge, 2003.
Dore, R. *City Life in Japan.* Berkeley, CA: University of California Press, 1958.
DTP/David Taylor Partnerships. *Active Engagement. A Study of Northwest Professional Sport Clubs' Involvement in Community Regeneration.* Warrington: NWDA, 2006.
Etzioni, A. *The Spirit of Community.* New York: Crown Publishers, 1993.
Football Task Force. *Investing in the Community. A Submission by the Football Task Force to the Minister of Sport.* London: Football Task Force, 1999.
Fukutake, T. *The Japanese Social Structure – its Evolution in the Modern Century.* Tokyo: University of Tokyo Press, 1989.
Harvey, D. 'The New Urbanism and the Communitarian Trap'. *Harvard Design Magazine* 1 (1997): 1–3.
Hirose, I. 'The Making of a Professional Football League: The Design of the J.League System'. In *Football goes East: Business, Culture and the People's Game in East Asia,* ed. W. Manzenreiter and J. Horne, 38–53. London: Routledge, 2004.
Horne, J. '*Sakka* in Japan'. *Media, Culture and Society* 18, no. 4 (1996): 527–47.
———. 'Soccer in Japan: Is *wa* all you need?' *Culture, Sport, Society* 2, no. 3 (1999): 212–29.
———. 'Professional Football in Japan'. In *Japan at Play,* ed. J. Hendry and M. Raveri, 199–213. London: Routledge, 2001.
———. 'Sport and the Mass Media in Japan'. *Sociology of Sport Journal* 22, no. 4 (2005): 415–32.
Horne, J., with D. Bleakley. 'The Development of Football in Japan'. In *Japan, Korea and the 2002 World Cup,* ed. J. Horne and W. Manzenreiter, 89–105. London: Routledge, 2002.
J.League. *J.League News: Official Newsletter 30.* Tokyo: Japan Professional Football League, 2004.
———. *J.League News: Official Newsletter, January, 31.* Tokyo: Japan Professional Football League, 2005a.
———. *J.League News: Official Newsletter 33.* Tokyo: Japan Professional Football League, 2005b.
———. *2005 J.League Guide* (English). Tokyo: Japan Professional Football League, 2005c.

———. *2005 J-League sutajiamu kansensha chosa hokokusho* [Report on the stadium survey of J.League spectators in 2005]. Tokyo: Nihon Puro Sakka Riigu, 2006.

Kawabata, Y. 'Sekkeizu of tsuita yume. NPO hojin Shonan Bellmare Supotsu Kurabu' [Dream with a blueprint – NGO Sportklub Shonan Bellmare]. *Sakka Hihyo* 17 (2003): 59–67.

Kimura ,Y. 'Oita Trinita, kanshudo no ketsujitsu to kongo' [Oita Trinita – the fruits of bureaucratic leadership and the future]. *Sakka Hihyo* 18 (2003): 70–5.

Kinohara, K. 'J.League Chairman Saburo Kawabuchi: Bad Days are Over, but J.League must Change with the Times'. *Japan Times,* March 9, 2001.

Koiwai Z. 'Sakka ni yoru machizukuri' [Town development though football]. *Toshi Mondai* 85, no. 12 (1994): 59–69.

Kozu, M. et al. *Puro supotsu to chiiki chakumitsu. Supotsu chiiki chosa in Niigata* [Professional sports and regional adherence. Sport region survey in Niigata] (2002). Tokyo: Hitotsubashi University. Online available at http://www.soc.hit-u.ac.jp/~kozu/activity.

Kubotani O. 'Supotsu shinko ni yoru kiban seibi. Genjo to kadai' [Basis maintenance by sports promotion]. *Toshi Mondai* 85, no. 12 (1994): 43–57.

Lützeler, Ralph, and Eyal Ben-Ari. 'Urban Society'. In *Modern Japanese Society,* ed. J. Kreiner, U. Möhwald, and H.D. Ölschleger, 277–303. Leiden: Brill, 2005.

Manzenreiter, W. 'Japan und der Fußball im Zeitalter der technischen Reproduzierbarkeit: Die J.League zwischen Lokalpolitik und Globalkultur' [Japan and football in the age of technical reproduction. The J.League between local politics and global culture]. In *Global Players. Kultur, Ökonomie und Politik des Fußballs,* ed. M. Fanizadeh, G. Hödl, and W. Manzenreiter, 133–58. Frankfurt/Wien: Brandes & Apsel/Südwind, 2002.

———. 'Nihon shakai no "ibentoka" to sakka' [Football and the 'eventisation' of Japanese society]. *Supotsu Shakaigaku Kenkyu/Japan Journal of Sport Sociology* 12 (2004a): 25–35.

———. 'Sport zwischen Markt und öffentlicher Dienstleistung. Zur Zukunft des Breitensports in Japan' [Sports between market and public good. The future of mass sports in Japan]. *SWS-Rundschau* (Journal für Sozialforschung) 44, no. 2 (2004b) (special issue: Sport): 227–51.

———. 'Fußball und die Krise der Männlichkeit in Japan' [Football and the crisis of masculinity in Japan]. In *Fußball: Die männliche Weltordnung,* ed. E. Kreisky and G. Spitaler, 296–313. Frankfurt: Campus, 2006.

Manzenreiter, W., and J. Horne. 'Global Governance in World Sport and the 2002 World Cup Korea/Japan'. In *Japan, Korea and the 2002 World Cup,* ed. J. Horne and W. Manzenreiter, 1–25. London: Routledge, 2002.

———. 'Public Policy, Sports Investments and Regional Development Initiatives in Contemporary Japan'. In *The Political Economy of Sport,* ed. J. Nauright and K. Schimmel, 152–82. London: Palgrave Macmillan, 2005.

Morisaki, K. 'Believe – keiyaku no shunkan' [Believe – the moment of a contract]. In *Niigata gensho. Nihonkai tenkoku no tanjo o megutte* [Phenomenon Niigata. On the birth of a football empire at the Japan Sea], ed. Sakka Hihyo, 195–235. Tokyo: Futabasha, 2004.

Morrow, S., and S. Hamil. 'Corporate Community Involvement by Football Clubs: Business Strategy or Social Obligation?' (Working paper, *Stirling Research Papers in Sports Studies* 1, no. 1. Stirling: University of Stirling, 2003).

Robertson, J. *Native and Newcomer: Making and Remaking a Japanese City.* Berkeley, CA: University of California Press, 1991.

Sawano, M. *Kigyo supotsu no eiko to zasetsu* [Glory and failure of corporate sports]. Tokyo: Seikyusha, 2005.

Sugimoto, Y. *An Introduction to Japanese Society.* Cambridge: Cambridge University Press, 1997.

Tsujiya, A. *Sakka ga yatte kita. Thespa Kusatsu to iu jikken* [Football has come – The experiment of Thespa Kusatsu]. Tokyo: NHK Shuppan, 2005.

Ubukata, Y. *J.Riigu no keizaigaku* [The economics of the J.League]. Tokyo: Asahi Shinbun Sha, 1994.

Uchiumi, K. 'Arubi ga seicho o tsuzukeru tame ni' [For that Albi can continue to grow]. In *Niigata gensho. Nihonkai tenkoku no tanjo o megutte* [Phenomenon Niigata. On the birth of a football empire at the Japan Sea], ed. Sakka Hihyo, 111–28. Tokyo: Futabasha, 2004.

Yamashita, T., and N. Saka. 'Another Kick Off: The 2002 World Cup and Soccer Voluntary Groups as a New Social Movement'. In *Japan, Korea and the 2002 World Cup,* ed. J. Horne and W. Manzenreiter, 147–61. London: Routledge, 2002.

NATIONS AND ETHNICITIES
'The nation and its fragments': football and community in India[1]

Kausik Bandyopadhyay

Introduction: football and community in the Indian context

Football has been one of the central components of popular culture in colonial and post-colonial India. Throughout the game's history it has been closely linked to various historical processes which have shaped the society and culture of the region since the late nineteenth century. These include imperialism, nationalism, communalism, regionalism, decolonization, partition, immigration, violence, diplomacy, inter-state relations, commercialization and professionalism.[2] The history of Indian football has also been inextricably linked with the formation of community connections and identities which have been strongly articulated through the game in different ways during different periods of time. Whilst the notion of 'community' is itself ambiguous and debatable, it can be meaningfully analysed – in the context of this essay – through concepts such as nationalism, communalism and sub-regionalism.[3] In India, football started as a marker of nationalist identity and community against British imperialism. This, however, gave way to a series of fragmentations in terms of new forms of community connections or identities. These related to social *differences* expressed through communal and sub-regional identities represented through club loyalties. Indeed, it is in relation to the expression of these differences that football thrived as a mass spectator sport in colonial and post-colonial India.

This essay examines the ways in which the notion of 'community' can be theoretically reconceptualized in the context of Indian football. By doing so, it will establish football's credibility as a viable theme in the study of national/regional/local identities in Indian social history and cultural studies. It will also bring forth the pertinent question of 'the autonomy of sport as a manifestation of indigenous popular culture, and local, regional and national negotiation and resistance in the face of global movements'.[4]

Football in India: the beginnings

It is reasonably clear that football came to India with the East India Company. The game's early pioneers were the officers and men of Trading Farms and Regimental Battalions, European professors of educational institutions, and naval men who used to play the game at ports such as Calcutta, Bombay, Madras and Karachi.[5] Tony Mason and Paul Dimeo, following the most overarching and widely popular theory of the 'games ethic' popularized by J.A. Mangan, explain football's introduction and organization in Calcutta primarily in terms of the British public school games-playing ethos[6] learnt by the educated Bengali lower-middle and middle classes at the British-run Anglo-Indian colleges.[7] The 'games ethic' concept – in common with the notion of 'muscular Christianity'[8] propagated by moral missionaries – had a firm belief in sport as an instrument of imperial moral persuasion. This belief was clearly discernible in the efforts of evangelicals such as Theodore Leighton Pennell and Cecil Earle Tyndale-Biscoe who used football in the North-west Frontier Provinces and in Kashmir respectively as a 'key weapon in the battle to win over local populations and to begin transforming them from their "uncivilized" and "heathen" state to one where they might be considered "civilized" and "Christian"'.[9] In Bengal, especially in Calcutta, Anglo-Indian schools certainly utilized sports including football as integral elements of their educational curriculum. To these early missionaries, as well as public school teachers, the game was a moral tool to inculcate 'a series of ... lessons, regarding hard work and perseverance, about team loyalty and obedience to authority and, indeed, involving concepts of correct physical development and "manliness"'.[10]

Despite the initial importance of middle-class schools and colleges in the development of football in India, their ultimate role in the widespread promotion of the game should not be overstated. Indeed, football's appropriation by the Indian public during the late nineteenth century was a distinctly complex process, especially in Bengal where the game came to be embroiled in identity politics and cultural resistance.

During the mid-to-late nineteenth century, the Bengali 'community' was stereotyped by its British colonizers as an effeminate non-military race.[11] The response to this was uniquely *cultural*. The Bengali people reacted to the stereotype through the promotion of a 'neo-traditional physical culture' to efface the 'self-image of effeteness'.[12] This promotion was led by a number of noted Bengali intellectuals and middle-class cultural nationalists who urgently led a resurgence in traditional Bengali physical culture and traditional indigenous games. This movement – led and popularized in Bengal by Nabagopal Mitra's *Hindu Mela* in the 1860s–70s – began to promote the rejuvenation of the ancient Hindu principle of physical culture.[13] However, the physical culture movement was marked by a conspicuous lack of any competitive element which exemplified modern western sports like football, cricket and hockey. Moreover, even if rigorous physical exercise was looked upon as a plausible weapon to counter British stereotypes of local physical weakness, it did not afford Bengalis the opportunity to compete with the their colonizers on even terms. Middle-class Bengalis quickly realized the futility of the traditional physical culture movement as a form of cultural resistance, and sought new ways to reassert their physical prowess and redeem their masculinity. Western sports, and especially football, provided the ideal tools. Dimeo has argued that by adopting modern sports in this fashion Bengalis followed a 'route of mimicry'.[14] However, he fails to identify that these sports were adopted explicitly as a form of resistance which would enable Bengalis to show their physical worth by competing with Europeans on an equal plane. Football's adaptation was, therefore, more of a cultural ploy than a simplistic form of mimicry.

In the 1880s and 1890s, football in India was solidly regarded as a cultural weapon to reassert Bengali/Indian physical prowess and masculinity. By the end of the nineteenth century the game had developed from being an occasional recreation for military men and a school sport/leisure activity among other Europeans to being an arena for competition and conflict between the British and the Indians.[15] To suggest that Indian football clubs of the 1880s and 1890s from their very inception began to reflect or represent nationalist instincts on the sports field is almost certainly overbold. However, by the turn of the century football in India can be described as a new and unique cultural nationalist force, although the approach of different clubs to the game was not always uniform.

It was the Mohun Bagan club which rose amongst its contemporaries to symbolize the clearest nationalist response to the injured 'cultural self' of Indians during this period. Originally founded in 1889 by a few idealistic North Calcutta gentlemen at Mohun Bagan villa, it proved, from its very inception, to be more than a simple sports club. It was an institution with the avowed objective to not only produce excellent sportsmen, but also to impart in them impeccable moral and social values. The ideals that the founders set before themselves were novel for Indians at the time.[16] The executives of the club saw to it that each member combined the development of the body with the development of their 'mind'. Little did the pioneers envisage, however, that the club would, through its epic victory over the East York Regiment in the 1911 IFA Shield final, bring about a national reawakening.

One club, one nationalism: football and nationalist community in colonial India

Within a span of three decades, football had become an important part of Bengali popular culture in colonial India. It transcended simple recreational practices and became a cultural weapon to fight British imperialism. At the turn of the century Bengali youth came to look upon football 'as an avenue through which they would be able to retrieve their sinking political prestige and establish their superiority over the semblance of power the Raj represented'.[17] Indeed, the sight of 'puny', barefooted, Bengali players matching heavily built and better-equipped Europeans soon took on the form of a cultural battle against foreign rulers. In the shifting socio-political context of the early twentieth century, when Bengal was engulfed by a spate of nationalist fervour in the wake of the anti-partition movement during 1905–08,[18] football came increasingly to be looked upon as a novel instrument of cultural nationalism in Bengal. The game became a weapon to use on the cultural battlefield of the *maidan*[19] and an emblem around which nationalist consciousness could be fostered. In the wake of vehement anti-partition agitation, Bengali looked towards the game with a new purpose. Any success against British teams on the football field began to be viewed as a victory of the spirit of nationalism over the evil of colonialism.

The trend of barefoot on-field battle against European civil and military teams was set in the context of political agitation and social unrest which grew in response to the partition of Bengal in 1905. From that year onwards, the Mohun Bagan club came to prominence with successive wins in the Cooch Behar Cup in 1904–05 and a Gladstone Cup success in the same season. From 1906 to 1908 the club won the Trades Cup three times in a row. This was in addition to winning the Gladstone Cup in 1908, the Cooch Behar Cup in 1907 and 1908, and the Lakshibilas Cup in 1909 and 1910. More importantly, Mohun Bagan began to achieve a series of victories against strong European sides during this period stirring up a passionate blend of nationalist fervour amongst the Bengali community.

The rise of Mohun Bagan to fame had a clear impact on the emotional involvement of Indian people with football. The Indian crowd became enmeshed with the on-field tensions of soccer encounters between 'their' team and various European outfits. People all over Bengal appreciated these victories in the context of a surge of anti-British sentiments in the political realm, and in July 1911 Mohun Bagan – comprising ten barefooted Indian players[20] – created sporting history when it defeated European civil and military teams one by one to lift the coveted Indian

Football Association (IFA) Shield.[21] The enthusiasm that Mohun Bagan's march to the final created was unique. It was 'the moment of departure'[22] in Indian football history when an Indian nationalism started appropriating a western sport to assert its distinctive identity. The crowd which attended the games was estimated to be between 80,000 and 100,000 strong. As one newspaper noted: 'The spectators who packed every inch of the Maidan simply defied calculation. They might have been eighty thousand or they might have been more.'[23] Thus when Mohun Bagan actually entered the final of the IFA Shield, signs of a great mass awakening in Bengal were quite visible. People became obsessed with the dream of beating the ruling British at their own national game. The dream became reality when Mohun Bagan defeated the East Yorks team 2-1 in the historic final of 29 July 1911.

Mohun Bagan's victory was hailed as a blow struck not only for Indian football but also for Indian nationalism. However, it is difficult to ascertain whether the 'nation' appealed to was Bengal or India. Most of the press reports, in celebrating the victory, used the terms 'Bengali' and 'Indian' interchangeably,[24] thereby indicating the ambiguous nature of footballing nationalism in colonial India. However, it is clear from the reports that Indian people – irrespective of class, caste or community – were supposed to connect with a victory over the British imperial ruling class.

Recent observations on the 1911 Mohun Bagan victory largely confirm the view that it had a strong impact on Indian society. Indeed, attempts have even been made to relate the Shield triumph to the moving of the capital of Indian from Calcutta to Delhi later in the same year. Ramachandra Guha, noted Indian sports historian, states:

> It was in the same year, 1911, that the British shifted the capital of the *raj* from Calcutta to Delhi. Recent memorialists of Mohun Bagan's victory have, alas, failed to notice this coincidence. *If* it is a coincidence, for it is highly likely that one was the cause of the other and that to pre-empt further humiliation the British adroitly and deliberately moved the seat of power from Bengal, away from its skilful footballers and its bomb-wielding nationalists. The link between sporting prowess and militant anti-imperialism was thus undermined, to be finally rent asunder by Gandhi and the Bombay capitalists.[25]

A similar interpretation is offered by Rudrangshu Mukherjee, a scholar-turned-journalist:

> The victory seems, in retrospect, to have been a triumph of the moral force which Gandhi extolled and advocated in *Hind Swaraj*. For Bengalis who had seen only a few years ago their land partitioned and their young men and women imprisoned and punished during the Swadeshi movement, the win over a white team in football seemed a moment of national pride. It appeared as some sort of recovery of dignity and self-respect in the year that Calcutta was to lose its status as the capital. It was the inherent inequality of the encounter in which the apparently weak trounced the obviously strong that made Mohun Bagan's victory the stuff of legends.[26]

In contrast to this assessment, Mason is more circumspect in his analysis of the events of 1911:

> Mohan Bagan's victory did not produce a bombardment of Fort William by Bengali athletes, nor did it provoke a military revolt against peace and order. It clearly injected some confidence into some of the native peoples of Calcutta and convinced them that they were as good as their masters. But it also seems to have reinforced admiration for those masters. Perhaps that is the essence of the mystery of hegemony.[27]

This view aside, however, it is largely accepted that in the aftermath of the Mohan Bagan victory football not only came to represent a novel cultural sporting nationalism for Indian people, but also contributed to the formation of a unique footballing identity. In the wake of the triumph, the game became a rallying point around which nationalist consciousness gained momentum. Indeed, in the first three decades of the twentieth century the *maidan* became an arena where spontaneous effusion of nationalist sentiment found ready expression as and when a native team – especially Mohun Bagan – played against British civilian or regimental sides. Playing and watching the game cut across the affiliations of indigenous caste, class and community in Indian society and provided a social bond for nationalist-minded Indians. Football as a cultural weapon to fight and defeat the British added a new dimension to the anti-British national consciousness of Indians, particularly in Bengal. Thus, parallel to the political struggle against an oppressive colonial power, there began a social struggle of national liberation organized around a specific cultural activity. In that context, the football *maidan* as a national cultural territory began to reflect an Indian nationalist impulse that found heroic expression in the effort of the footballers.

In the aftermath of Mohun Bagan's successes, football gradually came to present an outlet for the 'pent-up nationalism' of Bengali professionals and students. A large section of the Bengali community were affluent, educated, practical and decent, but were hesitant to actively take part in the freedom struggle. As such, they came to view the football field as an ideal place to confront British imperialism. Similarly, Bengali youth, many of whom were reluctant to participate in politics of direct confrontation, came to view football as a potent nationalist gesture and beating the British came to produce an immense emotional satisfaction for them. Urban and suburban middle-class Bengalis, who served the British as officials, clerks or professionals, could not show their anti-British resentment in public, and working-class people, who were not drawn into the fold of nationalist politics until the late 1920s, could only really express their nationalism is covert ways. This 'pent-up' nationalism of the Bengali middle and working classes thus found prolific expression through emotional outbursts experienced during Mohun Bagan's matches.

On the football field it was considered to be an act of great courage to shove an elbow or a fist into the face of a Sahib or a soldier, or kick him under the guise of tackling. Those who could get away with it were respected as great players. Footballers like Gostho Paul, Abhilash Ghosh and Balai Chatterjee earned glamour and fame in Bengali society for their reputation of successfully executing 'reverse hits' or *palta mar*. Off the field it was also claimed that some Indian spectators would deliberately pick quarrels with the 'superior' British. Sometimes these encounters would turn violent and afford the Bengalis the opportunity of giving the *gora* Sahibs a 'sound beating'. Indeed, the nationalist element within Bengali football culture during this period was often most obvious amongst spectators. Spontaneous effusion of nationalist feeling found prolific expression in specific forms of behaviours including pitch-side language; jokes and doggerels; erratic vocal outbursts; peculiar physical gestures; tearing shirts; throwing sandals and stones into the ground; torching papers and clothes; and, occasionally, spectator-violence.

For European scholars like Mason and Dimeo, Indian football victories over colonial masters were little but a sign of the success of British cultural imperialism.[28] They read in such football victories Indians' unwitting admiration for, acceptance of, and submission to, such cultural imperialism. Richard Cashman has raised a pertinent question as to whether we can analyse the spread of colonial sports solely in terms of the ideology of colonialism and the spread of the games ethic.[29] For him, the indigenous appropriation (domestication) of modern sports (cricket in his case) calls for more logical explanation.[30] Cashman's conclusion is that, 'while games are an effective vehicle for proselytization in some circumstances, they can be subverted in others'.[31] The appropriation of football in colonial India for nationalist purposes, as this section has shown, certainly suggests a colonial reformulation of the imperial model of the games ethic. It points to football's transformed role as an instrument of reaction, resistance and subversion configured in one club and represented by one national community.

Communalism on the maidan: football and communal identity in colonial India

By the early twentieth century, football came to provide a potential source of coalescence for Indian people irrespective of caste, class, religion or community affiliation. Players' and spectators' identities had the capacity to cut across traditional social categories and express a form of national communalism. However, the game could not hold on to this apparent unifying influence for long. Differences and conflicts based on social, religious, regional and sub-regional affiliations split the coherent footballing identity of the country into fragments. From the mid-1930s onwards, India's anti-British footballing nationalism came to be fractured and with the rise of the Mohammedan Sporting Club to football fame in the early 1930s rivalry in India football was no longer confined to Briton versus Indian. Instead it came to express divisions between Hindu and Muslim communities for the first time.

Muslim representation in Indian football began in the last decade of the nineteenth century when Mohammedan Sporting Club[32] rose in prominence thanks to the efforts of a number of Muslim individuals. The club, established in 1891, was quickly understood as a Muslim institution and gradually carved out a niche in the Indian football scene.[33] It would, however, be a mistake to argue that the club reflected divisive sectarianism at its inception. According to *The Mussalman*, in the aftermath of Mohun Bagan's famous Shield victory, the members of Mohammedan Sporting 'were almost mad and rolling on the ground with joyous excitement on the victory of their Hindu brethren'.[34] Another Muslim journal, *The Comrade*, of which Maulana Mohammed Ali was the founder and editor at that time said: 'We hereby join the chorus of praise and jubilation over the splendid victory of Mohun Bagan. The team did remarkably well throughout the tournament and won the Shield by sheer merit.'[35] Recounting Mohun Bagan's status as a team beloved by both communities, Achintya Kumar Sengupta wrote:

> Till then communalism had not entered the sports-field. Mohun Bagan then belonged to both the Hindu and the Muslim. The green galleries that burnt in the football stadium of the Calcutta that day carried the mark of both Hindu and Muslim hands. One brought the petrol and the other the matches.[36]

When Mohammedan Sporting Club began to emerge as a powerful team in Indian football in early 1930s, it was perhaps inevitable that the atmosphere around the club would change. Whilst its achievements were undoubtedly *Indian* success stories, Hindu football-lovers felt only a mixture of respect and fear for the club with no real sensation of joy.[37] The Muslim League, by then a force hostile to the Congress, was the ruling party in Bengal in the early 1930s and had the support of the British. Muslim nationalists could soon be seen holding the Congress flag in one hand and the black-and-white banner of Mohammedan Sporting in the other, and the Muslim League itself came to use the club as a cultural example of Muslim superiority in Bengal. From the second half of the 1930s, rivalry in Indian football was no longer confined to the British versus the Indians, but had extended to include Hindus versus Muslims, adding definite sectarian overtones to the sport.

In 1932 'a group of young, energetic, patriotic and progressive men' in Calcutta formed the New Muslim Majlis.[38] The main driver behind this development was Khwaja Nooruddin, cousin and brother-in-law of Khwaja Nazimuddin, who later played a heroic part in making the Mohammedan Sporting Club a premier football club. One of the immediate aims of the Majlis was to co-opt the Mohammedan Sporting Club and to develop it into the nation's premier club. The socio-political successes of the Majlis went hand in hand with the success on the football field achieved by the Mohammedan Sporting Club.

When the club went on to win the first division league in its first year at that level, the repercussions were overwhelming. The club souvenir published in 1935 noted:

In the 44th year of its existence we find the club not only makes its own history but history in Indian Football by winning the championship of the Calcutta Football League. When the Calcutta League, 1934, opened, the Mohammedan Sporting team were styled as the babes of the League owing to their promotion from the second division. From babes through the evolution of victory after victory and holding the top place on the League table they became the giants of the League and earned the coveted and unique distinction of being the first Indian team to win the League.[39]

The club souvenir also pointed to enormous enthusiasm that the victory brought in its wake:

With their progress in the League there was unbounded enthusiasm among the Muslim public of Calcutta and the team were responsible for increasing the gates at which ever match they played fourfold. But not only in Calcutta was this enthusiasm manifested. In the mofussil thousands followed each game with the greatest of interest, so much so that many used to walk miles to the railway station to meet incoming trains with Calcutta newspapers in order to get the results as soon as possible.

After their the team was lionized in the city of Calcutta and it was not for some weeks after that they could call an evening their own without having to attend some function in their honour. They were given a civic reception at the Town Hall when an address was presented to them by the Mayor of Calcutta.[40]

In 1935 when Mohammedan Sporting lifted the League for the second consecutive time, it was deemed to be a great achievement by Calcutta Muslims. The club souvenir thus recorded the immediate reaction to the victory: 'Tumultuous scenes were witnessed on the Calcutta ground after the match. The joy of the crowd was unbounded and each of the players were carried shoulder high while their bus was escorted in triumphant procession by thousands of Mohammedans wild with joy.'[41]

The success of Mohammedan Sporting in lifting the Calcutta football league had a mixed impact on Indian society. For some – irrespective of their caste, creed or community – it was a worthy victory for Bengalis alia Indians on the sporting field. Indeed, the supremacy the club mastered over British sides was hailed as a unifying Indian victory in many quarters. For some Hindus, however, the victory was a cause for concern as it represented a victory of Muslim confidence and superiority.

There were tributes and messages, as gathered from the club's souvenir, which clearly hailed Mohammedan's victory as a success for the Muslim community. The Mayor of Calcutta, A.K. Fazlul Haque, commented: 'The marvellous achievements of the Mohammedan Sporting Club on the football field have earned a name and fame for Muslims in the sporting world, of which the community may justly be proud.'[42] Syed Abdul Hafeez, a member of the Council of State, wrote in his message: 'The Muslims of the sporting world take pride in the initiation taken by the Mohammedan Sporting Club of Calcutta. The club came into existence to fulfil a long felt want of the sporting spirit of the community.'[43] Another Muslim gentleman, M. Rafique, spoke of the importance of the club's success in terms of a great community service:

Games and sports play a vital part in moulding and shaping the character and ultimately the destinies of individuals, no less than that of communities. The success of the Mohammedan Sporting Club will be a harbinger of greater successes in the *self-realisation of our great community in other branches of human endeavour*.[44]

After a second year of league success, the Mohammedan Sporting Club was clearly established as a symbol of Muslim identity and confidence across India. This is evident in the congratulatory messages it received from different corners of Bengal and the whole of the country.[45] As K. Nooruddin, one of the revivers of the club in the 1930s, remarked, 'Their spectacular performance, in recent years, is the turning point for the Mussalmans of Bengal in the field of sports.'[46] More importantly, in terms of how Muslim fans reacted to the victories, the club souvenir recorded the following:

> Ever since their [the club's] chances were rosy in the League last year and throughout this year, they have had the solid backing of thousands of supporters who rain, cloud or sunshine, have mustered to a man to see them play and encourage them.
>
> Club football fans would be amazed to see who some of these supporters are. Businessmen who leave their firms and shops to witness the games, old men who have lost interest in football for years, but who have had it resuscitated with the enthusiasm for Mohammedans.[47]

Commenting upon the Mohammedan Sporting Club's huge following during this period, Mohammad Nasiruddin, editor of *Saogat*, wrote:

> Calcutta maidan used to witness large gathering on the days of Mohammedan Sporting's match. The crowd comprised educated and uneducated youth and old men along with maulavis and maulanas. When space on the sidelines of the ground proved insufficient, diehard fans climbed upon trees and sat on the branches to witness the matches of their favourite club. Kaji Najrul Islam, the famous Muslim bard, called these over-enthusiastic fans 'branch-monkeys'.[48]

In the changing political situation in Bengal in the 1930s Mohammedan Sporting was discriminated against by the IFA. Despite the club's gallant performances against leading European teams, it was not given anywhere near the recognition accorded to Mohun Bagan after its victory in the IFA Shield in 1911. Key to the IFA's discriminatory attitude towards Salim and Mohammedan Sporting was the Muslim political ascendancy in West Bengal in the 1930s.[49] The Bengali bhadroloks began to feel threatened by the Muslim political ascendancy in Bengal in the mid 1930s.[50] With the accession of the Krishak Praja Party-Muslim League ministry led by Fazlul Haq in 1937[51], in almost every domain of the public sphere from higher education to administrative and political appointments Hindu bhadrolok preserves were under threat. It was this situation that led the IFA to oppose the dominance of Mohammedan Sporting and ultimately to look favourably upon British rule.[52]

This atmosphere of hostility failed to deter the club from registering its fifth straight league triumph in July 1938. These performances escalated tensions between the IFA and the club, and in 1938 Mohammedan Sporting again suffered from seemingly unfair treatment from the authorities. The central grievances of the club were 'maximum punishment for minimum offences, repeated bad referring, arbitrary decision with regard to the venue of matches and generally the tyranny of the majority of the council of the IFA against our club'.[53] Whilst Mohammedan Sporting did compete in the 1938 IFA Shield under extreme duress, the governing body's derisive attitude finally took its toll and forced the Mohammedans to withdraw from the Calcutta Football League in 1939. Interestingly, this withdrawal was not confined to the Mohammedan Sporting Club alone. East Bengal Club and Kalighat Club also joined together against the discriminatory attitude adopted by the IFA, which continued to favour the Mohun Bagan club.

Regardless of these administrative confrontations, victories by Mohammedan Sporting and other Muslim clubs over strong European and Hindu teams certainly instilled a spirit of self-confidence and pride in the Muslims of Bengal; the vast majority of whom, through years of persecution and humiliation, had lost faith in the future.[54] It can be argued, therefore, that the Mohammedan Sporting Club contributed significantly to an atmosphere which enabled the Muslim League to gather increasing popular support in Bengal.[55] The series of victories achieved by club, even in the all-India competitions, considerably increased the prestige of the party. The club's effect on Muslim fans was said to be consistently 'electrifying',[56] and a number of new Muslim sporting clubs in the districts and sub-divisional towns were established as a result.

Along with this new Muslim interest in football came a more aggressive form of support for teams such as Mohammedan Sporting. Indeed, the Muslims who were said to be 'rolling on the ground with joy' in 1911 at the victory of their Hindu brothers all appeared to disappear, and were replaced by a new breed of supporter who came to watch games carrying knives and bottles of soda water. Indians had never displayed such aggressive spirits on the Calcutta sports-field before. Das notes that 'reverses suffered by the Mohammedan Sporting Club in football matches enraged Muslim feelings which were expressed in sporadic violence against the Hindus',[57] and Nandy comments, 'with each victory, a communal wedge was driven deeper into Calcutta football if not into Calcutta society'.[58] Thus the transition of Indian football from nationalist force to promoter of separatist, communal identities was complete by the time of independence and partition in 1947.

The Quite India movement of 1942, the economic insecurity generated by the Second World War, the panic evacuation of Calcutta caused by the fear of Japanese bombs, the famine, restlessness among the country's youth, and the communal riots that broke out on the day of the call for 'direct action' by the Muslim League: the stress of all these events gradually reduced enthusiasm for football in India. Because of the riots, there was no competition for the Shield in 1946 and the Calcutta League was not played in 1947. Immediately after partition in August 1947, having finally achieved their wish of financially supporting and building a successful Muslim football club, the patrons of Mohammedan Sporting left for either East or West Pakistan. The club's fame and success was extinguished almost immediately, never to be revived in quite the same way again. Since independence, Mohammedan Sporting has not enjoyed another period of success like that experienced during the 1930s and 1940s and has only won the League championship on three occasions.

Confrontation and assimilation: host and migrant communities in Indian club football

In colonial India, Indians employed football to express first nationalist and later separatist, communal identities. The move from colonialism to independence, however, added a further fragmentary dimension to Indian football. In the aftermath of the Partition of Bengal that accompanied independence, large-scale Hindu immigration from East Pakistan (now Bangladesh) to West Bengal created a new socio-demographic tension which resulted in a distinct socio-cultural conflict in Bengali society. The sub-regional identity of the East Bengali Hindus clashed with that of the established Hindu settlers of West Bengal. To the West Bengali Hindus, who used to refer to East Bengali Hindus derisively as *Bangals*, the new immigrants disrupted the normal patterns of local life. Hence, they strongly disapproved of according them any prominent positions in local society, culture or business. The *Bangals*, with their common memory of a homeland culture and a shared experience of suffering and migration, fought hard to earn their living, economic strength, social position and cultural recognition to ensure survival in a hostile environment. They ultimately came to refer to locals as *Ghotis*. While the *Ghoti-Bangal* conflict certainly epitomized an ethnic rivalry in Indian society, the identities, however, seemed more 'instrumentalist'. That is that were more constructed than 'primordialist'.

The *Ghoti-Bangal* conflict certainly came to express itself in the football arena. As immigrants sought to preserve their cultural identity and integrity in a new society, they searched for new avenues to assert themselves. In this context East Bengali Hindus appropriated football as a cultural tool to establish their social identity and cultural excellence. Consequently, the *maidan* became a cultural space where the opposed identities of the *Ghotis* (settlers) and

Bangals (immigrants) came to be produced and reproduced through a bitter rivalry between Mohun Bagan, the club of the *Ghotis* and East Bengal, the club of the *Bangals*.

The differences between *Ghoti* and *Bangal* were clearly discernible in terms of dialect, manner, dress, food habits, rites and rituals and even appearance, transcending wider similarities of religion, language and a common cultural past. These mostly *cultural* differences, though not rigid, had the potential to create sharply distinctive *social* identities in times of heightened socio-political tension. The partition of Bengal in 1947, followed by a massive influx of East Bengali Hindu refugees into West Bengal, created the occasion for a sub-regional social conflict to flourish. In the aftermath of partition, the East Bengali refugees found in East Bengal a club of their 'own', representing their cultural 'self' to fight and win against the 'other' (West Bengali Hindus). As the latter mockingly named East Bengal 'the club of the *Bangals*', in turn the East Bengali Hindus renamed Mohun Bagan 'the club of the *Ghotis*'. Consequently, the *Ghoti-Bangal* rivalry on the *maidan* divided Bengali Hindu society into two camps during every match between the two respective clubs. Interestingly, as Moti Nandy writes: 'these two communities even divided the aquatic population in a symbolic manner – the prawn for the *Ghotis* and the hilsa for the *Bangals*. In the evening after a football derby, the prices of prawn and hilsa used to rise or fall depending on the result of the match.'[59]

Whilst the rivalry between East Bengal and Mohun Bagan was most pronounced after partition, it began when the East Bengal Club was formed in 1920 by East Bengalis keen to ameliorate the continuous discrimination waged against them by Calcutta's Bengali clubs.[60] By the 1930s, however, East Bengal had lost some of its exclusive sub-regional character and fielded no more East Bengali players than Mohun Bagan or any other club.[61] Even during this period, though, the name and banner of East Bengal continued to inspire the East Bengali population and they had a clear emotional attachment to the club. At the height of communal tension in Bengal on the eve of partition, the IFA was alarmed at the increasing spectator violence at Mohun Bagan vs. East Bengal matches. For example, a 1946 League match between the two which resulted in East Bengal's League triumph witnessed rampant hooliganism and violence.[62]

The degree of consistent rivalry between the two clubs before partition, however, should not be exaggerated. Hostility between supporters shifted from a fluid to a rigid/exclusive state only after the partition of Bengal in 1947. Hindu refugees started to arrive in large numbers in West Bengal from East Pakistan after 1947, and it was under the stress of such difficulties that Hindu refugees discovered in East Bengal Club a cultural institution which could represent them, with no small amount of success, on the sports field. 'For these ravaged and embittered masses', remarks Nandy, 'the one source of hope, pride and victory lay in the triumphs of the club named after their abandoned homeland'.[63] In a spell of five years between 1949 and 1953 the refugee influx witnessed dazzling performances from the famous 'Five Pandavas' of the East Bengal forward-line – Vengkatesh, Apparao, Dhanraj, Ahmed Khan and Saleh – leading the club to a series of successes in national level tournaments.[64] For the uprooted *Bangal* migrants, these victories soon became a cultural weapon to fight discrimination.

Press reports on matches between East Bengal and Mohun Bagan in the 1950s and 1960s confirm their importance through comments on the presence of exceptionally large crowds. The IFA Shield final between East Bengal and Mohun Bagan in 1947 had to be abandoned on the first day due to spectator violence.[65] In the Shield final between the two clubs in 1950, a huge police force had to be stationed at the ground to avert violence.[66] These skirmishes gradually extended to engulf the whole of the Calcutta *maidan*, so much so that the IFA decided to continue with the League only with regular assistance from the Calcutta Police in 1951.[67] East Bengal, however, objected to this decision and a bitter rivalry ensued between the club and the police. The matter assumed such a controversial dimension that the Chief Minister had to intervene to settle matters.[68] The Chief Minister also expressed concern over the question of the organization and control of the game in 1955. Disappointed with the IFA's role in the process, he proposed the formation of a central organization to control the game in Calcutta.[69] The very next year East Bengal along with a few other clubs filed a petition to the IFA against biased refereeing in the League. The referee's bias, according to the petition, was intended to favour one particular club. They demanded that the IFA must end the favouritism within a week.[70] Needless to say, the favoured club was Mohun Bagan.

Throughout the 1950s and 1960s, the rivalry between Mohun Bagan and East Bengal continued to prosper along sub-regional and cultural lines. Whilst the refugees, backed strongly by the Communists, waged a pitched battle against the Congress-led West Bengal Government on the political plane,[71] East Bengal led the onslaught on the cultural plane, i.e. on the football field. The situation became so alarming in the late 1950s that Dr B.C. Roy, then Chief Minister of West Bengal, suggested a change in club names which carried religious, regional or ethnic overtones.[72] Further, Football's politicization in the context of increasing spectator violence in the 1950s was a major source of discord between the IFA on the one hand and clubs like East Bengal, Mohammedan Sporting or Aryan on the other. The *Ghoti-Bangal* war on the football field and the political war on the streets of Calcutta merged in the 1950s and 1960s to produce an almost indivisible association between football and politics.

The configuration of Indian football along sub-regional lines took an aggressive turn in the 1970s. The war of liberation in East Pakistan and the emergence of Bangladesh in 1971 led to a fresh wave of immigration of Hindus into West Bengal. This added substantially to East Bengal Club's support base as the club served as a rallying point for the immigrants' shared cultural identities. Maybe as a result, the first half of the 1970s was a glorious period for the club.[73] More importantly, during the six years from 1970 to 1975, the club conceded only one defeat at the hands of Mohun Bagan.[74] Naturally, therefore, the supporters of the club dominated the *maidan* in this period.

The immigration of the early 1970s coincided with a period of intensive social tension and political turmoil in West Bengal in the wake of the anti-establishment Naxalite movement which used violence and terror as means to achieve its ends. The football field failed to isolate itself from this violence. As a result spectator behaviour began to undergo qualitative changes. As Surojit Sengupta, the footballer-turned-sports journalist, has remarked: 'in the context of the Naxal Movement in the early 1970s, political uncertainty and social depression often turned Calcutta's football ground hot and violent'.[75] Emotional bonding with a club rapidly acquired more extreme expressions as aggression became more pronounced and victories and defeats were met with equally hysterical reactions. Spectators routinely stood in queues for days at a time to obtain tickets to watch matches. Skirmishes and feuds were common during these long waits, and people would frequently become injured or fall ill. In the 1975 Shield final, East Bengal defeated Mohun Bagan 5-0. After the fourth goal was scored, one East Bengal supporter had a heart attack out of sheer ecstasy and had to be taken to hospital immediately.[76] For a 25-year-old Mohun Bagan supporter named Umakanto Palodhi, the ignominious defeat aroused so much dejection that he committed suicide. The suicide note he left said: 'By becoming a better Mohun Bagan footballer, I wish to take revenge of this defeat in my next birth.'[77] Two years later when East Bengal defeated favourites Mohun Bagan in a 1977 League encounter[78] a young Mohun Bagan supporter poisoned himself by drinking a bottle of pesticide.[79] The post-match report pointed to extremely unruly behaviour amongst the crowd and mentioned that East Bengal supporters after the match had become uncontrollable.[80] Matters between the two clubs eventually came to a head in 1980 when, during a relatively unimportant League match between the two teams at the Eden Gardens in Calcutta, clashes between supporters led to widespread violence in the stadium resulting in a stampede that cost 16 fans their lives.[81]

Whilst supporters of East Bengal and Mohun Bagan viewed their assumed cultural differences extremely seriously, the players never conformed strictly to the *Ghoti-Bangal* divide. *Ghotis* like Arun Ghosh earned fame playing for East Bengal while *Bangals* such as Gautam Sarkar rose to prominence as players for Mohun Bagan. Both later noted that the identification of the clubs with *Ghotis* or *Bangals* depended entirely on the extreme feelings of some supporters and a few club officials, and that players hardly played any role at all.[82] Since the early 1980s, the supporters' rivalry on sub-regional lines, too, began to fade away, as memories of partition and the old homeland grew weaker. As Dimeo notes:

> By the 1980s ... identity markers were becoming less distinct. The memory of East Bengal as 'home' was the preserve of a fading generation of migrants, their sons and daughters more at home in West Bengal. Inter group relationships became more common, dialects less pronounced, and cultural traditions passed away. There are cases of fans with East Bengali parents supporting Mohun Bagan. Thus, a liminal, in-between space developed that contravened the polarity of previous years.[83]

Whilst relations between East Bengal and Mohun Bagan have undoubtedly improved in recent decades, there is still a continuing and unique enmity between the two clubs. The tradition of a long-term rivalry, the consolidation of oppositional identities and the conventions of supporters' cultures and intensifications with their clubs have all helped sustain the excitement of the 'battle royal' of Indian football.[84] What still differentiates this rivalry from other Indian club rivalries is the intense emotional attachment of the clubs' supporters towards *their* club and vehement opposition to the *others*' club.[85] This oppositional perception of *self* and *other* continues to shape the most fascinating rivalry in Indian football.

Nation versus club: the dichotomy continues!

In the transition from colonialism to post-colonialism, football in India acted as a platform for social networks, community connections and identity formations of various types. Whenever the game mobilized or unified a community for a cause – be it national, religious or sub-regional – it always created intense club loyalty that led to the game's widespread social popularization as a mass spectator sport. The three clubs – Mohun Bagan, Mohammedan Sporting and East Bengal – while representing respective identities and commonalities of nationalism, communalism and sub-regionalism, also heightened the social viability and commercial prospects of football in India. The intense support bases of the three clubs sustained the mass craze around the game all over India until the 1980s when club teams from Punjab, Maharashtra, Kerala and Goa began to challenge Bengal's supremacy in domestic tournaments. This new challenge also signalled the beginning of new rivalries between club-based regional communities across India. With the launch of the new National League in 1996, these rivalries now have a perfect stage on which to be played out.

Since the fragmentation of Indian sporting nationalism in the 1930s, club loyalties in football have become dominant over national interests. Even in the peculiar amateur (semi-professional since the mid-1990s) set-up of Indian football, the clash of interests between India's leading clubs and the national team has been a constant problem for the game's administrators, resulting in India's dismal showing in international football over the last three and half decades. And now with the slow but steady commercialization of football in twenty-first century India, club communities are growing increasingly strong. The introduction of theme songs and websites; the promotion of merchandising such as club jerseys, flags and symbols; and the formation of local fan clubs and satellite communities are all aimed at strengthening and widening the geographical fan base of the clubs both within India and beyond. It is the responsibility of the All India Football Federation, the apex controlling body of football in India, and its affiliated

Football and Community in the Global Context 87

state units to ensure that the interest of the national team must not be destroyed entirely by the growing strength of these club communities: a situation which is likely to plague Indian football for quite some time yet.

Notes

1. This title is taken from Partha Chatterjee's celebrated work *The Nation and Its Fragments: Colonial and Postcolonial Histories* (Calcutta: Oxford University Press, 1995). Chatterjee used the title to denote a larger historical context of nationalism in colonial and postcolonial India. Sport, however, has no place in his scheme of understanding and representation of nation and its fragments.
2. For a broad discussion on some of these aspects, see Majumdar and Bandyopadhyay, *Social History of Indian Football*.
3. The discussion on these aspects in this essay has some resonance to the author's earlier writings on the subject. For details, see Bandyopadhyay, 'Race, Nation and Sport'; '1911 in Retrospect' and 'Ghoti Bangal o Bangalir Football'.
4. Mangan, 'Series Editor's Foreword', viii.
5. For a brief discussion on the beginnings of football in India, see Bandyopadhyay, 'Race, Nation and Sport', 1–4.
6. The accepted definitive study of public school games as moral training is Mangan's *Athleticism*.
7. Mason, 'Football on the Maidan', 144; Dimeo, 'Football and Politics in Bengal', 62.
8. For a reflective discussion on this theme in Asian context, see Mangan, 'Imperial Origins', 1–49.
9. Mangan, 'Soccer as Moral Training', 41.
10. Ibid.
11. In fact, throughout the nineteenth century, British imperialists, perhaps out of their deep dislike for the climate, topography and inhabitants of Bengal, made the Bengali a butt of satiric criticisms for his supposed physical effeteness – a stereotype that ran all through the period of Imperial rule. This colonial construction of 'effeminate Bengali' could be found in everyday British attitudes toward commonplace Bengalis, in their various speeches and most prolifically in their writings, viz. contemporary Anglo-Indian literature.
12. For an in-depth study of this concept, see Rosselli, 'The Self-Image of Effeteness'.
13. For a detailed history of this movement, see Bagal, *Hindu Melar Itibritta*.
14. Dimeo, 'Colonial Bodies, Colonial Sport', 84.
15. This transformation of football's social dimension has been elaborately discussed in Mitra, 'Nationalism, Communalism and Sub-regionalism', chapter 3.
16. *Mohun Bagan Club Platinum Jubilee Souvenir*, pp.1–5.
17. Mitra, 'Babu at Play', 46.
18. The best work on the anti-partition movement to date is Sarkar, *Swadeshi Movement in Bengal*.
19. A sports field.
20. Only Sudhir Chatterjee played in boots for the club.
21. Details on the results of all these matches can be found in *Mohun Bagan Platinum Jubilee Souvenir*, 15–17; also see Nandy, *Mohun Bagan 1911*.
22. I have taken this term from Chatterjee's, *Nationalist Thought and the Colonial World*, 54–84. Chatterjee, however, used the term in an entirely different context.
23. *Amrita Bazar Patrika*, 31 July 1911, 8.
24. Newspapers that stressed 'Bengali' identity were *Amrita Bazar Patrika*, *Nayak*, *Times of India Illustrated Weekly* and *Basumati*. On the other hand, *London Reuter*, *The Englishman* and *The Mussalman* reckoned the victory to be an 'Indian' one.
25. *The Telegraph* (Calcutta), 20 June 1998.
26. Mukherjee, 'Elegy on the Maidan', *The Telegraph*, March 5, 2002.
27. Mason, 'Football on the Maidan', 150–1.
28. Ibid.; Dimeo, 'Football and Politics in Bengal', 71. For a most authoritative discussion of British cultural imperialism on the sports field see Guttman, *Games and Empires*.
29. Cashman, 'Cricket and Colonialism', 259–60.
30. Ibid.
31. Ibid.
32. The Jubilee Club was established in 1887, a sporting organization for Muslims in Calcutta. The club changed its name twice in the next few years, first to the Crescent Club and then to the Hamidia Club.

Finally, in 1891, the latter became the Mohammedan Sporting Club. Mohammedan Sporting Club Records, Mohammedan Sporting Club, Calcutta.
33. The initiative of some Muslim youths, both of Calcutta and the suburbs, who felt the need of the Muslim youth to have its own sporting club, founded the Crescent Club in 1889. It is said, however, that the club had its predecessor in the Jubilee Club founded in 1887 in Calcutta at the initiatives of Khan Bahadur Aminul Islam, Maulavi Abdul Ghani of Malda and Maulavi Muhammad Yasin of Burdwan. In 1890, the club's name was changed again into Hamidia Club. In 1891, finally, the club came to be transformed into the Mohammedan Sporting Club. For further details on the origin of the club, see *Mohammedan Sporting Club*, 'History of the Club', 27, 35–9.
34. Quoted in *Mohun Bagan Club Platinum Jubilee Souvenir*, 25.
35. Ibid.
36. Sengupta, *Kallol Yug*, 66.
37. Comments of Muhammad Nasiruddin, the editor of *Saugat*, a periodical published from Dacca, quoted in Ritan, *Football*, 21.
38. Ispahani, *Qaid-E-Azam Jinnah*, 4; McPherson, *Muslim Microcosm*, 121.
39. *Mohammedan Sporting Club*, 36.
40. Ibid.
41. Ibid.
42. Ibid., 12.
43. Ibid., 25.
44. Ibid., 26. Emphasis added.
45. Hundreds of messages came from Muslim clubs and organizations in different parts of India including Shillong, Sylhet, Dacca, Rangpur, Tippera, Dinajpur, Jalpaiguri, Darjeeling, Purnea, Cuttock, Benares, Bombay, Bangalore and Calcutta. For details, see *Mohammedan Sporting Club*, 28.
46. Ibid.
47. 'Tribute from the Green Stands', in ibid., 34.
48. Comments of Mohammad Nasiruddin quoted in Ritan, *Football*, 20–1.
49. Majumdar and Bandyopadhyay, *A Social History of Indian Football*, chapter 5.
50. Ibid.
51. Led by Abdul Kasem Fazlul Haq, the Krishak Praja Party drew its strength from the mass following it enjoyed among Bengal's Muslim peasantry and intermediate shareholders.
52. Majumdar and Bandyopadhyay, *Social History of Indian Football*, chapter 5.
53. Ibid., 101.
54. Ispahani, *Qaid-E-Azam Jinnah*, 12.
55. Shamsuddin, *Atit Diner Smriti*, 154–8.
56. Momen, *Muslim Politics in Bengal*, 72.
57. Das, *Communal Riots in Bengal*, 170. Also see *Amrita Bazar Patrika*, 8 July 1946, 4; File-5/27/46 Poll (I), the IB Daily Summary Information of 8 July 1946.
58. Nandy, 'Calcutta Soccer', 318.
59. Nandy, 'Football and Nationalism', 249.
60. Historians of the East Bengal Club have all noted this aspect of discrimination waged against the East Bengali players and people and unanimously pointed to the exclusively regional character of the club at its birth and its impressive beginning in Calcutta football. For details, see Bandyopadhyay, *Cluber Naam East Bengal*; Dutta, *Glorious East Bengal*; Nandy, *East Bengal Club*; Pandit Mashai, *East Bengal Cluber Itihas*; Saha, *Itihase East Bengal* (all in Bengali).
61. A number of worthy footballers from eastern Bengal played for Mohun Bagan throughout the first half of the twentieth century. The list includes names such as Nagen Kali, Hemango Basu, Rabi Basu, Bagha Som, Sanmatha Datta and K. Datta. For details see Sen, *Kheladhular Bichitra Kahini*, 21–9.
62. *Amrita Bazar Patrika*, 7 July 1946.
63. Nandy, 'Calcutta Soccer', 319.
64. Thanks to this legendary forward-line, during this period East Bengal won both the IFA League and Shield three times (League – 1949, 1950, 1952 and Shield – 1949, 1950, 1951); Durand Cup and DCM Trophy twice (Durand – 1951–52 and DCM – 1950, 1952); and the Rovers Cup once (1949).
65. *The Statesman*, 5 October 1947.
66. *Amrita Bazar Patrika*, 17 September 1950.
67. Ibid., 31 May 1951.
68. Ibid., 22 and 23 June 1951.
69. Ibid., 29 June 1955.

70. Ibid., 22 June 1956.
71. For a useful study of the relationship between Communist political ascendancy in West Bengal and refugee politics, see Chakrabarty, *Marginal Men*.
72. See the *Amrita Bazar Patrika*, 17, 18 and 24 July 1957. The Chief Minister by these terms apparently referred to Mohammedan Sporting, East Bengal and the Rajasthan Clubs respectively.
73. East Bengal won the League title six times in a row from 1970 to 1975 – still a record. It won the IFA Shield in 1970 and then with a gap of a year in 1971 won every year from 1972 to 1976. The club bagged the Durand Cup in 1970 and 1972; Rovers Cup in 1972, 1973 and 1975; DCM Trophy in 1973 and 1974; and Bardoli Trophy in 1972 and 1973.
74. This sole occasion when Mohun Bagan got the better of their archrivals was in the 1974 Durand Cup semi-final. Mohun Bagan won the match by a solitary goal.
75. Interview with Surojit Sengupta, 25 August 2002. For Sengupta's fuller views on football culture that grew around the East Bengal-Mohun Bagan rivalry in India, see Sengupta, *Back Center*. Incidentally, Sengupta who was a worthy right-winger of East Bengal team in the 1970s, has recently left his job to take charge as the sports editor of *Khela*, the foremost sports vernacular magazine of Bengal.
76. *Ananda Bazar Patrika*, 30 September 1975.
77. Ibid., 1 October 1975. Also see Chakrabarty, 'Mohun Bagan-East Bengal Reshareshi', 118.
78. East Bengal won the match 2-0.
79. *Ananda Bazar Patrika*, 10 July 1977. The report said that the person was taken to the PG Hospital in a very critical condition.
80. According to the same newspaper report, 'total chaos resulted in the streets and different quarters of the city as the euphoric supporters ran wild with *mashals* (fire torch) in their hands from one place to another. There were several complaints against the jubilant crowd, which stopped private cars and scooters on the streets. Bricks were thrown into the ground and on another club's tent resulting in the injury of at least two dozens of people, three of them being rushed to Shambhunath Pandit Hospital. According to the police, eight persons were arrested on that evening.' *Ananda Bazar Patrika*, 10 July 1977.
81. The pre-match press reports suggested possibilities of chaos and violence on the match day. In fact, the Federation Cup final between the two teams on 8 May 1980 witnessed extremely unruly behaviour of not only the fans but also the players and club officials. See *Ananda Bazar Patrika*, 15 August 1980; *Khelar Asar*, 16 May 1980.
82. Sengupta, 'Nirapade Bhinna Clube', 184–9.
83. Dimeo, 'Team Loyalty', 106.
84. Despite radical changes in the Indian sporting map in the 1980s – organization of Asian Games at Delhi (1982), India's World Cup victory in cricket (1983) followed by Mini World Cup triumph two years later (1985), live telecast of World Cup football since 1982 and of European and Latin American league and cup matches (since 1987), the organizational laxity of All India Football Federation, and most important of all, the utter failure of the national and regional football bodies as well as the two great Calcutta clubs to adapt to the challenge of globalization, commercialism and professionalism till the mid-1990s – the intensity of rivalry between Mohun Bagan and East Bengal showed no signs of abatement. However, the rivalry faced a real challenge in 1997 when both the clubs came to be sponsored and marginally controlled by the same company, viz. the United Breweries Group. After this sponsorship deal there arose a large apprehension among the supporters of the clubs that their age-old enmity would come to an end. Yet what still continues to dominate Indian football is a desperate rivalry between the two Bengali outfits.
85. A most recent incident is conclusively revealing on this point: In late May 2003 Mohun Bagan Club, bogged down by internal strife and court cases, could not arrange for the money to retain its star players including the club's heart-throb Jose Ramirez Barretto, the Brazilian forward. Learning this from newspaper reports, one ardent supporter of the club decided to sell off his ancestral house and came to the club authority to know the formalities of payment. The club officials understandably refused the offer but take pride in it as a reflection of the club's continuing tradition and glory. As East Bengal, the foremost enemy of his club won all the five tournaments they participated in the previous season including the all-important National League title with a nearly all win record against Mohun Bagan, the fan could not bear the thought of a repeat of the same story next year. Hence, to retain the star forward who, he believed could only ameliorate the plight of the club against their arch-rival; he committed his only asset for the sake of the club. For details see *Ananda Bazar Patrika*, 3 July 2003. Rupak Saha narrates a similar incident of 1991 when an East Bengal fan mortgaged his house and took his wife's gold ornaments to rope in a few good players for the club in times of the club's financial crisis. For details, see Saha, 'Bangalir Football', 23–4.

References

Bagal, Jogesh Chandra. *Hindu Melar Itibritta.* [History of the Hindu Mela]. Calcutta: Maitrayee, 1945.
Bandyopadhyay, Kausik. 'Race, Nation and Sport: Footballing Nationalism in Colonial Calcutta'. *Soccer and Society* 4, no. 1 (2003): 1–19.
———. '1911 in Retrospect: A Revisionist Perspective on a Famous Indian Sporting Victory'. *The International Journal of the History of Sport* 21, no. 3/4 (2004): 363–83.
———. 'Ghoti-Bangal o Bangalir Football: Krirakhetre Ekti Samajik Dwanda'. In *Itihas Anusandhan-20*, ed. Aniruddha Roy, 496–504. Kolkata: Firma KLM, 2006.
Bandyopadhyay, Santipriya. *Cluber Naam East Bengal.* Calcutta: New Bengal Press, 1979.
Cashman, Richard. 'Cricket and Colonialism: Colonial Hegemony and Indigenous Subversion'. In *Pleasure, Profit, Proselytism: British Culture and Sport at Home and Abroad, 1700–1914*, ed. J.A. Mangan, 258–72. London: Frank Cass, 1988.
Chakrabarty, Manas. 'Mohun Bagan-East Bengal Reshareshi'. *Anandamela,* July 19, 2000.
Chakrabarty, Prafulla K. *The Marginal Men, The Refugees and the Left Political Syndrome in West Bengal.* Calcutta: Lumiere Books, 1990.
Chatterjee, Partha. *Nationalist Thought and the Colonial World: A Derivative Discourse?* London: Zed Books, 1986.
Das, Suranjan. *Communal Riots in Bengal.* New Delhi: Oxford University Press, 1991.
Dimeo, Paul. 'Football and Politics in Bengal: Colonialism, Nationalism, Communalism'. In *Soccer in South Asia: Empire, Nation, Diaspora,* ed. Paul Dimeo and James Mills, 57–74. London: Frank Cass, 2001.
———. '"Team Loyalty Splits the City into Two": Football, Ethnicity and Rivalry in Calcutta'. In *Fear and Loathing in World Football,* ed. G. Armstrong and R. Giulianotti, 96–107. Oxford: Berg, 2001.
———. 'Colonial Bodies, Colonial Sport: "Martial" Punjabis, "Effeminate" Bengalis and the Development of Indian Football'. *The International Journal of the History of Sport* 19, no. 1 (March 2002): 72–90.
Dutta, Jayanta. *Glorious East Bengal.* Calcutta: Sahitya Prakash, 1975.
Guttman, Allen. *Games and Empires: Modern Sports and Cultural Imperialism.* New York: Columbia University Press, 1994.
Ispahani, M.A.H. *Qaid-E-Azam Jinnah – As I Knew Him.* Karachi: Forward Publications Trust, 1966.
Majumdar, Boria. 'The Vernacular in Sports History'. *Economic and Political Weekly* 37, no. 29 (20 July 2002): 3069–75.
Majumdar, Boria and Kausik Bandyopadhyay. *A Social History of Indian Football: Striving to Score.* London: Routledge, 2006.
———. *Athleticism in Victorian and Edwardian Public School: The Emergence and Consolidation of an Educational Ideology.* Cambridge: Cambridge University Press, 1981 and London: Frank Cass, 2000 (with a new introduction).
———. 'Series Editor's Foreword'. In *Fear and Loathing in World Football,* ed. G. Armstrong and R. Giulianotti. Oxford: Berg, 2001.
———. 'Soccer as Moral Training: Missionary Intentions and Imperial Legacies'. In *Soccer in South Asia: Empire, Nation, Diaspora,* ed. Paul Dimeo and James Mills, 41–56. London: Frank Cass, 2001.
———. 'Imperial Origins, Christian Manliness, Moral Imperatives and Pre-Srilankan Playing Fields – "Beginnings" and "Consolidation"'. In *Sport in Asian Society: Past and Present,* ed. J.A. Mangan and Fan Hong, 1–49. London: Frank Cass, 2003.
Mason, Tony. 'Football on the Maidan: Cultural Imperialism in Calcutta'. In *The Cultural Bond: Sport, Empire, Society,* ed. J.A. Mangan, 142–53. London: Frank Cass, 1992.
McPherson, Kenneth. *The Muslim Microcosm: Calcutta, 1918–1935.* Wiesbaden: Sunny House, 1974.
Mitra, Soumen., 'Nationalism, Communalism and Sub-regionalism: A Study of Football in Bengal, 1880–1950'. M.Phil diss., Centre for Historical Studies, Jawaharlal Nehru University, 1988.
———. 'Babu at Play: Sporting Nationalism in Bengal, 1880–1911'. In *Bengal: Yesterday and Today,* ed. Nisith Ray and Ranjit Roy, 45–61. Calcutta: Papyrus, 1991.
Mohammedan Sporting Club. Calcutta League Champions 1934–35. A Souvenir. Calcutta: Mohammedan Sporting Club, 1935.
Momen, Humeral. *Muslim Politics in Bengal: A Study of Krishak Praja Party and the Elections of 1937.* Dacca: Franz Steiner Verlag, 1972.
Mohun Bagan Club Platinum Jubilee Souvenir. Calcutta: Mohun Bagan A.C., 1964.
Mukherjee, Rudrangshu. 'Elegy on the Maidan'. *The Telegraph,* March 5, 2002.
Nandy, Moti. 'Calcutta Soccer'. In *Calcutta: The Living City, 2: The Present and Future,* ed. Sukanta Chaudhuri, 316–20. Calcutta: Oxford University Press, 1990.

———. 'Football and Nationalism'. Trans. Shampa Banerjee. In *The Calcutta Psyche,* ed. Geeti Sen, 241–54. New Delhi: India International Centre, 1990.
Nandy, Paresh. *East Bengal Club, 1920-1970: Ponchas Bochhorer Sangram o Safalya.* Calcutta: Bichitra, 1973.
———. *Mohun Bagan 1911.* Calcutta: Karuna Prakashani, 1976.
Pandit Mashai (Ramesh Chandra Goswami). *East Bengal Cluber Itihas.* Calcutta: Book Garden, 1963.
Ritan, Lutfar Rahman. *Football.* Dacca: Bangla Academy, 1985.
Rosselli, John. 'The Self-Image of Effeteness: Physical Education and Nationalism in Nineteenth-Century Bengal'. *Past and Present* 86 (1980): 121–48.
Saha, Rupak. 'Bangalir Football'. *Desh,* August 28, 1993.
———. *Itihase East Bengal.* Calcutta: Deep, 2000.
Sarkar, Sumit. *The Swadeshi Movement in Bengal.* New Delhi: Peoples Publishing House, 1973.
Sen, Sachin. *Kheladhular Bichitra Kahini.* Calcutta: R.M. Gupta/Geetanjali Book Centre, 1983.
Sengupta, Achintya Kumar. *Kallol Yug.* Calcutta: M.C. Sarkar & Sons, 1950.
Sengupta, Surajit. *Back Center.* Calcutta: Sunny Publishers, 1986.
Sengupta, Tanaji. 'Nirapade Bhinna Clube'. *Desh* (Binodon sankhya), 1988.
Shamsuddin, Abul Kalam. *Atit Diner Smriti.* Dacca, 1968.
The Telegraph (Calcutta), 20 June, 1998.

NATIONS AND ETHNICITIES

Coming in from the margins: ethnicity, community support and the rebranding of Australian soccer

James Skinner, Dwight H. Zakus and Allan Edwards

Introduction

Australia is one of the few countries in the world that has four football codes operating full professional leagues and development systems. Of these codes Australian Rules football, an indigenously developed hybrid of other sport and football codes, is the most widely supported and revenue-rich league. The other codes are imports from Britain due to Australia's colonial past – rugby and soccer. Of these, and in terms of media, audience and revenue attraction, rugby league and rugby occupy the second and third places in terms of fan and media support. The development of these codes paralleled their historical evolution in Britain around the 'football split' between the professional- and amateur-based codes of rugby. The fourth football code, association football (hereafter soccer) occupies the most troubled and lowest fan, media and revenue support of all football codes.

For a country with a small population, the existence of four football codes, each with a national professional league, local semi-professional competitions, and with development systems and concomitant organizations locally, nationally and internationally represents a major accomplishment. Underlying this however is a fear by the top three codes that soccer might rise to challenge their positions and take players, fans, media attention and revenues away.

Soccer in Australia, however, occupies a paradoxical position in that it has the highest overall participant rates, yet is ranked fourth of the four codes in popularity and resources. That is, it is seen as a marginal code in respect of the media attention, professional leagues and salaries, opportunities for players in Australia, its sponsorship and revenue generation opportunities, and its position in global football successes. This marginalization, until very recently, resulted from government policy (and athe contradictions it set in train), attitudes in media reporting, reactions by other sport leaders and a xenophobic discourse. To understand this position and the future of soccer in Australia, one needs to understand its history and its fundamental connection to ethnic communities and populations.[1]

This essay looks at that history and soccer's direct relationship to various ethnic communities and populations. This discussion provides the basis for examining the position and development of the sport over time, with particular emphasis on the evolution of the National Soccer League (NSL), and how recent structural changes to the sport seek to bring it in from the margins.

The historical position of soccer in Australia

As with most western sports in Australia, their arrival was due to British colonizing of greater parts of the world, especially during the nineteenth century. The sports of the military, government, free settlers and of upper-class colonizers were brought from the mother country. The English, and in particular the Scots, fermented the early game of 'football'. Although the first recorded match of soccer was not until the late 1880s,[2] a number of communities across Australia formed clubs and regularly played the sport by this time. The early development of soccer in Australia as an Anglo-Australian code was due to this group. These developments also set up the first differentiation of soccer to rugby and Australian rules, where soccer was denigrated as a 'pommie' game.

Soccer did attract a playing and spectating following. Records of overseas clubs and national teams show strong support for the games played in Australia. In the early twentieth century, and indicative of a colonial country, immigration was (and continues to be) necessary for the growth of the nation. When Australia formed in 1901 one of the first national policies was the Immigration Restriction Act that set out a 'White Australia' position for future settlement; that is, immigrants from English-speaking countries were preferred and sought. As is also known, with hindsight, that the pool of potential immigrants cannot be so restricted. Some would suggest Australia's current government continues an unofficial 'White Australia' policy against refugees from Asia, Africa, the Middle East and other non-English speaking milieux despite a 'multi-culturalism' policy outlined from the 1970s onwards. However, in earlier days, the non-Anglo-Australians became the 'other' within exacerbated xenophobic attitudes and behaviours and it is in this broader context that immigrants entered the picture in their masses.

While there were influxes of immigrants in the pre-confederation period around the 1880s, between 1910–14, and then the 1920s, it was following the Second World War that significant numbers arrived from outside of English-speaking settings. Further, many of these people had suffered the horrors of war, genocide and displacement, horrors which were not alleviated upon arrival in Australia as many immigrants worked in isolated rural areas, for low pay, and received further prejudicial treatment. Their position as the 'other' abetted the distinction of their culture, language and life as different and as a point to attack (or at least to be treated as lesser). Concentrations of new immigrants, mostly males in the first instance, forced the new peoples to seek their fellow compatriots for survival.

Ethnic enclaves grew, in both rural and urban landscapes, as immigrants sought solace in those with the same cultural identity and because of economic necessity. The activities and associations formed often included sport activities, clubs and competitions as a feature of these groupings and because most post-Second World War arrivals came from Eastern Europe, soccer was the dominant sport of choice. These immigrant communities contributed to the expansion of the code in Australia and were the mainstay of its success; however, because of their marginal position in Australian society this also contributed to soccer's further marginalization.

The biography of the late Australian soccer icon, Johnny Warren, provided an 'insider's' view of the code in Australia. The title of the book, *Sheilas, Wogs, and Poofters*, highlights the marginalization of the code and Anglo-Australian opposition to it.[3] The labelling of soccer as 'wogball' – a racist, ethnically-stereotyped description of the code – helped further marginalize soccer in mainstream white Australia.

Warren's biography, however, is not the only source outlining the marginalization of soccer with the 'mass arrival of six million immigrants between 1945 and 1990'.[4] The number from mainland Europe was greater than those from the United Kingdom, Ireland and New Zealand. Of these the major nationalities were: Italians, Greeks, Yugoslavs (Croatians and Serbs), Poles, Dutch, Germans and Maltese. As noted above, ethnically and nationally-based communities formed which helped people adapt to life in Australia and their common cultural bases became part of the way their sporting and sport club formations operated and developed. Again, for many of these, 'immigrants'' soccer became a defining cultural characteristic in their new country.

Conflict with existing ethnic groups in Australia (i.e., between Anglo-Australians and more recent immigrant populations) fermented on several fronts. The first was in terms of the federal government's poor attempts at multi-cultural policy, when the country continues to exhibit a xenophobic attitude and way of dealing with non-Australians. Though this policy sought to ameliorate and integrate different racial and cultural (ethnic) groups, the entrenched attitudes and behaviours of the 'white Australia policy' failed to go away. This became evident in terms of soccer as government pressure to reduce its organizational and governance issues led to direct federal government intervention into the sport.

The second conflict or paradox resulted from the incoherent structure and the operations of governing bodies for soccer at state and national levels in Australia. From its early days soccer witnessed several new governing bodies for the sport, broadly divided along ethnic lines. Also, conflict surrounded ethnically-based soccer clubs wanting to compete as clubs with particular identities (and with a European style of play) as opposed to the more 'rational' Anglo-Australian district level structure of competitions (and a UK style of play). This split also concerned money and resources, as ethnically-based clubs were well-funded and wealthy, while other clubs struggled. Ethnically-based clubs were also able to import talent from overseas, further strengthening their success (although it did lead to a FIFA ban on Australian soccer). Finally, the attempted 'de-ethnicization' of soccer in the 1980s and 1990s further marginalized ethnically-based clubs and split the code. The struggles were not merely around the violence and ground disturbances of old ethnic rivalries; it was about the 'whiteness',[5] power and future development of the sport on Australian lines.

A third paradox surrounds the marginalization of supporters from ethnic minorities within the modernization of the game. Although those seeking to market and promote soccer as a successful sports commodity have prioritized developing the Anglo-Australian market, ignoring strong ethnically-based market segments does not seem a wise move. It is these populations who have, after all, sustained the sport in Australia as well as producing many of the 400 ex-pat players around the world. Likewise, moving the television contract from the Special Broadcast Services (SBS) network, or 'Soccer Bloody Soccer' as it is popularly known in Australia, to the cable-only Foxsports network, downplays the historic sustenance of the sport in Australia. How much the recently formed Football Federation of Australia (FFA) moves soccer from its 'immigrant' roots into the mainstream football marketplace in Australia remains to be seen.

Developing new soccer futures has not been a smooth or steady progress and we now consider wider societal pressures on soccer. As is evident, these pressures have not always resulted in positive results; in fact, they often resulted in the further marginalization of the sport and retarding Australian soccer's success nationally and internationally.

Repositioning and rebranding the elite game

Established in 1977 the National Soccer League (NSL) was the first truly national premiership competition of any sporting code in Australia. Since its inception however, the NSL was a highly volatile league plagued by problems and controversies. Several issues have combined to make soccer such a difficult product to develop at the elite level in Australia. The failure to retain or attract high quality players, tension between clubs and supporters stemming from 'traditional' European political, racial and cultural conflicts, financial instability and poor senior-level management were all prominently reported in the sporting and business sections of the Australian media as key factors.[6]

Initially, the Australian Soccer Federation (ASF) banned clubs unwilling to forego their traditional, ethnically and nationally-based names and symbols. As a consequence, the Victorian Greek Soccer club, South Melbourne Hellas, adopted the shortened title South Melbourne.[7] However, in 1983 the ASF retreated from this position because it could not attract enough clubs or sponsorship. Between 1977 and 1982 crowd numbers stagnated as the public failed to embrace the code and the national league was again characterized by divisions along ethnic lines.[8]

In an attempt to attract greater interest in the code and increase attendance at matches, the NSL switched to the summer months in 1989–90. In the winter, the airwaves were, and still are, dominated by the Australian Football League and the National Rugby League on free-to-air television and the radio (plus Rugby Union on the FoxSports cable network). The shift was seen as a way of not directly competing with these codes while at the same time aligning the league with the European season. The problem was that the code now had to compete with the increasingly popular international summer sports of cricket, tennis and basketball which had also moved to the summer season.

By 1990 however it became apparent that soccer in Australia was not being embraced by mainstream society and its associations with ethnic division were marginalizing its wider support. As a consequence, in 1990 Dr Graham Bradley was appointed by the ASF to report on the state and future of the sport. Bradley's report suggested that Australian soccer was seen as a 'game for ethnics'.[9] Bradley recommended a re-adjustment of the management structure of the ASF and emphasized the need for the development of a highly successful national team, a prestigious National Soccer League and an active junior base in all states.[10]

As a consequence of the Bradley report, in 1991 an operational review of Australian soccer was undertaken. In 1991 14 teams composed the NSL, seven from Sydney, four from Melbourne, two from Adelaide, and one from Wollongong (a rural New South Wales city). The composition of the league was changed to reflect a greater national presence. The revamped league consisted of six teams from NSW, four from Victoria, three from South Australia and one from Queensland,[11] which, it was hoped, would assist in 'de-ethnicizing' the code. The change however had limited impact in removing the associations with, and stereotypes about, soccer's ethnic base that the wider (white) general public attached to the game.[12] Consequently, in 1992 the ASF banned names with ethnic or national associations at all level of competition, a formal ruling which compelled all teams playing in the NSL to abandon their traditional names.[13]

Attempting to reposition the NSL into the mainstream Anglo-Australian community was a difficult task, made even more challenging as other issues continued to plague the code. During 1993 and 1994 Australian soccer was the subject of a series of rumours concerning the administration of the player transfer system. It was suggested that large amounts of money from overseas clubs were being transferred to unknown parties. In order to counter the increasingly suspicious public perception about the transfer system the ASF, in June 1994, appointed Donald Gerald Stewart, a former judge of the Supreme Court of New South Wales, and a former head of the National Crime Authority, to conduct a formal inquiry into Australian Soccer. Justice Stewart's report was never published by the ASF itself as it was considered embarrassing to personnel within the ASF; but it was subsequently published by the Senate (Australia's Upper House in the Federal Government), which severely criticized the transfer system and noted that Australian players were being exploited by NSL clubs.[14]

In 1996 a new strategy was devised to garnish mainstream support. In advance of the 1996 season the ASF became Soccer Australia (SA) with David Hill appointed as the new chairman. The renaming was employed to signal a new era in the code, a name that was not associated with the problems and controversies of the past. One of Hill's first directions was to instruct the clubs to remove symbols of European nationalism from their clubs' logos, including team uniforms, club flags, stadium names and letterheads. The Italian club Marconi Fairfield was ejected from the league in August 1996 after refusing to remove the Italian flag colours from its boomerang logo and Sydney and Melbourne Croatia were also expelled for failure to remove their national symbol. This measure provoked indignation from other clubs and the entire soccer community.[15]

To avoid conflict between ethnic minority communities, their clubs and SA, David Hill attempted to broker a compromise. Hill realized that such powerful clubs could not be expelled from the league without significant negative public relations fallout which would undermine the league. If the clubs agreed to modernize their logo designs and reconfigure their traditional colours, SA said that it would retreat from its position to expel Marconi and Sydney and Melbourne from the 1996 season.[16] However, the position taken by David Hill and SA did not stop the rivalries and tensions between different ethnic communities being expressed in the game. The Bad Blue boys, a group of Croatian supporters from Sydney United (Sydney Croatia changed its name to Sydney United) defied the directives of SA and continued to bring their national flags and chant C-R-O-A-T-I-A at games, causing tensions between supporters and the security guards. Similarly during a match between Parramatta and Sydney in 1997, confrontation between Parramatta (Greek) fans and Sydney (Croatian) fans erupted.[17] Despite Hill's efforts it was clear that the majority of support in Australian soccer still continued to be divided along ethnic and national lines.[18]

Hill's tenure at the helm of SA was short-lived and underlying tensions remained. His template for change was met with high levels of resistance and he created many enemies within the organization and the wider soccer community. The 'Bobby Despotovski incident' highlighted the persistent nature of ethnic tensions despite Hill's attempts to 'de-ethnicize' the NSL in the 1990s. Perth Glory striker Despotovski was accused of making gestures towards the crowd that were derogatory and provocative to elements of the Melbourne Knights crowd. The violence following this incident ultimately resulted in Despotovski and his Perth Glory coach Bernd Stange being physically assaulted as they attempted to board the team bus.

The financial woes of the Carlton Soccer Club and Eastern Pride further smeared the NSL's reputation.[19] After questionable business planning reliant upon revenue from international player transfers, Carlton went into receivership and removed from the NSL competition. The Eastern Pride, based in the financially marginal Gippsland region in Victoria, temporarily had all their points deducted by SA for failing to pay its $50,000 NSL affiliation fee. These points were later reinstated after new SA Chairman Tony Labbozzetta brokered a peace deal but further difficulties relating to the payment of player wages also fuelled speculation that the Australian Professional Footballers' Association (PFA) was planning a rebel league. Although the PFA's CEO Brendan Schwab went so far as to register the trademark 'Australian Premier League', negotiations between the SA and PFA eventually resolved the issue. These agreements covered both the NSL and international representative teams but some senior ex-patriot players, such as Harry Kewell, often under pressure from their overseas clubs, were still reluctant to represent Australia in 'minor' international competitions.[20]

This is a symptom of the critical underlying problem for Australian soccer. The international labour market for soccer players is a classic example of the skill stratification that emerges when leagues are in competition for playing talent. The tradition and history of soccer in Europe and the UK, along with social, financial and market forces, make European and UK clubs a central destination for mass player migration from across the world.[21] This represents a major problem as Australian soccer talent gravitates towards these leagues. In April 2006 there were 117 Australian players plying their trade with overseas clubs.[22] This talent drain must also be understood in conjunction with the effect of easy consumer access to the UEFA tournaments and major domestic competitions via pay television. Australian soccer fans face a relatively small cost differential when choosing to 'upgrade' their consumption choice to a higher quality sports-entertainment product, such as the Champions League,[23] which in effect, further marginalizes the game in Australia due to its perceived inferior quality.

The corporate or consumer attractiveness of the NSL, aided by continual changes to the composition of the league, suffered. After going through the process of developing criteria for the selection of only 12 clubs for the 2001–02 NSL season, SA reversed their initial decision to cut the Brisbane Strikers and Canberra Cosmos from the league. Under fear of an internal revolt from state federations and board members, SA chairman Tony Labbozzetta oversaw the readmission of these clubs, resulting in a 14-team competition for the 2001–02 season.[24] This, coupled with Australia's inability to qualify for the World Cup, meant that SA and the NSL continued to face major challenges to sustain elite level soccer in Australia. Consequently in *Australian Soccer's Long Road to the Top*, Michael Cockerill commented that 'Australia's place in this increasingly complex football world remained uncertain'[25] something reflected in its further marginalization within FIFA.

Continued and extensive media publicity surrounding alleged mismanagement and corruption in SA eventually resulted in the Australian Sports Commission in 2003 establishing an Independent Soccer Review Committee. The committee published a report on the governance of Association Football in Australia, named the Crawford Report. Chaired by David Crawford, who in 1993 conducted an independent review of the management and governance issues confronting the Australian Football League, the committee undertook a programme of national consultation including over 230 written submissions, 32 meetings with stakeholders, 42 meetings with members of the public, and a number of meetings involving consultants Ernst & Young and international experts. Following the consultation process the committee identified the following major challenges: (1) ensuring the governing bodies are independent and capable of acting in the best interests of the sport as a whole; (2) separating governance from day to day management by implementing an effective governance and management structure; (3) ensuring that all stakeholders have the opportunity to be heard, that is, changing memberships and voting structures at national and state levels; and (4) restructuring the relationship between SA and the NSL.[26]

In Crawford's (2003) examination of appropriate membership and voting structures he made two key suggestions. First, when addressing the structure of soccer the report suggested that it was essential to 'ensure equitable representation of members and interest groups in voting for the people charged with the responsibility of running the game'.[27] Furthermore, it was deemed that 'appropriate representational structure for membership of SA is a mixture of state bodies and special interest groups'.[28] This approach would cause some significant changes to what existed: state voting rights would be linked to registration numbers; state affiliates would receive extra votes based on membership; the NSL voting rights would be reduced to one vote; and a wider range of interests would be represented under the umbrella of 'special interest groups' now receiving votes. This approach was intended to reduce the overall voting numbers from 61 to approximately 22, streamline the decision-making process and reduce internal politicking.[29]

The debate of how responsibility for the governance of the code should be shared between the national body and its affiliates provided the basis of the next challenge. A brief overview of the roles of each body suggested that the national body would have dual responsibilities. This would include the development of the elite component of the code as well as its grassroots development, where now state affiliates of the national body would primarily take responsibility for the development of the grassroots game. The committee, in reviewing other sports, noted that some sports had established agreements between the national body and state bodies that outline their common and separate responsibilities within their sport. These types of agreements were considered by the committee as being the basis for each body understanding its responsibilities and expectations within the national structure and the committee believed soccer would also benefit from adopting this approach. These agreements would cover such aspects as: membership registration and servicing; development programmes; high performance programmes; marketing and sponsorship; competition scheduling; and other areas of mutual interest.[30] One of the major roles for state affiliates, according to Crawford,[31] would be the provision of grassroots member services. This clear delineation of roles would, it was hoped, reduce duplication of services and simplify the governance structure.

The findings of the report clearly articulated an argument that the key to the future success of soccer in Australia was the governance of the professional aspects of a sport. The revenue streams that could be derived from this component had the potential to far exceed any other component of SA. Crawford believed that:

> the NSL has a better chance of success if it is allowed to operate as a stand-alone body ... however, because Soccer Australia has responsibility for the wellbeing and development of the game at national and international levels, there is potential for overlap between the objectives of Soccer Australia and a stand-alone NSL.[32]

To overcome this it was recommended[33] that SA establish the NSL as a separate entity operating under a license for three main reasons. First, a separate board would be more responsive to the needs of the professional game; second, the professional side of the sport required board members with a different skill set; and finally, SA would be shielded from any potential NSL shortfalls.[34] The agreement would clearly articulate the requirements and responsibilities that each entity would have.

The majority of reforms and recommendations have been implemented by the National and State Football Associations. Restructuring of the governance of the associations and the voting rights given to groups not previously represented (e.g., referees, women's players, etc) led to a more democratic approach. Following the recommendations of Crawford[35] further change occurred in 2004 when the governing body SA changed its name to the Football Federation of Australia (FFA). This led to the somewhat forced resignation of the entire SA board and the formation of a new board chaired by Frank Lowy – Australia's second wealthiest man with a sharp business acumen and an unbridled passion and enthusiasm for the code (and, interestingly, a long-standing association with Jewish soccer clubs).

Under the guidance of Lowy and newly appointed Chief Executive Officer John O'Neill (the former CEO of the Australian Rugby Union) the FFA achieved financial stability. The former NSL was also renamed the A-League and the FFA announced a new eight-team competition to revitalize soccer in Australia. Licences to compete in the League were opened to a competitive tender process and only provided under strict guidelines. At the conclusion of the process seven teams from across Australia and one from New Zealand were selected. These were: Adelaide United FC; Central Coast Mariners FC; Melbourne Victory FC; Newcastle Jets FC; Perth Glory FC; Queensland Roar FC; Sydney FC; and the New Zealand Knights FC based in Auckland. The A-League attracted corporate support with Hyundai as major sponsor and games are televised on the FoxSports cable network. Additionally, a AUD$3 million dollar television advertising campaign was also launched, with the theme for the campaign being 'Football, but not as you know it', a strategy clearly aimed at reducing the historical ethnic associations attached to soccer. We can see here a familiar pattern of modernization and reorientation of the game to new, television, audiences and a rejection of traditional representative roles for clubs in favour of more 'rational' market approaches. The slogan in Australia even echoes that of the English Premier League more than a decade before which claimed to be a 'whole new ball game'.

The success of these initiatives, further enhanced by Australia's successful qualification for the 2006 World Cup and advancement to the second round, can not be underestimated in raising the profile of soccer in Australia. Since the 1974 appearance of the Socceroos (the Australian national soccer team's promotional name) in the World Cup Finals in Germany there has been a four-yearly cycle of public anticipation and excitement followed by disappointment and disinterest due to the Socceroos' inability to qualify. Many commentators have suggested that the World Cup qualifying system that Australia must navigate has further marginalized the game in that country. The potential for qualification was made particularly difficult in 2002 as FIFA reversed its initial directive of allowing the first-placed Oceania team (the region in which Australia sits within FIFA's structure) direct access to the finals rather than having to play-off against the fifth-placed South American team.

This reversal, and more broadly Australia's World Cup marginalization, stems in part from the lack of influence the Oceania region holds in the FIFA Executive. Limited voting power and the apparent lack of allies in the FIFA executive has meant the only way for Oceania to achieve anything for itself is to continually 'lobby' the other confederations. Even then, as history shows, decisions have not been binding and can be overturned at the whim of the executive. The ease with which Australia dealt with the Oceania qualification games for Germany 2006 clearly indicated that the country was too dominant in that federation region. By defeating Uruguay (who had finished fifth in the South American confederation) on penalties to advance to the finals, soccer's advocates in Australia argued that the national team should no longer be marginalised from the world stage through an 'unfair' qualification process.

Although the Asian Football Confederation (AFC) historically rejected all advances from Australia to join (Oceania was founded for such reasons when the four founding teams of Oceania had no where else to go), at their executive meeting in Kuala Lumpur in March 2005, the AFC unanimously endorsed the proposal for Australia to join. The AFC was convinced that Australia's inclusion in Asia would not just be a commercial success, but it would make the region stronger and provide the AFC with greater political influence within FIFA.

The combined success of the inaugural A-League season, World Cup qualification, and the shift from Oceania to the AFC has also created greater commercial interest in soccer. This is evidenced through the FFA recently securing an AUD$120 million, seven-year deal with FoxSports which will provide greater media exposure and cash flow for all A-League clubs until 2013. The deal is approximately 20 times greater that the initial one-year deal for the 2006 A-League season and gives FoxSports the rights to 90 A-League fixtures every season, six Socceroos matches (World Cup final matches are excluded as the rights to this event are held by SBS), and 98 games across the Asian region at both club and international level. It is argued that such a deal positions the sport 'firmly into the mainstream of Australia's sporting consciousness both in terms of income and exposure of the home-grown product'.[36]

Concluding comments

Early signs suggest that the A-League is playing its role in providing a link between the game's huge participant community and the new-found success of the Australian representative team, and in doing so the FFA is driving the repositioning of soccer into Australian sport's mainstream. Match, television and online audiences suggest that the on and off-field quality of the A-League resonates and engages a significant section of the Australian sporting community outside of its marginalized ethnic origins.

Total crowd attendance for the first season of the league exceeded one million with approximate average attendances in the order of 11,000–12,000. Although by European and South American comparisons these attendances may seem small, within the Australian context it positions the A-League as a serious competitor against the other football codes. FoxSports also report solid broadcast audiences with averages comparable with Rugby Super 14, despite the Rugby competition's relatively long history. The A-League's web traffic is also placing it in comparable space with the other football codes: in October 2005 the A-League family of websites received more than 850,000 hits, which compares favourably with the AFL number of 961,000 in September – the peak month of the AFL season.[37]

Membership of the AFC and playing in AFC competitions will transform and change soccer in Australia as it will allow the newly formed FFA to complete the pyramid of the Australian game. That pyramid, whose base is made up of the 1.5 million plus players and volunteers will be made whole by the immediate introduction of a raft of strong, regular, meaningful matches and competitions. Previously, the mainstream Australian sporting public only had a meagre diet of irregular, 'friendly' international matches for the Socceroos, some equally irregular and often one-sided qualifying matches in Oceania, and one truly meaningful sudden death qualifier in Australia just once every four years. The Socceroos played six Asian Cup qualifying matches in 2006, and in 2007 reached the quarter finals of the Asian Cup. Half of these qualifying matches were in Australia, and they fell on FIFA reserved dates making it much easier for Australian overseas players to be available.[38]

This programme of regular, scheduled, high quality, meaningful qualifying and competition matches against strong Asian opposition (as well as the opportunity for the top A-League Clubs to play in the Asian Champions League – equivalent of the European Champions League) makes much more compelling soccer for commercial partners. This creates the potential for more dollars to be driven into the top end of the game, in turn, providing greater revenue to be invested into the grass roots development of soccer. At a time when Australia as a nation is attempting to forge greater economic and cultural ties with Asia, the alignment of the FFA with the AFC has the potential to enhance this involvement and integration.

It should be noted that the FFA still has a great deal to overcome in order for soccer to secure the long-term support of the mainstream Australian sporting communities. It is necessary for the FFA to continue to nurture the historical relationship between soccer and its ethnically-based origins, but not to the detriment of mainstream community support. There is therefore the need for a balance to be struck between maintaining traditional audiences, by not alienating football communities based around nationality and ethnicity; whilst also attracting new ones by moving away from distinctions based on ethnic and national lines. As such there is a need to develop a sense of 'communitas' by developing a family of fans.[39] By moving in this direction the FFA will continue to widen community access and provide the opportunities for clubs to promote social integration as Australian soccer attempts to 'come in from the margins'.

Notes
1. Skinner, Zakus and Edwards, *Football Communities*.
2. Mosely and Murray, 'Soccer'.
3. Warren, Harper and Whittington, *Sheilas, Wogs, and Poofters*.
4. Mosely and Murray, 'Soccer', 222.
5. Farquaharson and Marjoribanks, 'Representing Australia'.

6. Macdonald and Skinner, 'The Long and Winding Road'.
7. Radnege, *Encyclopedia of Soccer*.
8. Mosley, *Ethnic Involvement*.
9. Westerbeek, Smith and Deane, 'De-ethnicization and Australian Soccer'.
10. Shilbury and Deane, *Sport Management in Australia*.
11. Ibid.
12. Hughson, 'Football, Folk dancing and Fascism'.
13. Hughson, 'Soccer support'.
14. Dabscheck, 'Socceroos Strike a Deal'.
15. Westerbeek, Smith and Deane, 'De-ethnicization and Australian Soccer'.
16. Ibid.
17. Hughson, 'The Boys are Back in Town'.
18. Giulianotti, *Football*.
19. Macdonald and Skinner, 'The Long and Winding Road'.
20. Ibid.
21. Maguire and Stead, 'Border Crossings'.
22. www.footballaustralia.com.au.
23. Macdonald and Skinner, 'The Long and Winding Road'.
24. Ibid.
25. Cockerill, *Australian Soccer's Long Road to the Top*, 166.
26. Crawford, *Report of the Independent Soccer Review Committee*; Skinner and Carroll, 'The Crawford Report'.
27. Crawford, *Report of the Independent Soccer Review Committee*, 14.
28. Ibid., 15.
29. Skinner and Carroll, 'The Crawford Report'.
30. Ibid.
31. Crawford, *Report of the Independent Soccer Review Committee*.
32. Ibid., 28.
33. Ibid.
34. Skinner and Carroll, 'The Crawford Report'.
35. Crawford, *Report of the Independent Soccer Review Committee*.
36. Smithies, 'Code Kicks $120million Goal', 73.
37. www.footballaustralia.com.au.
38. Ibid.
39. Skinner, Zakus and Edwards, *Football Communities*.

References

Cockerill, M. *Australian Soccer's Long Road to the Top*. Port Melbourne: Lothian Books, 1998.
Crawford, D. *Report of the Independent Soccer Review Committee into the Structure, Governance and Management of Soccer in Australia*. Canberra: Australian Sports Commission Publication, 2003.
Dabscheck, B. 'The Socceroos Strike a Deal'. *International Review for the Sociology of Sport* 37, no. 1 (2002): 79–95.
Farquaharson, K., and T. Marjoribanks. 'Representing Australia: Race, the Media and Cricket'. *Journal of Sociology* 42, no. 1 (2006): 25–41.
Football Federation of Australia. (2006). http://www.footballaustralia.com.au.
Giulianotti, R. *Football: A Sociology of the Global Game*. Malden, MA: Blackwell Publishers, 1999.
Hughson, J. 'Football, Folk Dancing and Fascism: Diversity and Difference in Multicultural Australia'. *Australia and New Zealand Journal of Sociology* 33, no. 2 (1997): 167–86.
———. 'Soccer Support and Social Identity: Finding the Third Place'. *International Review for the Sociology of Sport* 33, no. 4 (1998): 403–9.
———. 'The Boys are Back in Town: Soccer Support and the Social Reproduction of Masculinity'. *Journal of Sport and Social Issues* 24, no. 1 (2000): 8–23.
Macdonald, R., and J. Skinner. 'The Long and Winding Road'. *The Sport Management Association of Australia and New Zealand Newsletter* 2, no. 2 (2001): 21–2.
Maguire, J., and D. Stead. 'Border Crossings: Soccer Labour Migration and the European Union'. *International Review for the Sociology of Sport* 33, no. 1 (1998): 59–73.

Mosely, P. *Ethnic Involvement in Australian Soccer: A History 1950–1990.* Canberra, Australia: National Sports Research Centre (NSRC), 1995.
Mosely, P., and B. Murray. 'Soccer'. In *Sport In Australia: A Social History,* ed. W Vamplew and B. Stoddart, 213–30. Melbourne: Cambridge University Press, 1994.
Radnege, K. *Encyclopedia of Soccer.* South Yarra: Hardie Grant Publishing, 2001.
Shilbury, D., and J. Deane. *Sport Management in Australia: An Organisational Overview.* Melbourne: Deakin University, 1995.
Skinner, J., and J. Carroll. 'The Crawford Report'. *The Sport Management Association of Australia and New Zealand Newsletter* 7, no. 2 (2003): 1–2.
Skinner, J., D.H. Zakus, and A. Edwards. *Football Communities Research Report.* A report commissioned by the Football Federation of Australia. Gold Coast, Australia: Griffith University, 2005.
Smithies, T. 'Code Kicks $120million Goal with TV Deal'. *The Courier Mail,* April 21, 2006.
Warren, J., A. Harper, and J. Whittington. *Sheilas, Wogs, and Poofters: An Incomplete Biography of Johnny Warren and Soccer in Australia.* Sydney: Random House, 2002.
Westerbeek H., A. Smith and J. Deane. 'De-ethnicization and Australian Soccer: The Strategic Management Dilemma'. *International Journal of Sport Management* 6, no. 3 (2005): 270–88.

COMMUNITY AND THE INSTRUMENTAL USE OF FOOTBALL
Anyone for Football for Peace? The challenges of using sport in the service of co-existence in Israel[1]

John Sugden

Social and political context

Those wishing to use sport to promote social reform need first to carefully dissect the nature of the sport experience in its natural setting and broader social and historical context. The conflict in Israel and Palestine has deep historical roots and widespread and complex contemporary manifestations. For the purpose of this paper, only a brief outline of the key socio-political and demographic features that are the most pertinent to F4P can be outlined.

The state of Israel was controversially created in 1948 in the long shadow of the Second World War. While this can be seen as a major achievement for the hitherto nation-less and persecuted Jewish people, in equal measure it can be viewed as a disaster for the Palestinians on whose land the fledgling state took shape.[2] In 1948 only 160,000 Arabs remained in Israel, the rest, some 640,000 fled, mainly to neighbouring Jordan, Syria and Lebanon (today the Palestinian Diaspora number in the region of 3.5 million). Approximately 2.5 million Palestinians live in the Occupied Territories (West Bank and Gaza), some of the most densely populated places on earth. Perhaps rightly so, the situation of the Palestinians within the Occupied Territories, the plight of the Palestinian Diaspora, and the Israeli State's engagement with these external factors attract most global attention. However, often forgotten by the international community, and the main concern of this essay, is the status of relations between the Jews and the Arabs who remained within the state of Israel after 1948.

The late and highly respected Palestinian academic and activist, Edward Said believed that co-existence, not separation, is the way forward if a lasting peace is to be achieved in Israel. He points out, 'we cannot coexist as two communities of detached and uncommunicatingly separate suffering ... the only way of rising beyond the endless back-and-forth violence and dehumanisation is to admit the universality and integrity of the other's experience and to begin to plan a common life together'.[3] Likewise, Naim Ateek, a senior Christian-Arab cleric, argues that any lasting peace in the region must be based upon reconciliation which itself is dependent upon mutual recognition of, and respect for, different cultural traditions and the history of oppression and suffering that underpins those traditions. 'Before the process of peacemaking can begin, a change in attitude of Israeli Jews and Palestinians towards one another is necessary. They need to face each other with candour, to create the new attitudes that will be the foundation for peace and stability in the region.[4]

By the year 2000 Jewish Israelis numbered approximately 5.5 million, made up of a mixture of migrant first generation European and Americans, Ethiopian Jews (Falash Mura) and more recent arrivals from the former Soviet Union. While in terms of religious persuasion the majority of the Jewish population consider themselves to be secular, a significant minority are devoted adherents to the Hebrew faith. This religious orthodoxy is a key dimension of Israel's fractured political make-up. The number of 'Palestinian-Arab-Israeli' citizens is approximately 1.2 million, roughly 18% of the population. This too is an exceedingly complex identity. The order of its wording changes depending upon the political consciousness of the individual bearing it. It is further complicated via the religious and ethnic suffixes that can be added: Muslim (Sunni and Shiite), Christian, Druze, and so forth, not to mention more tribal affiliations, such as the Bedouin and Circassians (nineteenth-century migrants from Eastern Europe's North Caucuses), which also inform the mapping of the county's sectarian geography.

F4P is based in Galilee in the north east of the country, a region with towns and villages with names such as Nazareth, Cana, Tiberias and Megiddo, evocative of the region's biblical past. Modern Galilee's population (1.146 million) makes up 17% of the overall population. Two-thirds of the Galilee's residents are at the bottom of the socioeconomic scale. About half of them – 46% – are Arabs, mostly Moslem, but with a large minority of Christians. The unemployment rate in the Galilee is some 50% higher than the national one. In the more rural areas of Galilee, Jews and Arabs live in separate towns and villages, whereas in the larger urban areas, such as Akko and neighbouring Haifa, the two communities live in separate enclaves. Travelling between them it is clear to the observer that the Jewish communities are considerably better off than their Arab counterparts who feature disproportionately in the ranks of the region's socio-economically deprived. Official statistics confirm this is the case.[5]

Sport and football in Israeli society

Outside of the Middle East, good examples of how sport can contribute to peace processes can be found in South Africa and Northern Ireland. In the former case, sport was one of the most important fronts in the struggle against apartheid, albeit most significantly in terms of an international *boycott* of sports events involving that regime. In the post-apartheid era, sport has a new role as a medium through which the diverse and formerly antagonistic elements of the 'rainbow nation' are reconciled and harmonized,[6] although this is neither unproblematic nor uniform across all sports. In Northern Ireland, where sport was once a theatre for the expression of cross-community animosity, it is now formally recognized as a key element in the peace process. However, as research carried out in Northern Ireland tells us, the view that 'any sport and all sport' is a universal social good is extremely naive.[7]

Like everything else in Israel, sport is highly politicized. It is an important sphere of civil society and is terrain contested between Jews and Arabs and the various factions within each community. The politically contested dimension of Israeli sport has increased in proportion to the growing numbers of Israeli-Arabs who choose to participate.[8] Until relatively recently, other than at the margins, in sectarian places and spaces, for Arabs in Israel, football was another contested aspect of mainstream civil society wherein they were losing out. Traditionally professional football in Israel has been linked to mainly Jewish political parties and political associations, including trades unions. In addition, as Ben-Porat has argued, along with other state-sponsored sports and sporting organizations, after 1948 football was an integral part of the process through with the cultural façade of the (Jewish) state of Israel was constructed.[9] This made it difficult for Israeli Arabs to participate at the highest levels. It also helped to exacerbate problems for Israel's participation in international football competitions, leading the world governing body FIFA to the radical step of taking Israel out of the AFC (Asian Football Confederation) to avoid confrontation with regional Arab states, and placing them first within the OFC (Oceania – Australasia and the South Pacific), and latterly within UEFA (Europe) for future World Cup qualification purposes.[10] As we shall see, the decision made by FIFA in 1998 to readmit Palestine into the 'FIFA family' – even though Palestine is not recognized internationally as a nation-state – has led to problems for some talented Israeli Arab Palestinians who now have to decide to which football 'nation' they should owe allegiance.[11]

However, in the wake of the post-1967 modernization of Israeli society and the advance of post 1980s globalization, things began to change with evidence of a professional/commercial performance pragmatic at work through which professional football became more open to the participation of Arab players and Arab-owned teams. 'The globalisation and liberalisation of Israeli society since the 1980s and the waning power of the political parties (the former patrons of soccer) have facilitated the commercialization of the game, introducing a profit motive and economic rationality of both players and owners.'[12] In other words, it is good business to recruit the best players, regardless of their race or ethnic/national identity because this produces better teams and more success. The net result of this is, perhaps impelled by relative impoverishment and the perceived riches available in professional sport, more and more Arabs are taking up opportunities to play and watch football in settings that were formerly the almost exclusive preserve of the Jews, although exclusions remain. This tendency has been encouraged by breakthroughs made by both Jewish and Arab players from Israel who play in the most prestigious professional European leagues. It is for these reasons that Sorek has been able to argue that football more than any other sporting sphere has the potential to be an 'integrative enclave' in Israel.[13]

This advance does not come without the creation of other problems, nor is it uncontested. Precisely because more Arab players, teams and their fans are now taking part, football also offers more opportunities for racial and ethno-national confrontation. For instance, 'death to the Arabs' and other, unprintable and more profane, racially vicious chants are sometimes heard coming from the exclusively Jewish terraces of Beitar Jerusalem, the team which is consistently at the top of the NIF's (New Israel Fund) weekly racism incitement index. The NIF index was introduced in 2004 into the Israeli football league in recognition of the increase in sectarian-related incidents in and around the country's football stadiums. As well as working with the NIF, the IFA (Israeli Football Association) is also consulting with representatives from The FA (the English Football Association), who with their long, although not unproblematic,[14] experience of dealing with racism in English football are helping them to devise anti-racist strategies which are most suitable for the local context.[15]

Linked to the theme of equity and inclusion, given that one of F4P's objectives is to get more girls and women involved, another important contextual issue is concerned with the relatively underdeveloped state of women's sport in Israel. As one report puts it:

> In general terms it might be said that women have never had the encouragement to take up competitive sport in the same way that men have. Research has shown that in Israel only about 25% of the participants in competitive sport are women, a number much lower than the average in the western world, and even lower than the average in the word as a whole.[16]

This view is confirmed by the results of a survey carried out in 2000 by the Israel Women's Network which revealed that of all registered athletes in 15 major sports only 24% were female. Football showed the worst imbalance where, out of a total of 32,000 registered players, only 1,000 were female, barely more than 3%. In terms of who runs sport in Israel the situation is even worse as women are virtually invisible with less than 10% representation and once more the worst culprit is football. Even though Israel inaugurated a women's league in 1998, the Israeli Football Association (IFA) has no female representatives on the governing body.[17]

In 1995 the Ministry of Education in Israel adopted the 'Brighton Declaration on Women and Sport' requiring government and volunteer organizations to promote gender equality in sport and to establish special programmes to ensure due representation of women at all levels and in all entities.[18] It would appear that there is still a long way to go. As will be illustrated later in the essay, however, in addition to pointing to male privilege, any explanation for the under-representation of women in sport in Israel must take account of a complex range of local factors, not the least of which are religious in nature.

Project history and development[19]

The first formal phase of the F4P project began modestly in 2001 when six volunteer coaches from the University of Brighton and one staff leader conducted a week-long coaching camp in the Arab town of I'blin. The timing could hardly have been worse as operations began during the height of the second *Intifada* (uprising). The key difference between this and other popular anti-Israeli protests was that it spilled out of the Palestinian Authority and drew in Palestinian Arabs living as citizens within the state of Israel. They took to the streets to protest against the brutal means being used by the Israeli authorities to quell the unrest in the Palestinian Authority as well as to draw attention to their perceived lack of civil rights within Israel itself. In response to such protests, in Israeli-Arab towns such as Nazareth and Sakhnin (both now partners in the F4P project), the security forces reacted very aggressively as a result of which many Arab-Israeli citizens were arrested and some were killed or seriously injured.[20] This grievously damaged already fragile cross-community relations between Arabs and Jews within Israel in general, and in the region of Galilee in particular. The increasing use of suicide bombers as a strategy for resistance by a variety of Palestinian extremist groups exacerbated a growing cross-community mistrust and polarization.

For the 2001 football project, the original plan had been to partner I'blin with a nearby Jewish municipality, but with lines of communication all but down, and in the wake of a bus bombing in the neighbourhood, the ensuing security situation caused the Jewish community to withdraw their children from the project at the eleventh hour. The 2001 project went ahead nonetheless in I'blin, involving 100 Muslim Arab and Christian Arab children (10–14 years old). This reflected the sectarian geography of the town of I'blin where Moslems and Christians lived in separate neighbourhoods. As we have seen, community divisions in the region are more complex than simply between monolithic blocs of Arabs and Jews and rifts and tensions within the Arab community in Galilee was a dimension of the problem that the UK team had not previously appreciated or accounted for. This in itself was an important learning experience. In the face of all of the odds, and despite the absence of a Jewish partner, the fact that the project took place at all was a considerable achievement, demonstrating that, from a logistical point of view – fund raising, volunteer recruitment, planning, travel, provision of equipment, programme execution, and so forth – such programmes could be successfully mounted.

Building upon this qualified success, the following year a second project took place involving a slightly expanded team of eight coaches and two staff leaders. This time, in addition to I'blin the cooperation of the Jewish communities of Misgav and Tivon was secured allowing

150 Arab and Jewish children, including 20 girls, to share the coaching and playing experience. The inclusion of girls training separately but alongside the boys was not universally approved of and this issue was to emerge later as one of F4P's biggest challenges.

Local volunteer coaches and community sport leaders were more involved in the planning of the 2002 event and participated fully in the coaching project. The involvement of local people and their increasing sense of partnership/ownership was perceived as a very important development and a key area in terms of the project's longer term sustainability.

In 2003 F4P once more doubled in size, involving 12 UK coaches and three leaders running three simultaneous projects, in six different locations, working with 300 children and 30 volunteer coaches from six communities widespread throughout Galilee. For the first time, the 2003 event also involved a pre-project training day during which, once they had arrived in Israel, the UK volunteers and leaders worked alongside their Arab and Jewish colleagues in preparation for the forthcoming week's programme. Once the project proper started, parallel with the football coaching, there was a programme of 'off-pitch' activities whereby those age groups of children who were not involved with the football engaged with a variety of community relations activities designed and led by local leaders and volunteers. Some of these were recreationally based while others required more of an intellectual input.

By this time the British Council in Israel had grown to become a key partner with the University of Brighton in the development, management, fund raising and administration of F4P. This is a well established global organization with a proven commitment to social and cultural development and education. The special circumstances of Israel's conflict ridden society meant that the British Council there had added community relations work to its portfolio of activities. In F4P they saw an opportunity to promote this dimension of their mission through sport while at the same time drawing on the expertise and excellence of volunteers trained in UK Universities. In return, from its main offices in Tel Aviv and Jerusalem and its sub office in Nazareth, the British council were able to furnish F4P with a local administrative hub from which year-round planning and networking could take place with communities taking part in the project. The British Council were also key in getting the Israeli Sports Authority (ISA) involved in the project. The ISA soon became the most important factor in developing and communicating with the growing network of participating communities and it is largely through them that the longer term sustainability of F4P has been so much enhanced.

All who had been key participants agreed that the 2003 project was a great success. However, during the post-project evaluations, and in anticipation of facilitating a further project in 2004, some significant issues emerged. Firstly, it was determined that, even though the football coaching had been much appreciated by the children, F4P had to ensure that what they were achieving was more than simply improvements in football skills. The team felt that they needed to do more to ensure that the content of that football programme was clearly underpinned by values and principles that fed a broader community relations agenda and that those values and principles were appreciated by the local coaches and experienced by the children in practice.

Related to this, it became clear that the 'off-pitch' activities had not been universally successful. Getting youngsters to play together is one thing, but placing them in situations where they had to talk about and confront some of the more sensitive features of their divided society is far more problematic. Engagement with this kind of work requires levels of training and expertise that neither the UK team nor most of the local facilitators possessed. The F4P team concluded that at this stage of the project's development, this kind of intervention was beyond the remit of the project. If not done well, there was a danger that bad feelings engendered in some of the 'off-pitch' activities would undermine the positive work taking place within the football programme.

Rather than ignore this issue F4P determined to rethink the ways in which they used the on-pitch activities and set out to design a soccer coaching manual that would provide opportunities for social contact across community boundaries; promote mutual understanding; and engender in participants – children and coaches alike – a desire for and commitment to peaceful coexistence. In addition, of course, F4P aimed to enhance soccer skills and technical knowledge, but this was very much secondary to the broader community relations aims. The resulting coaching manual emphasizes neutrality, equity and inclusion, respect, trust and responsibility and contains a series of football practices and exercises through which children's learning and understanding of these principles and values can be made manifest. A pilot version of the F4P Coaching Manual was produced in March 2004 (Lambert, Stidder and Sugden, 2004) and was used in the next phase of the project in Israel in July later that year.[21]

The 2004 main event was more than twice the size of anything that had been done previously. It involved 700 children from 16 communities widespread throughout Northern Israel. In its execution, a team of 28 student-volunteer coaches and seven leaders from the UK worked alongside 60 local, Jewish and Arab-Israeli volunteers at seven different project sites, including a girls-only project in Tiberias on the banks of the Sea of Galilee.

The initiation of a girls-only project staffed entirely by female coaches and translators was in response to F4P's own evaluations and feedback from local sources who favoured the inclusion of girls but were also sensitive to regional and religious customs and traditions with regard to gender issues. It can be problematic taking values germane to Western societies and attempting to articulate them through sport in Oriental and other non-western cultures. Even if desirable, crude attempts to impose self-defined 'universal' values are unlikely to work. The desire to achieve equity and inclusion, while at the same time being respectful of local customs and religious traditions, can raise tensions and problems which can only be resolved through adopting a pragmatic approach and the introduction of the girls-only project should be viewed in this light.

The 2005 F4P programme was the largest and most ambitious since its inception in 1999–2000. Broadly, it followed the pattern of the 2004 project, with a training week for Jewish and Arab coaches from Israel and UK volunteers held at the University of Brighton during March 2005, followed in July by the main project in Israel. This consisted of a parallel series of eight, five-day long coaching projects involving 18 different communities and approximately 1,000 Jewish and Arab children. The July project followed what was becoming a familiar pattern beginning with a training day for local coaches, followed by four days of coaching with the F4P Manual. On day one of each project the children from the separate communities were placed in mixed coaching groups of 12 (n=12). They were mixed according to community identity and football ability ensuring that not only did Arab and Jewish children play alongside one another, but also that when it came to competition time, teams would be evenly matched. As had happened in each of the preceding years, the 2005 enterprise came to a close with a grand finals day and awards ceremony (involving all participants), followed the next day by a feedback evaluation morning for all coaches and all community representatives.

Women's problems

The main topic of concern with dominated the 2005 evaluation meeting was a huge controversy that had blown up around female inclusion in the project. As with previous years, one of the eight project teams consisted of female coaches who were trained to work at a girls-only project. Within the broad objective of the project to promote mutual understanding, tolerance and peaceful co-existence through football, there was a specific commitment to equity and inclusion (one of the principles underpinning the F4P model). Compared to most of Europe and North America, Women's football is underdeveloped in Israel and there are some particular challenges to be met in trying to move forward in terms of gender equity. In different ways, both Orthodox Jewish opinion and more conservative Muslim views were ill disposed towards women and men mixing in any sporting activity. At the outset F4P knew that it was not possible to integrate girls with boys in the various project locations. Even having girls playing separately from boys on the same project site was disapproved of, especially if some of the coaches were male. As organizers were about to learn, in the most extreme cases, even having women playing sport while men looked on was not tolerated. Nevertheless F4P were strongly committed to gradually and pragmatically inching forward our gender equity agenda.

As a matter of principle and to set an example project workers made sure that six of the projects would have at least one female coach. However, despite working in soaring temperatures, the female coaches were required to dress 'modestly' to ensure that not too much bare flesh was revealed. In addition, for the second year running F4P decided to have a girls-only project, staffed entirely by women coaches and helpers and drawing female participants from the communities of Sakhnin (Arab) and Tiberias and Akko (both Jewish).

As had happened the previous year, when the finals day was held in the Arab town of Nazareth, plans were made that the girls' finals would be held at the same time and in the same place as the boys' competition. Two days before the finals were scheduled to be held the overall UK project coordinator and a representative from the British Council in Israel were summoned to meet with the Deputy Mayor of Um el Fahem. He reported that his offices had been strongly petitioned by local religious leaders not to allow the finals to go ahead because of the anticipated involvement of girls engaging in physical activity in a setting shared by boys and men.

Um el Fahem is a large town right on the boarder with the Palestinian Authority. The skyline clutter of flat-roofed three and four story extended family homes, interrupted by gilded mosques and minarets reveals the town as unmistakably Arab. Um el Fahem is built on a series of hills overlooking the notorious Green Line – the ominous and controversial security barrier which the Israeli authorities have built to separate the state of Israel from Palestine. The town is 90% Muslim and has a reputation both for radical political activism and religious fundamentalism. When F4P were there the town's former Mayor, Sheik Read Salah, who is also leader of the Northern Branch of the Islamic Movement of Israel, languished in prison, charged by the Israeli authorities with channelling funds to a number of proscribed militant Arab organizations, among them Hamas (Islamic Resistance Movement).

Um el Fahem also happens to have some of the best community football facilities in the region – the town's football stadium is called 'The Stadium of Peace' – and was the only town which felt able to offer them for our purposes. Nazareth and Nazareth Ilit, both less controversial venues, had initially offered good facilities, but had, for various reasons, withdrawn those offers. The prospect of including Um el Fahem as a community partner and using their facilities for the training and finals days caused considerable debate, especially since the town was regarded with considerable suspicion in certain Jewish circles. In the context of decades of extreme violence, given Um el Fahem's reputation for Islamic radicalism, such suspicion is easily understood. However, the very fact that Um el Fahem had joined the project and in doing so showed a commitment to the underlying values of cooperation and peaceful co-existence, was viewed very positively. Um el Fahem was partnered with the neighbouring Jewish community of Megiddo – better known by its biblical name, Armageddon, site of many ancient and not so ancient battles and the biblical location for the final reckoning (an interesting setting for a peace project!). Although they were no more than ten miles apart, hitherto Megiddo and Um el Fahem had little or no contact with one another. The Arab town was viewed with great suspicion by its Jewish neighbours and for their part many of Um el Fahem's residents believed that Megiddo was located on occupied Palestinian land. It was generally felt that getting two such communities engaging in any form of cooperation was of itself a major achievement. Organizers felt that having the co-educational finals day in Um el Fahem would give out a strong, positive signal and set a good example for others to follow.

F4P had partially anticipated problems in involving girls in Um el Fahem and decided to place an all male coaching team there. Another problem emerged, however, in that one of the Jewish volunteer coaches/translators from Megiddo was female. F4P organizers negotiated with the local coordinators and it was agreed that so long as she wore track-suit bottoms, tied her hair back and wore a hat, – presumably so that from a distance she might be mistaken for a man – she could continue to participate. However, what had not been considered was the impact of the co-educational training day which had been held in Um el Fahem at the start of the 2006 project, when as many as 20 women coaches and translators would be seen working alongside men on the training ground outside of the main stadium. Local religious leaders, who had considerable political power in the town, had put enormous pressure on the Mayor's office and it had been decreed that unless F4P remove the girls from the finals, the tournament would not be allowed to go ahead for fear of triggering a riot.

Apologetically the Deputy Mayor explained that this had been brought to his attention after the training day when male and female coaches were seen practicing together. Even though it was explained that in the finals the girls would be playing separately from the boys, the fact that there would be men watching, and girls would be playing without being fully covered up meant that within a strict interpretation of Shar'iah law the principles of Islam would be violated. The details of this are made clear in the following *fatwa* issued by Sheikh Faysal Mawlawi, deputy Chairman of European Council for Fatwa and Research:

> The requirements to be met for a Muslim woman to practice sport relate, at all scales, to her duty to cover the '*awrah* (parts of the body that are not supposed to be exposed to others; vis-à-vis women, her '*awrah* is from the navel to the knee; as for men, it is all of her body except the hands, feet and face). Thus, if there is a sport that a woman can practice while adhering to this requirement, then it is permissible for her so long as all other religious requirements are fulfilled ... (in addition) They must not intermingle with men in any way that brings them physically close together and there should be no kind of photographing or television that may broadcast these scenes.[22]

What had already been facilitated and what had been planned for the finals was clearly in violation of virtually all of the tenets of this interpretation. With less than 48 hours to go before the commencement of the finals day and with no other comparable facility available, faced with this *fatwa*, under protest F4P agreed to move the girls' finals to the nearby Kibbutz Barkhai where they could play 'behind closed doors'. In return F4P insisted that the girls were allowed to return to the stadium after their finals to participate fully in the awards ceremony – which most of them did, standing out in the bright red Three Lions t-shirts donated to us by The FA which they had been asked to wear especially for the occasion so they would not be missed when they entered the stadium. In another token act of subversion F4P gave the job of refereeing one of the two boys' final matches to one of the project's women coaches, a former senior international for the Republic of Ireland who had been capped several times. (The other boys' final was refereed by Brendan Batson, one of England's first high profile, black professional footballers, who now campaigns tirelessly in the cause of anti-racism in football and works on a consultancy basis for The FA)

Despite such rearguard actions, this remained a deeply frustrating experience and an uncomfortable compromise, especially given that one of F4P's core principles is equity and inclusion. To say the least it did not go down very well with most of the girls themselves and was met with hostility by the all-female coaching team and all the rest of the coaching staff. However, it was either compromise or cancel the tournament altogether and F4P believed that this would have been even more damaging to our cause. Interestingly, it was a decision that suited some of the Orthodox Jewish parents as much as their devout Muslim counterparts as they too objected to their daughters playing in the same spaces as Arab boys and men. The whole episode has complicated the thinking for future FAP tournaments.

Conclusion: war stops peace!

Wednesday, July 12, 2006. The British Airways jet banked over Cyprus ready for its slow descent across the South Eastern Mediterranean into Tel Aviv's Ben Gurion International Airport. Football for Peace 2006 was about to begin. The main party of 40+ volunteer coaches and support staff were scheduled to fly out the following day. I was the advanced guard and was arriving a day early to check final arrangements and visit the stadium in Jerusalem where the F4P football festival was to be held the following week.

I was nervous. Not because of the flight but because of breaking news coming out of Israel that there had been skirmishes between Hezbollah guerrillas and the IDF (Israeli Defence Forces) along the border between Israel and Lebanon. There had been several fatalities and two Israeli soldiers had been captured. The IDF was already engaged in serious action further south, in the Gaza Strip, where there had been a large mobilisation in the wake of the kidnapping of another Israeli soldier by Palestinian militia. The action in Gaza was some distance from the main centre of our operations in Galilee, but the more recent events along the border with Lebanon were much closer and could jeopardise the 2006 enterprise.

Things had not improved while I had been in the air and, by the time I was deposited at my hotel in Jerusalem, Hezbollah had begun responding to Israel's incursion into Lebanon by firing Katushya missiles at towns and villages in Northern Galilee. One of the first places to be hit was the resort town of Nahariya were the UK coaches were to have spent a couple of days enjoying rest and relaxation at the end of the 2006 project. That evening I was supposed to be having a leisurely dinner in a Jerusalem restaurant with Caron Sethill, the Assistant Director of the British Council in Israel, who is one of F4P biggest supporters. Instead she picked me up at the hotel and we sped North for a hastily convened meeting in a road-side diner just South of Haifa, Israel's third largest city. My heart sank when as we drove and listened to the radio it was reported that missiles had struck Haifa. This meant that virtually all of the communities that had been lined up to host F4P projects were well within missile range. I knew then that irrespective of the outcome of our meeting it would be both impossible and irresponsible to allow F4P 2006 to go ahead.

For the six years that F4P had run we had always said that we might one day have to abort the project at the eleventh hour if the security situation demanded it and now that time had arrived. It was a gloomy meeting as I sat with Jane and Caron from the British Council and Gazi and Offer from the Israeli Sports Authority examining our options, but all of us knowing that there was only one course of action to take. Everybody had worked so hard to prepare for this year's event which was to have been the biggest ever: twenty two communities; eleven projects; 1000+ children; a F4P peace convoy on the way to the finals festival in Jerusalem's Betar stadium which was also to feature an exhibition match between a UK team and a team of TV celebrities. Expectations were huge which meant that the disappointment would be equally big, both for the partner communities and for the UK volunteers.

Even as we talked the main party was gathering at London's Stanstead Airport, but I had told the party leaders not to check anybody in until they had heard from me. A decision could not be delayed. We had a duty of care to the children who had signed up to the project and at a time when they and their families had been warned to either stay in or close to air raid shelters it would have been inconceivable of us to try and bus them around to play football. Likewise we had similar responsibilities for the UK student volunteers and, desperate though I was to see the project go ahead, I could not countenance taking them into a region that was rapidly deteriorating into a war zone. I borrowed Jane's mobile phone and called the party leaders at Stanstead and told them that the project was being postponed.[23]

Any doubts that F4P had made the wrong decision were soon dissipated as in the following days the border skirmish had developed into a fully fledged war between the IDF and Hezbollah and Katushya missiles were raining down across the Galilee hitting many of the host communities for the project such as Akko, Afula, Nazareth, and Tiberias.

However, even though the 2006 project had to be postponed, there had been some valuable lessons learned and some fundamental questions raised about doing a project like this in a place like that. Among the learning for a project such as this are the following points:

(1) Despite what the legendary Liverpool FC Manager, Bill Shankley, may or may not have said, football is not more important than life and death;
(2) In a war zone self-preservation is the overriding motive for action both for the victims of conflict and for would-be peace-makers;
(3) In a region experiencing serious internecine conflict, culturally focussed peace initiatives can work only when preceded by military and political accommodations;
(4) Culturally focussed peace initiatives work best within maturing peace processes;
(5) Complex political and social problems are usually unresponsive to simplistic solutions;
(6) Approaching conflict resolution in a segmented and piecemeal fashion is unlikely to achieve sustainable results;
(7) Adopting a stance of impartiality/neutrality is difficult to sustain when a context of injustice prevails and intensifies.

In addition to these observations the following important questions should be noted:

(1) Can conflict resolution and co-existence be promoted between Jewish and (Palestinian) Arab citizens within Israel while conflict between Israel and the Palestinian Authority and between Israel and neighbouring Arab countries rages?
(2) Should we be engaging with sporting initiatives in the 'abnormal' society that constitutes the State of Israel?
(3) Should we be developing partnerships with institutions of the Israeli State such as the Israeli Sports Authority and Ministry of Education?
(4) How to respond to those who say that the central role played by the British Council in the project leads to the conclusion that Football for Peace is just another exercise in British neo-imperialism?
(5) Is mobilizing a westernized, left-liberal agenda to encourage the equal participation of women in sport in countries with strong and conservative religious traditions another form of cultural imperialism?

As ever, sociologists are usually much better at identifying social problems than finding solutions and these are all very hard questions to which there are no easy answers. Faced with such imponderables and in the light of what happened in 2006 F4P could not be blamed for shelving the project indefinitely as yet another – albeit small – failed peace initiative in the Middle East. However, the project has also had to consider the disappointment of their Jewish and Arab partners when the project had to be cancelled; and it has to consider the children and grown ups that lost opportunities to make new friends and broaden horizons because camps could not be run. This does not mean that we should ignore the questions and issues highlighted above. Rather, they become part of the reflective and critical framework within which Football for Peace will continue to evolve.[24]

Notes
1. This chapter is based on material published in a book about the Football for Peace project, edited by John Sugden and Jim Wallace, published by Meyer and Meyer in 2007. The author is one of the organizers of Football for Peace.

2. Said, *End of the Peace*.
3. Said, *End of the Peace*, 208.
4. Ateek, *Justice and Only Justice*, 168.
5. Sa'ar, 'Government's Financial Neglect'.
6. Keim, *Nation Building at Play*.
7. Sugden, 'Sport and Community Relations'.
8. Sorek, 'Arab Football in Israel'.
9. Ben-Porat, 'Commodification of Football in Israel'.
10. Sugden and Tomlinson, *Fifa and the Contest for World Football*, 239.
11. Taylor, 'For Occupied Palestine'.
12. Ben-Porat and Ben-Porat, '(Un)bounded Soccer',433.
13. Sorek, 'Arab Football in Israel'.
14. Back, Crabbe and Solomos, *Changing Face of Football*.
15. The FA, 'United they Stand'.
16. Israel, 'Story of Sport in Israel', 2.
17. Israel Women's Network, 'Women in Sport'.
18. Ibid.
19. Those interested in more detail about the Project's early beginnings should consult Whitfield's, *Amity in the Middle East*.
20. Said, *End of the Peace*.
21. Lambert, Stidder and Sugden, *Football for Peace*.
22. Islam on Line, 'Islam's Stance'.
23. Sugden, 'Field Notes'.
24. Football for Peace returned to Galilee in December 2006 and successfully conducted a residential project for 300 Arab and Jewish children five miles south of the Lebanese border'.

References

Ateek, N. *Justice and Only Justice,* Maryknoll, NY: Orbis, 1989.
Back, L., T. Crabbe, and J. Solomos. *The Changing Face of Football: Racism, Identity and Multiculture in the English Game.* London: Berg, 2001.
Ben-Porat, A. 'The Commodification of Football in Israel'. *International Review for the Sociology of Sport* 39, no. 4 (1998): 421–36.
Ben-Porat, G., and A. Ben-Porat. '(Un)bounded Soccer: Globalization and Localization of the Game in Israel'. *International Review for the Sociology of Sport* 39, no. 4 (2004): 421–36.
Islam on Line. 'Islam's Stance of Women's Practicing Sport'. 2004. www.islamonline.com/ggi-bin/news.
Israel, S. 'The Story of Sport in Israel'. *The Jewish Agency for Israel,* 2000. www.jafi.org.il/education.
Israel Women's Network. 'Women in Sport'. 2002. www.iwn.org.il.
Keim, M. *Nation Building at Play: Sport as a Tool for Integration in Post-apartheid South Africa.* Aachen: Meyer and Meyer, 2003.
Lambert, J, G. Stidder, and J. Sugden. *Football for Peace Coaching Manual.* Unpublished, University of Brighton, 2004.
Sa'ar, R. 'Government's Financial Neglect may Cause Collapse of Galilee Communities'. August 22, 2004. www.haaretz.com.
Said, E. *The End of the Peace Process.* London: Granta, 2002.
Sorek, T. 'Arab Football in Israel as an "Integrative Enclave"'. *Ethnic and Racial Studies* 26, no. 3 (May 2003): 422–50.
Sugden, J. 'Sport and Community Relations in Northern Ireland and Israel'. In *Sport and the Irish,* ed. A. Bairner, 238–51. Dublin: University of Dublin Press, 2004.
Sugden, J. Extract from field notes, July 12, 2006.
Sugden, J. and A. Tomlinson. *Fifa and the Contest for World Football. Who rules the Peoples' Game?* London: Polity Press, 1998.
Sugden, J. and J. Wallace, eds. *Football for Peace? The Challenges of Using Sport for Coexistence in Israel.* Aachen: Meyer and Meyer, 2007.
Taylor, E. 'For Occupied Palestine, Just Turning up is a Struggle'. *The Guardian,* September 8, 2004: 33.
The FA. 'United they Stand on Both Sides of the Line'. *Communiqué,* Issue 12 (2005): 3.
Whitfield, G. *Amity in the Middle East.* Brighton: Alpha Press, 2006.

COMMUNITY AND THE INSTRUMENTAL USE OF FOOTBALL
Vamos, Vamos Aceirteros: soccer and the Latino community in Richmond, California[1]

Ilann S. Messeri

Visit any number of soccer complexes or fields in the United States and you might be surprised by what you see. During games the parking lots will be crowded with an impressive fleet of SUVs: the type of automobile that has largely become synonymous with youth soccer and 'soccer moms' in the United States. The distinguishing difference between each vehicle will probably be the colourful writing on their windows, which is intended to cheer on different teams. The passengers of the vehicles will be coaches, parents, players and friends, all coming to participate in one of the United States' largest and most popular youth sports. If the sheer number of SUVs is not surprising enough, one may be astonished by the size of some of these complexes, which can include more than 40 soccer fields, baseball fields, football fields, small stadiums, or any number of other athletic arenas.

Before the games, most teams go through their set routine, which can include any number of exercises in various styles. Some teams opt for highly organized and synchronized warm-ups, whilst others choose to use more spontaneous methods. Some coaches, players and spectators have dubbed different styles of warm-ups as being European, Brazilian, English, French, Italian or other country- or regionally-specific names. Before the opening whistle of the game, most teams will perform some sort of 'cheer'. Large numbers of these are rather generic and common, but others are elaborate and in some cases even include songs.

During games, which frequently occur simultaneously in fields adjacent to one another, you may notice that many teams have access to the most technically advanced equipment, be that in terms of their boots, balls, uniforms or warm-up outfits. For those who are used to a different style of play, the games themselves may be surprisingly physical, both for boys and girls. Perhaps most surprisingly of all, however, especially when considering the global nature of soccer and the United States' claim to diversity, you will notice the homogeneous social and ethnic make-up of the teams. Many are nearly all white and of the same socio-economic class.

Youth soccer in the United States is largely a white suburban sport where minority teams and players are frequently marginalized. However, there are some urban communities, largely made up of immigrant families, where soccer is a primary focus. This paper will focus on one such community. Specifically, it will explore the role of soccer within the Latino and Hispanic communities of Richmond, California, which are marginalized and impoverished immigrant communities. By using ethnographic methods, related literature, anecdotal evidence and structured interviews this essay will show the importance of soccer within the communities of Richmond. It will also explain the various roles that soccer plays within the community, and explore whether the possibility exists for using soccer to operate as a tool for socio-economic development. However, in order to fully understand these processes one must first have a general understanding of youth soccer in the United States, from its political undertones to its relative role in the sphere of American youth sports, and of Richmond itself.

Youth soccer in the United States

Youth soccer in the United States has long been a sport for the 'culturally dominant'. Unlike the game in other countries, soccer in the United States has become dominated by the suburban white middle to upper-middle classes. Andrews' study on the game notes 'that [soccer in the USA] presently enunciates the dominant rhythms and regimes of suburban existence every bit as naturally as the single family home, ballet classes, sport utility vehicles, lawn sprinkler system, *The Gap*, and the imperious Martha Stewart'.[2] In short, American soccer has largely become a homogenous, extremely competitive and wholly commodified sport. Unfortunately, these characteristics negatively affect urban non-white populations who also wish to participate in the sport. More specifically, the suburbanization of youth soccer in the United States has created an arena in which minorities are largely excluded from the playing field.

There are numerous different levels of youth soccer in America, ranging from non-competitive recreational leagues to the highly competitive and arguably politicized Olympic Development Program (ODP). Club soccer is the primary medium through which different skill levels are channelled. However, unlike youth club soccer in the rest of the world, the American game has no affiliation with professional clubs or the MLS (Major League Soccer). Instead clubs are divided into geographical regions, where some are merely neighbourhood teams, whilst others represent entire cities or even multiple counties. It should be mentioned that there has been a recent movement to begin creating youth club teams and academies in conjunction with professional teams in the US. However, this has not yet happened, and in order for it to occur numerous rules would have to be changed within the general structure of club soccer and within the MLS itself.

Within youth club soccer there are usually three or four different skill or competitive levels, with the lowest being the non-competitive, non-travelling, recreational level, commonly referred to as 'house' soccer or Class IV. This is usually made up of players of multiple ages. Class III soccer is the next level, and is considered to be semi-competitive, involves minimal travel and is usually 'age-pure' meaning that all players are either the same age as one another or younger than the specified age limit. The next level is Class I, which is considered to be highly competitive, includes a large amount of travel and is age pure. Teams at this level are selected at try-outs, where only the best players make the team. Lastly in certain states, and at older ages, there are Premier Leagues for Class I teams. These are the most competitive leagues in youth soccer and usually require the most amount of travel. For the purpose of this essay, and in terms of American youth club soccer, I will focus primarily on Class I soccer due to it being the only level of club soccer that creates opportunities for players to be exposed to both college and ODP coaches.

Youth club soccer has largely become, as Andrews describes, a sport governed by and for America's suburban population. The clubs not only serve as soccer teams for suburban children, but they have also become status symbols for families, with the wealthier and more exclusive clubs symbolizing the status and competitive nature of their members. Andrews argues that 'soccer [in the United States] has been appropriated as part of the innately competitive, socially differentiating, and highly stylized lifestyles, through which individuals attempt to seek membership of the valorised suburban middle class',[3] and due to its suburbanization, youth club soccer in the United States has long been made up of a relatively homogenous player pool.

There are numerous ways in which youth club soccer prohibits urban minority participation, but perhaps none as important as the sheer expense of the Class I game. If one wants to be on a Class I club team you must first try-out, or audition, for a spot on the team. Even ignoring the blatant discriminatory practices which can occur during such try-outs, one often has to pay a small fee to merely attempt to make the team. If you do make the team you are then required to pay a sum that can reach thousands of dollars in order to be an active participant of the team. It should be noted that whilst these fees may or may not include team uniforms, they most certainly do not include personal equipment, and when competing against players who often have the latest equipment, it is hard to not want or perhaps need the same. Further expenses include travelling and tournament costs. Many tournaments, particularly the more competitive ones, are at distant locales, often involving a fair amount of travel, and whether that travel is by plane or automobile the cost is usually paid by players' families. Tournament fees include the cost of joining the tournament itself and possibly accommodation for the course of the event. These fees and others add up to an experience that can be very expensive, a fact which is often cited by observers as the primary reason why many urban minority groups do not play Class I soccer.

Nevertheless, there are a few impoverished groups who do wish to participate in competitive American youth club soccer, and among those groups is the Latino community of Richmond. Frequently, the costs of particular clubs, and the cost of Class I soccer in general, prohibits these groups from gaining the best experience and exposure that competitive club soccer has to offer. When speaking of exposure, I refer to the fact that many colleges which recruit for soccer teams do so almost exclusively at highly expensive Class I tournaments and ODP events. This creates a system in which qualified impoverished players are not seen, and consequently do not get recruited by universities and colleges.

Through this structure, Class I club soccer serves as a feeder into the highly politicized Olympic Development Program (ODP). It should be noted that whilst I do not intend for this essay to be an attack upon the ODP and its merits, there are certainly problems inherent with a system that draws upon a form of soccer largely dominated by one particular group. Impoverished minorities are often overlooked or not seen altogether throughout the process of selecting ODP teams, and this is seemingly in direct conflict with the ODP's philosophy to 'identify players of the highest calibre on a continuing and consistent basis, which will lead to increased success for the U.S. National Teams in the international arena'.[4] Put simply, the ODP does not always identify the best players, and the majority of players they miss are impoverished minorities.

In summary, there are three specific and interconnected ways in which impoverished players, particularly minority ones, are disadvantaged when compared to others within the United States competitive youth club system. The first is the suburban nature of the system. Not only are the participants of youth club soccer heavily suburbanized, but the directors of programmes, top clubs and other important individuals/agencies are also either located in suburban areas, or are sympathetic to suburban needs. This leads to a system where many of the poorer teams and players are largely ignored, and as a result a bifurcation occurs between those at the dominant end of the spectrum within US youth club soccer and those at the lower end. The second disadvantage is in large part created by the first, namely the cost of participating in Class I soccer clubs or programmes. It is clearly exclusionary for clubs to be so expensive to the point where youth soccer becomes unaffordable for many families. The final disadvantage is again in large part the result of the previous two: that not enough impoverished and minority players are exposed to both ODP and college coaches. Tournaments are undoubtedly the best way to be exposed to these coaches. However, as a result of tournament fees and travelling costs the numbers of tournaments that impoverished clubs attend are rather minimal, and they usually tend to be only small local ones.

Fortunately, there is another agency for youth soccer in the United States: namely, school soccer. The type of youth soccer in which this essay is particularly interested is high school soccer, especially as this is the dominant form of youth soccer amongst Richmond's Latino and Hispanic communities.

When comparing the two different systems of youth soccer, it is evident that Class I club soccer is generally more competitive and skilful than high school soccer, and while players usually participate in both programmes, club soccer tends to draw on a wider geographical area and larger populace than the high school game. High school teams are almost entirely comprised of attendees of the high school that the team represents, with a few exceptions being made in specific cases of continuation schools or students attending schools without a sports programme. This is what makes high school soccer so unique, especially with regards to Richmond. Teams are almost exclusively made up of local residents, and in some ways come to 'represent' their local community or communities. In essence, the structure of high school soccer means that Richmond High's team is free from many of the constraints of club soccer, and in some ways this has led the team to be more successful than more formal youth soccer clubs in the area. However, an exploration of soccer in Richmond alone would not be sufficient without some description of the actual community.

Richmond's Latino community

Richmond is commonly described as an impoverished city, neighbouring more affluent communities in the eastern part of the San Francisco Bay area. It frequently finds itself under heavy media scrutiny, more often then not due to its high crime rate. A recent study cited that Richmond is the twelfth most dangerous city in the United States and the most dangerous city in California.[5] Due to its high crime rate and its relative infamy, Richmond has become a city largely avoided and ignored by its more affluent neighbours, save for the occasional high profile court case or local news story about violent crimes. However, the common – and often official – perception of Richmond and the 'reality' of the place do not always match.

A great deal of the crime that occurs in Richmond takes place in a small area of the city: an area separate from the place which is the focus of this essay. Specifically, the majority of crimes in Richmond happen in an area called the Iron Triangle or, geographically speaking, North Richmond. This area is a particularly dilapidated, impoverished and ignored area of Richmond, and while there are Latino citizens living there, the majority of the Latino populace is heavily centred elsewhere. One could argue that the Iron Triangle is largely responsible for Richmond's infamous nature, not least because it is the most acute example of the social and economic neglect which the city has experienced.

It is interesting to note that the US Census Bureau's statistics for Richmond are somewhat in conflict with more common perceptions of the city. According to the census, Richmond's Latino and Hispanic residents make up 26.5% of the population of Richmond, with the total population being approximately 99,216 people.[6] The two other most populous racial categories are White, with 31.4%, and Black, with 36.1%. However, the racial breakdown of students at the two main public high schools in Richmond – John F. Kennedy High and Richmond High – presents a different picture. With the number of students from both schools combined, one finds that 52% of the student body is Latino, whilst only 3.7% is White.[7]

There are a variety of hypotheses that could explain this inconsistency. It may be that the Latino population is much younger than the white population, and thus a larger number of them are currently attending schools. Alternatively, it could be that white citizens of Richmond are more affluent and many of their children attend private schools. It could also be the case that the 2000 Census did not count all of the Latino citizens in Richmond, causing an under-estimation of numbers. A combination of these three suggestions is most likely, meaning the Latino population in Richmond is probably younger than other groups, attends public schools in large numbers and is heavily marginalized allowing for many Latino people to not be counted on the official census.

A key feature of the Latino community in Richmond is its heavily centralized nature. According to the US Census's tract maps, most Latino residents live along or close to 23rd Street, in essence supplying this study with an even more specific region than Richmond itself. 23rd Street is physically indicative of this phenomenon, with numerous shops and restaurants catering to the surrounding Latino community. It is also a somewhat impoverished area, devoid of both money and municipal resources like parks and other facilities that promote communal activities. Richmond High is located on 23rd Street and draws the majority of students from the immediate local district. The student body of Richmond High is 60.5% Latino.[8]

One could suggest that there are some aspects of the traditional *gemeinschaft*-type community within the Latino populace of Richmond. There are certainly strong personal ties and evidence of commitment to primary groups. In some respects the Latino and Hispanic community within Richmond could almost be said to constitute their own small city. As stated above, there are numerous businesses catering for the specific needs of the community and it is not uncommon for residents to run into people they know many times per day. Soccer most certainly helps in this respect. It introduces people to each other, and often creates relationships that are developed off the field. Soccer is one of the primary leisure activities within the community and thus it is one of the ways in which relationships are created and built upon.

Soccer in Richmond

Within the greater San Francisco Bay area, Latinos in Richmond are known to be, as one newspaper put it, 'passionate about [soccer] – even fanatical – but the perception is that the obsession can go over the top'. Others have said, 'in Richmond, the Latino communities treat soccer like life and death'.[9] These quotes not only illustrate the passion the Latino community has for soccer, but they also represent what neighbouring areas think of Richmond soccer. Aside from the well-known passion displayed by the Latino community, soccer in Richmond also has a somewhat dubious and even infamous reputation. Much of it stems from incidents such as the one on 20 November 2004 in which the coach of an under-10s Richmond team attacked the referee after he was unable to prove that all of his players were the right age.[10] Perhaps the best description of soccer in Richmond is that the community is so passionate about soccer that their judgment can sometimes be clouded, which can lead to decisions that are not always in the best interest of their reputation.

Soccer is undoubtedly the primary leisure activity amongst the Latino and Hispanic community in Richmond, and the same can be said for Latinos in the greater San Francisco Bay area. It engenders a great deal of passion amongst the community, and is firmly entrenched as a cultural activity. In many respects soccer is a link to the populace's former countries and past lifestyles, and may even provide an escape from the ongoing attempts to integrate into a new country. Moreover, soccer is seen as being so important to this community that companies have used it as a marketing tool directed at Latinos; so much so that the primary cable company in the area annually plans, organizes and stages one of the largest adult amateur soccer tournaments in the area where companies like Toyota and Anheuser-Busch Inc. advertise their products, and where local Latino radio stations promote themselves and report on the tournament.

At the national level soccer is also used as a promotional tool to the Latino populace. Recently, Major League Soccer tried to create a strong connection with Latinos in the US by implementing a new franchise that is essentially the 'little brother' of a popular club in Mexico.[11] This club, Chivas USA, located in Los Angeles where there is a large Latino population, was almost solely formed for MLS's Latino fan base with the hopes of garnering further support for the league from this passionate soccer audience.

This example shows the importance that soccer plays amongst the various Latino communities across the USA; an importance that many corporations readily acknowledge and are willing to use. For Richmond's Latino community, and for many other Latino communities throughout the country, soccer is more than a leisure activity: it is a cultural activity that provides not only a link to their past life or their parents' past life and country, but it also helps to serve as a form of integration into a new and foreign culture. All of the interviewees consulted for this essay said soccer is undoubtedly a part of Richmond's Latino community's culture, that it is imbedded within their families and within their past, and unequivocally a part of their cultural heritage.[12]

To help understand soccer's role within Richmond it is useful to consult Massey's analysis of Mexican migration to the USA. The study focused on a population of Mexican migrants in the US, and found that soccer clubs are one of the most important voluntary organizations to which migrants can belong. Massey states that 'although [a soccer club's] manifest functions are recreational, its latent functions are to strengthen and expand the social connections within the network, thereby supporting the migrant enterprise'.[13] Whilst it is clear that Richmond's Latino population and Massey's migrant population are somewhat different, they are still similar enough that one can find many parallels when comparing them, and the role of soccer is just one such similarity. Massey goes on to explain that:

> Indeed, the practice field has become an obligatory place of reunion for all out-migrant *paisanos*. It is the place where dates are made, work obtained, friends located, new arrivals welcomed, and news of the town exchanged ... This weekly reunion not only breaks up the routine of work, but it also provides a regular forum for communication and exchange.[14]

All of the interviewees for this paper agreed that soccer not only strengthened social networks and brought Richmond's Latino community closer together, but also in some cases created new networks and relationships that were developed off the field. This demonstrates that in the broadest terms, soccer clubs in Richmond perform functions similar to Massey's Mexican soccer clubs.

Unfortunately, Massey's study only investigated one particular soccer club, and in Richmond there is no club that is similar to that enjoyed by the study's migrants. Instead there are a number of different mediums in which soccer is played, and while most of them have similar effects to those of Massey's soccer club, there are also other mediums for soccer in Richmond aside from clubs and different roles that soccer plays within the community.

There are three different agencies for soccer which will be discussed, with the most focus going to the two youth programmes in the area: namely school soccer and club soccer. The other agency is adult soccer, which is somewhat less developed and organized than youth soccer, but, nonetheless, still important.

Adult soccer in Richmond is not nearly as common as youth soccer, and usually involves games of a relatively unorganized nature. 'Pick-up games', meaning unorganized games that are open to just about anyone passing by, and can be found in the evening at various parks throughout Richmond. These games are usually made-up of people that know one another and often have some sort of relationship outside of soccer, and can happen on a regular basis. Before the game begins the players socialize and warm-up at the same time, and after the game ends some players will go out and spend the rest of the evening together, maybe at a local restaurant, bar or cafe. It is these unorganized and sometimes impromptu games which most closely resemble Massey's soccer club, particularly in terms of the similar communal effects these games can produce.

There are also a few organized and competitive adult teams based in Richmond which play in leagues centred in either San Francisco or in the eastern part of the greater San Francisco Bay area (the East Bay). However, these teams do not tend to play an important role within the Latino community.

More important to the Latino community of Richmond is youth soccer. It is a more popular activity at the organized level, and frequently adults participate as coaches, managers and/or spectators. As previously mentioned there are two types of youth soccer in Richmond, namely club soccer and school soccer. The shortcomings of youth club soccer for the Latino community have already been discussed. However, it is instructive to revisit these problems at a local level and discuss them with Richmond's Latino community in mind.

Youth club soccer in Richmond is part of the ACCYSL – the Alameda Contra Costa Youth Soccer League – which is comprised of numerous different clubs within Alameda and Contra Costa County; namely the Albany Berkeley Youth Soccer Club, the El Cerrito Soccer Club, the Mersey Soccer Club, the Richmond United Soccer Club, the San Pablo United Youth Soccer Club and the ACCYSL Mavericks. Of these six clubs, Richmond's Latino youths primarily play for the Richmond United Soccer Club, San Pablo United and the ACCYSL Mavericks. Additionally, some young people from Richmond also play for teams within the West Contra Costa Youth Soccer League (WCCYSL). However, participation within that league among Richmond's Latinos is relatively small when compared to the ACCYSL, and therefore will not be discussed within this essay.

The Richmond United and San Pablo United Youth Soccer Clubs are relatively new to the area, and have teams for both boys and girls from the ages of 6–16. They primarily have teams of two different skill levels, namely Class IV and Class III. On the other hand, the Mavericks, which has teams for both boys and girls between the ages of 10 and 19, is primarily a club for Class I teams.

It should be noted that there are many young Hispanic and Latino residents of Richmond who do not play for a club, but instead play recreationally with friends, either at parks in pick-up games, in their yards, or sometimes even on the sidewalk or on the street. Some may even choose to play for adult teams, or more commonly for their school team. In the United States these players are sometimes referred to as 'street players', which should not be confused with actual people who play in the street. Rather, the term in the US is usually designated for people who do not have much experience with organized soccer. In addition to these so-called 'street players', there are also those young people in Richmond who play club soccer, but do not play for any of the previously mentioned clubs. Instead they play for some of the more elite clubs in the area. Certainly most of the players from Richmond would not be able to afford to join these clubs in the traditional way, namely by paying the club fees. Thus if they are considered to be good enough, elite clubs will usually offer them scholarships, and sometimes even give out other perks to attract the players. In Richmond, many of the best players migrate to wealthier clubs instead of playing for local ones with the hopes of being on a better team, have better coaching and of being better exposed to the mechanisms of progression within the system of soccer in the United States.

This situation can leave local clubs at quite a loss. Not only does it drain local talent from these clubs, but it also obviously weakens their ability to compete within the competitive structure of youth club soccer. Additionally, the level of support from the community for these local club teams is relatively small. At any given game, be it for San Pablo, Richmond or the Mavericks, the spectators are usually limited to a few of the players' parents, and perhaps some friends, who are usually responsible for bringing the players to the games and taking them home. It should also be noted that each individual team within the clubs usually have to raise their own finances, causing teams without a financial donor or some form of fundraising to be extremely limited in their ability to travel and attend tournaments.

Whilst youth soccer clubs in Richmond certainly have their limitations, they can also provide certain services that are beyond the reach of other soccer programmes within the US. The clubs provide minorities, particularly young Latinos and Hispanics, with a certain level of integration into American culture and its lifestyle that is not necessarily readily available within their own communities. US youth club soccer is undoubtedly run largely by and for white suburban populations, but by being involved within this system and by playing teams and players from outside their community, this allows players from Richmond to experience a lifestyle and culture distinct from their own. Additionally, club soccer is also the best way for players to be seen by scouts, particularly those from colleges and universities. As one interviewee put it, 'club soccer actually got me more exposed to college coaches, which is the big difference between school soccer and club soccer, and by going to Marin [a wealthier and better club team] I was able to get even more exposure than I would have had I stayed at a club in Richmond'. This statement provides insights into both the benefits of club soccer and its drawbacks. Club soccer undoubtedly provides players with more opportunities for advancement than other systems of soccer in the US, but usually those opportunities go primarily to those who need them least. This means that opportunities frequently go to white, suburban, middle- and upper-class players: ones who can afford to be at the very best clubs which have the best coaching, participate in the best tournaments and provide their players with the most exposure to both college and, in some rare instances, professional scouts.

The exclusive nature of club soccer is certainly one of the reasons that many within Richmond's Latino and Hispanic communities prefer school soccer, and in particular high school soccer. All but one of the people interviewed for this essay believed that high school soccer was more popular and important to the players in Richmond than club soccer; with the one exception citing that club soccer is likely to provide good players with greater exposure.

A comparison of club youth soccer with high school soccer is striking, almost to the point where the two are more than just different variations of the same sport. Club soccer is a far more technical game, whereas high school soccer, particularly within the league (the Alameda Contra Costa Athletic League) and section (the North Coast Section) that Richmond High School plays in, has become a far more physical game based largely on athleticism and strength. This difference makes it somewhat odd that Richmond players should prefer high school soccer. Their unarguable strong point as both players and as teams is their technical ability, which usually surpasses that of their opponents. Nevertheless, high school soccer teams in Richmond usually enjoy greater success at a higher level than the area's club teams. There are numerous reasons for this. Some have been discussed previously, like the costs of club soccer etc., while other reasons may have more to do with the high school soccer system than the actual teams that Richmond produces and the support that high school soccer in Richmond, particularly Richmond High, gets from the local community. Almost all of the interviewees pointed out that Richmond High School's soccer team gets much more support from the local community than any club or club team, a fact that not only alludes to the importance of the team itself within Richmond, but might also point to the failings of the local clubs.

There are anywhere between one and three different soccer teams at any given high school, depending on the number of students at the school, the numbers who want to play and how much funding the soccer programme gets from the school, fund raising and boosters. These teams are broken up into three different skill levels, with Varsity being the highest and most competitive. The middle level team is Junior Varsity, in which only students between grades 9–11, if they make the team, are allowed to play. The lowest level team is the Frosh or Freshmen Team, which is for grades 9 and 10 only. Whilst Richmond High School has a relatively large student population, and well over 100 students participated in the most recent try-outs for the soccer teams, the programme only has enough funding for two teams: Varsity and Junior Varsity.

Unlike the local clubs, most of the funding for the school teams comes from the school, the school district, fundraising from businesses or donations from the community. This means that high school soccer at Richmond High is relatively cost free for players and their families. In addition to the relatively large sums of money local community members and businesses provide, the school team also receives various other forms of support from the community. Indeed, the number of spectators at Richmond High's games is fairly large, especially when compared to club soccer. At a recent playoff game there were nearly 500 people present, most of whom were cheering for Richmond. Clearly, the Richmond High teams attract a larger audience than any local club as they draw on the families of the school's large student population, whereas club teams usually only draw upon the families of the players of that specific team. It is also important to remember that while many members of the community hold strong allegiances to various different professional clubs or national teams from their 'home' countries, Varsity high school soccer is the highest level of live soccer readily available to many people in Richmond.

This is perhaps a central reason why Richmond High School's soccer team gets so much support from the community. As Bar-On's discussion of soccer in Latin America suggests, local professional club teams, and even national teams, in many ways foster a sense of community through common local support.[15] In Richmond, where there is no local professional club team, individuals either have to support their favourite club and national team from afar, or turn to Richmond High where the community can become significantly involved with the school's teams. I do not mean to suggest that support for Richmond High replaces supporters' former allegiances to their favourite professional clubs or national teams. Rather, because of supporters' relative inability to interact with faraway teams in any manner other than watching games on television, Richmond High's soccer team becomes a natural outlet for their support. This becomes even more prominent when individual supporters either have family or friends who go to Richmond High School, and can be further magnified if those friends or family members play for the school's teams.

This is only one example of how Richmond High's soccer team, and soccer in general, creates a stronger community in Richmond. Through common support for the team, the community not only enriches the players' experience as well as their own, but also make new and important connections with one another, as well as finding another common rooting interest that help to strengthen previous bonds. Additionally, members of the community and parents of the players frequently work at the games in Richmond, either as security, working the ticket booth or by selling refreshments at the games.

Further networks within the community are created and strengthened through the Richmond school teams' community service work. Throughout the course of the 2005–06 school year the team served as security for the annual Virgin de Guadalupe Pilgrimage, helped to clean Richmond High's campus numerous times, and held dances for the community at the school as a fundraising event. While being in charge of security for the Virgin de Guadalupe Pilgrimage, where a procession of around 5,000 people marched from Richmond High to a local church where mass was held, the players were able to interact with the community in a unique and different manner from that of a 'normal' student athlete. Indeed, the fact that the players were entrusted to look after such a popular and important religious ceremony signifies the amount of respect and esteem that the community holds for soccer at Richmond High.

There are certain stipulations, rules and minimum levels of academic achievement that the players must abide by and reach in order to be able to play for soccer teams at Richmond High. These rules, which include a minimum grade point level and certain behavioural guidelines that players must meet when representing the team, the community and the city, help to provide a better image of the city and community in general. While club teams usually do have sets of rules which players must follow, these rules are often much more lax and not nearly as rigidly enforced as those of high school teams. The way the school team behaves and performs both on and off the field when playing away games definitely creates a reputation for the team, the community and even the city. For a long time Richmond High School's team had a poor reputation. Many opposing teams vocally expressed negative feelings about playing at the school, and some even refused to play games there. However, with past changes in both the school's administration and the coaching staff of the team, starting approximately around the school year of 2000–01, the reputation of the school has begun to improve, as has the reputation of the team.

On top of reshaping Richmond and the Latino community's image, two former Richmond High soccer players and coaches have begun to work closely with the local school district (West Contra Costa Unified School District) in order to improve the public schools within Richmond. This is by no means a mandatory service. These former student-athletes have volunteered themselves in order to inform members of the school board and district about the problems and needs of Richmond's schools. Through this process, these former players are not only 'giving back' to their own community, but they are also trying to improve it by increasing the general level of education at public schools and the resources given to them.

The relationship between Richmond High soccer and the local Latino community is one that is relatively unique compared to that of neighbouring cities. It is by no means a one sided relationship: the community supports the team, and in turn the team gives something back to the community. Through this relationship the community is strengthened. The accomplishments of Richmond High's teams elicit pride within the community, and in turn members of the team help to clean up the high school, serve as security at important events and serve on a school district's committee with the hopes of bettering local education. As part of these relationships, networks within the community are both made and strengthened.

It should be pointed out that soccer in Richmond is not all positive. The game in many ways helps to maintain the status quo, with perhaps the best example of this being how entirely gendered the sport is within the Hispanic and Latino community. Both school and club soccer programmes have teams for girls, but these do not get the same support as boys' teams and are therefore usually far less competitive. Most of the people interviewed for this essay acknowledged this problem, and many pointed out that girls are usually discouraged from playing soccer at young ages.

Conclusion

The Hispanic and Latino communities within Richmond are undeniably passionate about soccer, sometimes to a fault. The game plays such an integral role within the community that one would be hard pressed to find any other activity which elicits the same reaction. Soccer in Richmond breaches national boundaries: it is a sport that the community plays and enjoys together, regardless of nationalities. Most certainly some nationalistic pride remains, and some teams in the area are built upon those ideas. However, more often than not a certain pride for the city of Richmond and for the team itself overrides those nationalist pretences. There are some rivalries amongst teams in Richmond, and others with surrounding Latino communities, but when a team comes to represent Richmond, or more precisely the Latino community through Richmond High

School, the community comes together in common support for a team that they can truly call their own. While this may sound overly romantic, one cannot dispute both the passion for soccer in Richmond, and the nature of the relationship between the high school's soccer team and the community. Where other teams in Richmond have failed to garner support, Richmond High has been relatively successful.

It is now important to consider the more formal potential soccer has within Richmond. The power of sport is undeniable, and in Richmond, amongst the Hispanic population, soccer is the most popular athletic competition. Therefore, within that relatively impoverished community, we can ask whether soccer can be used instrumentally as a tool for social and economic development. This is clearly a possibility, but in order to fully explore the issue and arrive at a definitive conclusion much more extensive research is needed. Perhaps Richmond High's soccer programme is already heading in that direction. Recently the programme has applied for and received state grants to build a new field and locker room, and the field will be open for community use. This could provide an early indication of how soccer in Richmond could become a catalyst for physical and social regeneration.

It would be wrong to simply ignore the benefits that club youth soccer can offer. The system is undoubtedly intended for wealthier white upper and middle suburban classes. However, that does not mean that Latinos in Richmond, and in the US generally, cannot benefit from playing within the system. More often than not, club soccer is generally of a higher skill level than high school soccer, and it offers a myriad of opportunities that high school soccer does not. Not only is it the best way to be exposed to college and professional scouts, but it can also serve as a form of integration into an otherwise alien lifestyle, if that integration is wanted.

Nonetheless, soccer in Richmond is clearly dominated by its high schools. Club soccer has its place, but it is not nearly as popular amongst the community, or as successful on a competitive level. High school soccer plays an integral role within Richmond's Hispanic and Latino communities, creates new social networks between people, strengthens existing networks and can also become a focus for communal practices. As stated earlier, it should be noted that the effects of soccer are not all positive within Richmond. It can disrupt existing networks, create animosity between people and does not always serve the purpose that it should. Ultimately, however, soccer is the primary leisure activity amongst the Latino and Hispanic communities of Richmond and is part of past heritages and present cultures of large numbers of people.

Notes

1. Sanchez Jr, 'Richmond High Players Build Soccer Bond'. *Esta Barra Quilomerra* roughly translates into 'this loving crowd'. It is part of a song that Richmond High School's soccer team sings before every game. The full song and translation follows: *Vamos, vamos Aceiteros, vamos vamos a ganar, que esta barra quilomera, no te deja de alentar. Veni, veni, canta con migo que un amigo vas a encontrar, que con la mano de Juan, toda la vuelta vamos adar*; 'Let's go Oilers, we're going to win, because this loving crowd won't let you down. Come and sing with me, a friend you will find, because with the help of Juan, everything will turn out fine.'
2. Andrews, 'Contextualizing Suburban Soccer', 31.
3. Ibid., 32.
4. 'US Youth Soccer', http://www.usyouthsoccer.org/programs/odp/index_E.html.
5. Morgan Morgan, ed. *Crime City Rankings*.
6. US Census, 2000. http://www.census.gov
7. West Contra Costa Unified School District (WCCUSD) School Accountability Report Cards, 2003–2004. http://www.wccusd.k12.ca.us/schools/sarc
8. Ibid.
9. Nevius, 'Soccer Can Succeed in Richmond'; Nevius, 'Richmond Team Breaks The Mold'.
10. Camps and Sturrock, 'Coach Accused of Beating Ref'.
11. Delgado, 'Sport and Politics', 41–54.

12. All of the interviewees were older than 18 and were either from Richmond or were domiciled nearby. They included several former players of local high schools and local leagues, a coach of a local high school and league teams, and the founder of a local league.
13. Massey, 'The Social Organization of Mexican Migration', 105.
14. Ibid., 106.
15. Bar-On, 'The Ambiguities of Football', 1–16.

References

Andrews, David L. 'Contextualizing Suburban Soccer: Consumer Culture, Lifestyle Differentiation and Suburban America'. In *Football Culture: Local Contests, Global Visions,* ed. Gerry. P.T. Finn and Richard Giulianotti, 31–53. London: Routledge, 2000.

Bar-on, T. 'The Ambiguities of Football, Politics, Culture, and Social Transformation in Latin America'. *Sociological Research Online* 2, no. 4 (1997): 1–16. http://www.scoresonline.org.uk/2/4/2.html.

Camps, Mark and Carrie Sturrock. 'Coach Accused of Beating Ref Dispute Allegedly Arose Over Eligibility of 10-Year-Olds'. *San Francisco Chronicle,* November 21, 2004.

Delgado, Fernando. 'Sport and Politics'. *Journal of Sport & Social Issues* 23, no. 1 (1999): 41–54.

Massey, Douglas S. 'The Social Organization of Mexican Migration to the United States'. *The Annals of the American Academy of Political and Social Science* 487, no. 1 (1986): 102–13.

Morgan, K O., and S. Morgan, ed. *Crime City Rankings.* 11th edition. Lawrence, KS: Morgan Quitno Press, 2004.

Nevius, C.W. 'Soccer Can Succeed in Richmond'. *San Francisco Chronicle,* January 15, 2005.

Nevius. C.W. 'Richmond Team Breaks the Mold'. *San Francisco Chronicle,* March 12, 2005.

Sanchez Jr., Ricardo. 'Richmond High Players Build Soccer Bond'. *Contra Costa Times,* February 16, 2006.

POSTMODERN COMMUNITY AND FUTURE DIRECTIONS
Fishing for community: England fans at the 2006 FIFA World Cup

Tim Crabbe

Introduction

In recent years, there has been a significant and well documented re-alignment of the English game's social configurations.[1] As suggested elsewhere in this collection, the 'watershed moment' has principally been associated with the Hillsborough stadium tragedy of 1989 and the subsequent report by Lord Justice Taylor in 1990. This led to a requirement for all-seat stadia for matches involving clubs in the top two divisions of English professional football and saw the widespread reconstruction of stadia and relocation of a number of club grounds.[2] The main implication of this development for match-going supporters was the removal of large, mass standing areas, or terraced 'ends', which were less constrained, easily accessed, more favourably priced and consequently popular amongst the most regular, passionate and vociferous fans. The closure and rebuilding of these 'ends' has allowed clubs to further develop corporate facilities, family enclosures and to reconfigure the location of different social groups of supporters within stadiums which has contributed to a breakdown of many historic patterns of support and match day rituals.

In this essay some broader consequences of these transitions are considered. Specifically, the impact of these developments on the patterns of support associated with the England national team at the 2006 FIFA World Cup is presented. This is done within the context of a theoretical framework which acknowledges the process of change within football as the product of more fundamental social transformations which have had a profound impact upon the ways in which we have come to understand the concept of community. As such, after outlining a theoretical framework with which to make sense of these changes the essay will seek to capture a 'sense' of football's fan communities within the particular social context of a World Cup finals tournament which, it is suggested, are emblematic of the more ephemeral, temporal and fluid forms of community which increasingly characterize our times.

Liquid games: contemporary social theory and the 'new' football

When tied in with the creation of the FA Premier League[3] and wider evidence of a transformation in the ways in which the game is consumed,[4] the changing nature of English football can be related to broader economic, political, social and cultural changes which extend well beyond the game. Indeed contemporary social formations have increasingly been the subject of new forms of theorizing which have emerged in the context of a loss of faith in the efficacy of existing social theories and their attendant methodological approaches to deal with the complexities of our times. In this sense the emergence of a series of fresh and related concepts – variously termed late modernity; reflexive modernity; postmodernity and liquid modernity – can be understood as the consequence of a specific historical event which is in the process of superseding 'early' or 'solid' *modernity.*

Just as Max Weber suggested, in *The Protestant Ethic and the Spirit of Capitalism*,[5] that the 'Puritan ethic' played a key role in bringing about the monumental historical transition of traditional society to industrial capitalism, and by definition, 'solid' modernity, now it is widely argued that we are experiencing another epochal shift in social relations. In his work Weber revealed how the newly emergent industrial state redefined 'moral' problems requiring public attention as technical and administrative ones, which required bureaucratic solutions. By contrast, the work of sociologists such as Giddens, Bauman, Lash and Beck[6] shows that today, whatever the terminology used, contemporary social formations have become increasingly *individualized* through a discourse which stresses the narrative of 'reflexive selfhood'.[7] In 'liquid modernity', it is argued that we have become 'hedonistic sensation seekers' governed by the 'will to happiness'[8] rather than the coercive impact of the past.[9]

Post or 'liquid' modernity then has come to be seen as the product of an amalgam of post-Second World War social, political and economic changes that has been accompanied by a cultural transformation, bringing with it, for those who have the financial resources, 'new freedoms, new levels of consumption and new possibilities for individual choice'.[10] In the process it is argued that the 'solid' taken-for-granted social class systems of yesteryear with their centralized, hierarchical authority have gradually been deconstructed and superseded by a mediatized and technology driven society of horizontal social networks.[11]

For Delanty,[12] in their deconstruction of classical sociological understandings of community, postmodern theorists have then rejected the principles of sameness and locale which are often argued to be necessary for any community formation. From this perspective, people's continuing lust for community is born more of a sense of its passing and absence than its presence. Accordingly, rather than something that is imposed or 'lived with', in contemporary writings, community has come to be seen as an experiential formation which is more likely to be 'chosen' reflexively. For Giddens, this new sense of reflexivity extends itself into our conception of who we are, whereby 'the *self* becomes a reflexive project'.[13] For if in solid modernity people's perception of their place in the world was not ascribed, they at least generally knew where they stood.: the respective directors' and players' entrances, directors' boxes and terraced 'ends' at football stadiums denoted a hierarchy based on patronage, history and class 'status'. By contrast, in liquid modernity these symbolizations become blurred and uncertain, with class and locality becoming less significant determinants of identity and consumption choices. Instead of simply inheriting their place in the world, people are now compelled to *find* one and are judged responsible for their choices.

In the face of these new modes of consumption and performance, academic writers on the sociology of football have begun to develop and re-focus their own interest. From Ian Taylor's assessment of the advance of market relationships within the game[14] and Anthony King's thesis on the new consumption of football[15] to Steve Redhead[16] and Richard Giulianotti's[17] concerns with postmodernization and the emergence of the 'post fan', this has proved increasingly fertile ground. For whilst Robson has argued that football remains 'the practical medium par excellence of the continuing expression and celebration of the core practices and concerns of embodied masculinity in a specifically working class variant',[18] it is clear that this sense of an enduring football 'identity' and associated notions of community are now increasingly contested.

Post modern community, football and the 2006 FIFA World Cup

As a product of the 'solid', modernist, Victorian sports project, football has only latterly, if spectacularly, embraced the social changes referred to above and adapted to the individualized, consumerist terrain of contemporary social formations which these developments reflect. Today, just as the centrality of 'the local' pub and 'corner' shop within the social fabric of working-class neighbourhoods have given way to the city centre bar and supermarket, so then have 'football clubs' increasingly sought to transform themselves. In many cases this has involved them being physically lifted out of those neighbourhoods to new sites away from residential areas, or at least the rebuilding of stadiums according to new design aesthetics which reflect the more instrumental blueprint for the out-of-town shopping mall rather than the piecemeal expansion of the Victorian industrial landscape.

Yet it is precisely in this context that Scott Lash[19] has provided an alternative framework for understanding the concept of community whereby he argues that reflexive post modern communities are characterized by:

- peoples desire to 'throw' themselves in
- a wide stretch over time and place
- the continuing problem of their own creation and re-invention
- abstract and cultural representations

For our purposes what this analysis suggests is a clear *desire* for community and the continuing resonance of the concept in the face of shifting social and cultural formations, reflecting a 'need' to *perform* ones' belonging which can be readily applied to the new landscapes of football.

Breaking with the deconstructive linguistic approach of post structuralists such as Foucault, Lacan, Derrida and Barthes which sought to leave concepts such as identity and community redundant, the French sociologist Michel Maffesoli has offered a reinvigorated concept of community which is perhaps closest to that of Lash. His focus relates to the emergence of 'emotional communities' which are characterized more by their aesthetic than the geographic and symbolic formations more classically associated with community studies.

Maffesoli considers community in terms of the quasi-religious, emotional movements which arise out of 'tribes' rather than the 'masses' or the 'crowd'. For he sees mass society, structured around class-based forms of consumption, as being in decline having been replaced by more heterogeneous forms of consumption and informal friendship networks. He invokes the idea of the postmodern 'tribe' which, in the context of football, can congregate in non-territorial spaces such as internet chat rooms, post match phone-ins and fanzine letter columns as readily as football stadium concourses and stands. Such 'emotional' communities are considered to be characterized 'by fluidity, occasional gatherings and dispersal'.[20] Ultimately they are regarded as having no foundation or moral purpose beyond the relations of sociability and performance of identity that constitute them. They exist merely in the temporary groupings and channels that we slip in and out of as we navigate our own highways through life.

It is easy to see how this notion of the postmodern tribe might be invoked in the context of football. Indeed both Armstrong[21] and Giulianotti[22] have made use of the concept in relation to their considerations of the forms of sociation related to the notion of 'football hooliganism'. But the performativity that can be found in the playgrounds of football reveals a whole series of Maffesolian *neo-tribus* and Scott Lash's 'post-traditional' *Gemeinschaften* which extend well beyond the constraints of the rather narrow social formulations surrounding the categorization of the 'hooligan'.

Nowhere is this temporal togetherness more pronounced than in the gatherings of football fans that surround the staging of international football tournaments. Since the Euro 96 tournament finals in England, by far the most populous set of fans from outside the host country have been England supporters who have travelled in growing numbers, culminating in estimates of some 170,000 England fans in Germany to follow the national team.[23] Whilst the England team has long attracted a vociferous and committed following, the sheer volume of this support is a new phenomenon. Indeed Mark Perryman has argued that at the Euro 88 finals also staged in Germany, England had the smallest travelling support with around '7,500, compared to 12,000 Irish, 20,000 Danes, 25,000 Italians and around 30,000 Dutch'.[24]

The rapid growth of England's travelling support, particularly since the 1998 World Cup finals in France, is in many ways symptomatic of the wider changes in the game discussed previously, and the ways in which people now seek out, perform and celebrate their sense of community. For in accordance with other elements of the leisure industry and the conceptualization of liquid modernity, football entertainment is now 'produced' for an increasingly fragmented supporter base. The World Cup is no longer merely a test of international footballing standards: in England at least, it has become a defining, almost ubiquitous presence within the national psyche. Equally, the staging of the event has been re-imagined to embrace the proliferation of interest, providing ever widening circles of opportunity for consumption, facilitated through the organizers' determination to create a carnivalesque atmosphere – a kind of 'planet football'.

Whilst it has long been common for football fans to 'dress up' for matches and even for non-attenders to sport the colours of their national team on matchdays, at the 2006 FIFA World Cup finals, many German fans quite freely embraced the 'party' style throughout the tournament. On any day and across the country, it was common to find people with football shirts, jester hats and Hawaii style flower necklaces in black, gold and red. This performance of identity extended far beyond the conventional constituencies of fandom, with little obvious gender or social class distinctions as men and women, girls and boys embraced the tournament, displayed their allegiance and came together in civic spaces to share a communal engagement with the national teams' performances on giant screens and in local bars.

Such displays extended far beyond the tournament hosts though as groups of fans visiting from different countries could be found roaming the streets of the country's cities with flags, whistles, air horns, drums, and playful parodies of national costumes or signifiers – including French fans with live cocks, Mexicans with sombreros alongside the host national colours. Yet what was striking in those cities which hosted England's matches was that whilst the fans of many other countries seemed to 'pass through', appearing on match day and departing or disappearing into the background afterwards, the English style was characterized more by the pure exuberance and power that comes from weight of numbers. England fans simply took over the central spaces of their host cities for days at a time and appeared to be found everywhere, at all times. Yet rather than misinterpreting this presence as some uniform re-assertion of a particularized sense of national identity it is vital to understand that this presence was itself played out in a plurality of ways.

In the following section a sense of this plurality is presented through a proximate presentation of the variety of ways in which different groups of fans experienced the World Cup, both together but separate. The account builds upon a long-standing ethnographic engagement with various constituencies of England fans dating back to the Euro 96 tournament staged in England.[25]

However, what follows is not an ethnography as such, but instead draws upon this ethnographic experience to facilitate access whilst mobilizing the proximate but critical awareness of the flâneur[26] to capture the fluid, intertextual and sometimes fleeting encounters that characterize international football tournaments.

Fish in the sea: England fans in Cologne

In Papa Joes bar in Cologne's old town on 20 June 2006 the 18 men in early middle age who had just flown in for 24 hours of partying around England's game with Sweden were showing an almost stunning lack of interest in the festivities surrounding them. Dressed in linen suits, chinos, shirts and loafers they would more easily be mistaken for a group of journalists than football fans. This was the face of the corporate event – staff, clients, friends and hangers-on who, despite the private jet, pre-booked tickets, regular supply of beer and champagne, had the demeanour of 'seen it all before' cool distance. With one of the group offering to swap his higher category ticket with another of the party on the basis that he wasn't really that bothered about football – the trip was all about a freebie rather than watching England.

Indeed for some it almost appeared to be a duty, accompanying the boss, in his role as school master leading a day trip – visiting the museum … because he wanted them to; telling people when they were leaving the latest stop off; leading the group like a tour boat with the company logo through the various 'shoals' of fans in the old town; pre-booking drinks at a well to do bar beside the stadium, a meal at the city's premier restaurant after the match and entry to the VIP frequented 'Diamond' nightclub before jetting home in the early hours.

… Meanwhile, on the other side of the Rhine, a makeshift campsite had emerged in the context of the sheer weight of numbers of England fans and the inability of the city's hotels to accommodate them. A mile long stretch on the banks of the river had been transformed with thousands of fans moving in amongst crop fields despite the complete lack of adequate sanitary provision. In a way the whole area experienced what Eric Dunning and his colleagues might have referred to as a de-civilizing spurt, with fights breaking out in shower cubicles and a collapse of the etiquette surrounding a respect for the segregated use of gender specific toilets. In a desperate effort to 'get clean', some fans swam in the river before being driven back by the presence of sewage and dead rats. So unclean had one of our informants been that he accessed the hospitality at a local brothel merely to get a shave and a haircut!

The suffering was short lived though with maybe two thirds moving on by the following evening, the day after England's game with Sweden, as the convoy headed south for Stuttgart. For many of these fans the whole experience was wound up with a masculinized understanding of fandom as an endurance, something which you had to go through and 'take like a man', with some getting trawled off or caught in the netting of the local police force, whilst for others self-deprecatory survival was the best to be hoped for.

They came from all sorts of backgrounds, overwhelmingly English, but with the principle common feature that they had absolutely no intention of going to any great lengths to get to matches. Their World Cup was about travelling with the army, enduring hardship, trials and tribulations along with the enjoyment and camaraderie of being in the city of the game and amongst those going to see it. In the main, these fans were not even interested in asking the price of tickets on the black market. Yet, reflecting an understanding which sits in stark contrast with the corporate experience, and celebrating their presence as ambassadors of 'the home of football' one fan put it that it was they, who did not go to the games, that were 'the real fans'.

The mackerel in the sea, they knew their place, and willingly followed the crowd to the organized fanfests. Strolling through the old town in Cologne between the afternoon's Germany v Ecuador match and England's evening fixture, a crowd of England fans could already be found gathered outside, jovially chanting 'Get the Germans out, get the Germans out' to the tune of *Chirpa chirpa cheep cheep*. It was almost as though this *was* the match venue as they sought to take up their place in the fanfest, in all their garishness, ready to generate an alternative match day atmosphere.

Yet amongst the thousands revelling in their new found status as the soul of the global game were the vestiges of England's more notorious cohorts of hardmen, 'casuals' or what Patrick Slaughter has referred to as the 'old boys'.[27] There's was a kind of resignation born of wisdom that their time is over, elderly dolphins aware that there will no longer be the adrenalin buzz of 'steaming in' and surviving behind enemy lines. Their appearance has not changed much but the demeanour is more restrained. Still prepared to stand their ground and have a go if challenged by rival sharks, they know they are now in the background rather than the foreground, a former attraction who swim to the side of more populist varieties.

Sitting with Wolverhampton Wanderers' Subway Army watching the Argentina v Holland first round group match, they revealed themselves as a group of regular campers but one that carried a presence and latent threat as they sauntered into the campsite bar to watch the game. With their own offspring now in tow their normality was both striking whilst also suspended through a ritualized rejection of the shiny replica shirts and formal merchandise which symbolically unites the wider mass of supporters on the campsite. Yet whilst on previous adventures the conversations might have been characterized by 'incidents', scores to settle and new faces, here the subtext remained unspoken, conversation focused on travel arrangements, returning home and charging mobile phones. Separate from, but always close to, the other fish in the sea, they had not been to England's game the previous night.

For the most part, the antipathy and conflict which had previously been such a core feature of England football fan culture has now become a performative parade, characterized by the singing of provocative plays on war time reference points and the sale of related merchandise. Yet this itself appears to be wrapped up in the need for some sort of approval. The identification of other willing participants enabling a performative communion in the rejection of political correctness and dalliance with deviance. The fragility of this performativity was revealed in the self-reflective apology from one fan noticing others' non-engagement but also in the extent to which it has increasingly been exploited commercially through a proliferation of T-shirts, plastic 'Tommy' helmets and blow up bomber planes playing on the current popularity amongst England fans of the song 'Ten German bombers'.[28]

The commercial exploitation of travelling fans by independents and other fans, or 'grafters', has itself become an increasing feature of the international football tournament scene in recent years.[29] At one level this is all about low-level street trade centred on the sale of T-shirts, counterfeit merchandise and tickets and which involves a whole series of un-glamorous operational difficulties relating to personal tensions, transportation of merchandise, the passing of counterfeit notes and the fear of arrest or attack. These 'fans' endure their own hardships, earning enough to pay their way through a scavenger-like negotiation of deals that nevertheless distinguish them from the 'mug punter'. However, these street traders sit at the bottom end, sometimes crossing into, a much more sophisticated food chain centred on the illicit ticket trade which includes a number of levels of operation including:

- 'High level' sources with direct access to tickets
- 'Players' who obtain 'bundles' of tickets from football industry employees and corporate sponsors
- 'Middle men' and 'gangsters' with connections to organized crime and physical force
- 'Salesmen' with established clients who they deal with regularly and who provide an easy and safe outlet.

At tournament time, those involved in the process meet up in a designated hotel where they stay and sort out the deals. It can be a very lucrative trade even for the salesmen, with our contact expecting to realize a 100% return on his investment having passed on for £2,200 one Category A hospitality package, including tickets for England v Trinidad and Tobago, obtained for £400. Yet, whilst the trade can be rewarding, when there is a ticket shortage, a salesman may have to pay over the odds in order to get a ticket for a valued and reliable client and as such the key stress is felt by the salesmen who manage the forces of supply and demand. The 'players' are in the strongest position, facing the least risk as they do not have to pass tickets to end users. Beyond the financial incentives though, the 'players' bring with them access to the excitement of a fast-paced, glamorous jet set 'community', characterized by hotels, hospitality, entertainment and populated by larger than life characters … the sharks, preying on the other fish in the sea.

Also in search of the good life are the international party people, the disparate varieties of tropical fish coming together to perform behind the glass of the global lens – songs providing a kind of connective thread between different shoals. This togetherness was carried into Cologne's night clubs on match days where mainstream north European and predominantly English popular music was played as face-painted fans of various nationalities waved flags across the dance floor. Many wore the colours of several countries and even exchanged shirts, English fans joining in with 'Oom-pah' tunes and German fans singing along to Oasis in a kind of mobile display of internationalism. Yet this was a communion of the dance floor but which extended no further. It was temporal, revealing a longing for togetherness which is more difficult to achieve in other contexts but which is enabled in the context of the brevity of a World Cup finals tournament.

On the day of the France v Togo game on 23 June, the shared national language and staging of a football game seemed to melt the problems associated with colonial pasts as Togo and French fans came together for photos, singing each others songs 'Allez les Blue, Allez Togo' in unison, 'Planet Football' providing an uncomplicated platform on which to perform this kind of unity. Its power is its ephemerality, which allows people to come together and display their unity momentarily and then separate without any difficulty, trauma or sense of guilt.

Here, through football, the marketplace comes to colonize the idea of community and sell it to an audience who are willing to be standardized into a series of temporal collectivities as represented in Table 1.

Table 1. England's World Cup party people.

Type	Description
Corporates	For whom football is the latest free access 'event' to be wined and dined at. Strangely subdued, even disinterested, the tournament is presented on a plate in a pre-packaged format.
Barmy Army	'Stag parties' and students wearing synchronized fancy dress and matching T-shirts to define both their togetherness and separation from the 'crowd'.
Survivalists	Ticketless and without accommodation they endure and survive the trip. Camping, sleeping rough and 'blagging' they share a passion for football as a vestige of working-class cultural values.
Grafters	There to exploit the chance of an 'earner' as well as to enjoy the party. Ticket touts, street traders and dealers who follow the fish.
Shirts	Loyal and dependable 'customers' with tickets and travel obtained through orthodox channels. The tournament is long anticipated and well planned in advance, passing off without trouble or incident.
Internationalists	With a love of the beautiful game they travel for the football and don't mind which matches they see. Keeping well away from the mass of England fans the tournament provides an opportunity for staged cultural exchanges.

Conclusion

The sense of temporality and consumerist desire for community invoked in this essay builds on Zygmunt Bauman's notion of the 'cloakroom community' which provides a metaphor for the gatherings conjured by consumer society. Paraphrasing his illustrative description of the social rituals of theatre goers we can see how:

> [Supporters at] a [football tournament] dress for the occasion, abiding by a sartorial code distinct from those codes they follow daily ... [This] makes the [fans] look, for the duration of the event, much more uniform than they do in life outside ... During the [tournament] all eyes are on the [fans]; so is everybody's attention ... After the [final whistle], however, the spectators collect their belongings ... and when putting their street clothes on once more return to their ordinary mundane and different roles.[30]

In this sense, people might be seen to 'perform' all the aspects of community and commonality around football for the time they are together 'as one', but do not necessarily knit themselves into deep reciprocal relationships as a result. In such contexts, rather than solid thick ties we might see football as providing a momentary stopping place, more for gestures than consequences, where uncomplicated surface lives are manufactured only for the time being and are paraded as a *performative community*. During the tournament, supporters wish to be identified with one another through their attire and demeanour, as fans. Regardless of their chosen 'shoal' or 'tribe', the uniforms, ritualized performances and shared moments of celebration and endurance all mark out a sense of collective endeavour and belonging.

Yet after the match, away from the tournament, indeed, often even before a match is finished, the singing dies away and coats begin to cover up shirts as individuals turn their backs and make their way home, like disturbed rats scuttling for cover, eager to be ahead of – separate from – the crowd in the rush to get home. For the most part people move away from the tournament on their own or in small groups rather than with the masses, often relying on their own private transport and fighting with the traffic to get *away* first and most easily. For those that hang around and stretch out their communion with fellow supporters, the connections are ever more parochial, muted, private and ultimately overwhelmed by other considerations such as social arrangements for the night ahead, family commitments and the inevitability of separation.

In contrast to Maffesoli's focus on the search for belonging then we can also see in these relations a society marked by increasing 'individualization'.[31] It could be argued that here football supporters were not attempting to hold on to, or recreate, the *Gemeinschaft* type communities which Tönnies[32] described, but rather were finding ways to satisfy their own personal needs for security without taking on the reciprocal obligations that define 'community' in the writings of communitarian thinkers.

In this light, even the sense of 'community' and belonging which emerged out of the campsite alongside the Rhine could be read as a performance, with identity being 'performatively constituted by the very "expressions" that are said to be its results'.[33] Whilst Presdee[34] has suggested that this kind of leisure incorporates some of the important features of Bakhtin's classic carnival with its oppositional status and the subversion of the dominant hegemony, this might over-emphasize the oppositional nature of such activities. The kind of anti-corporatist, traveller-oriented behaviour that for many now goes with following England away may be 'seriously wild' in the ways that it exceeds and disrupts what most people describe as 'normality', but this is performed not to oppose and resist anything as such. Rather than a transgressive liminal performance, it can be seen as a mode of performativity dedicated to an almost childlike feeling of freedom and irresponsibility where individuals are able not only to perform their identity, but also to experience an atmosphere of intensified engagement with other like-minded people.

In many ways, rather like the street cruising culture described in *New Perspectives on Sport and 'Deviance'*,[35] the performative communities associated with the England national football team are reminiscent of Michel Maffesoli's *neo-tribus*[36] and Scott Lash's 'post-traditional' *Gemeinschaften*.[37] They are 'mobile and flexible groupings – sometimes enduring, often easily dissoluble – formed with an intensive affective bonding'. Their glue is their incumbents' individually constituted, though insatiable, appetites to connect with others. Indeed, these gatherings are unequivocally *not* about community in the orthodox sociological meaning. That fans may have shared experiences and long-lasting friendships with one another in different contexts is neither here nor there since the self-constitution of a 'community' of 'fans' takes place between autonomy and fragmentation.[38]

Consequently the spirit of the imaginary togetherness that this 'fandom' creates is much more important to its incumbents than its actuality. As such its disorganization is made to the measure of liquid modern times: a momentary stopping place more for gestures than consequences, of uncomplicated surface lives manufactured only for the time being.

Whilst not denying the lasting friendships that can flow from these gatherings, the kind of identity-making associated with England fans is largely concentrated on performing rather than building anything solid as such, and in this way it thrives on its ambivalence; it is always about performing 'identity' rather than expressing who you *are*. To this end, the World Cup sustains the liquid modern individual's predilection for the palimpsest reinvention of him or herself; that is, the capacity of individuals to erase traces of the past and assume new ready-made identities.

Notes

1. Crabbe and Brown, 'You're Not Welcome Anymore'.
2. See Ian Taylor, 'English Football in the 1990s'; Williams and Wagg, *British Football and Social Change*.
3. Conn, *The Football Business*.
4. Brown *et al.*, *Football*.
5. Weber, *Protestant Ethic*.
6. Giddens, *Modernity and Self-Identity*; Bauman, *Community*; Lash, *Critique of Information*; Beck, *Risk Society*.
7. Giddens, *Modernity and Self-Identity*.
8. Bauman, *Postmodernity*.
9. Bauman, *Intimations of Postmodernity*, back cover.
10. Garland and Sparks, 'Criminology, Social Theory and the Challenge of Our Times', 16.
11. Castells, *Information Age*.
12. Delanty, *Community*.
13. Giddens, *Modernity and Self-Identity*, 32.
14. Taylor, 'English Football in the 1990s'.
15. King, *End of the Terraces*.
16. Redhead, *Post Fandom*.
17. Giulianotti, *Football*; Giulianotti, 'Supporters, Followers, Fans and Flaneurs'.
18. Robson, '*No One Likes Us, We Don't Care*', x.
19. Lash, 'Reflexivity and its Doubles'.
20. Maffesoli, *Time of the Tribes*, 76.
21. Armstong, *Football Hooligans*.
22. Giulianotti, *Football*.
23. http://news.bbc.co.uk./1/hi/programmes/panorama/5219906.stm Accessed 1 August 2006.
24. Perryman, *Ingerland*, 57.
25. Back, Crabbe and Solomos, '"Lions, Black Skins and Reggae Gyals"'; Back, Crabbe and Solomos, *Changing Face of Football*; Crabbe, 'The Public Gets What the Public Wants'; Crabbe, 'England-fans'.
26. Bairner, 'The *Flâneur* and the City'.
27. Slaughter, 'A Day Out with the 'Old Boys'.

28. Set to the tune of *She'll be coming round the mountain*, the song invokes the Second World War Battle of Britain through repetition of the line 'There were ten German bombers in the air', followed by a second verse of 'And the RAF from England shot them down'.
29. Sugden, *Scum Airways*.
30. Bauman, *Liquid Modernity*, 200.
31. Beck and Beck-Gersheim, *Individualization*.
32. Tönnies, *Community and Association*.
33. Butler, *Gender Trouble*, 23.
34. Presdee, *Cultural Criminology*.
35. Blackshaw and Crabbe, *New Perspectives on Sport and 'Deviance'*.
36. Maffesoli, *Time of the Tribes*.
37. Lash, *Critique of Information*, 27.
38. Delanty, *Social Theory*.

References

Armstrong, G. *Football Hooligans: Knowing the Score*. Oxford: Berg Armstrong, 1998.
Back, L., T. Crabbe, and J. Solomos. '"Lions, Black Skins and Reggae Gyals": Race, Nation and Identity in Football'. *Critical Urban Studies Occasional Paper*. London: Goldsmiths College, Centre for Urban and Community Research, 1998.
———. *The Changing Face of Football: Racism, Identity and Multiculture in the English Game*. Oxford: Berg, 2001.
Bairner, A. 'The *Flâneur* and the City: Reading the 'New' Belfast's Leisure Spaces'. *Space and Polity* 10,2 (2006): 121–34.
Bauman, Z. *Intimations of Postmodernity*. London: Routledge, 1992.
———. *Postmodernity and its Discontents*. Cambridge: Polity Press in association with Blackwell, 1997.
———. *Liquid Modernity*. Cambridge: Polity, 2000.
———. *Community: Seeking Safety in an Insecure World*. Cambridge: Polity Press, 2001.
Beck, U. *Risk Society: Towards a New Modernity*. London: Sage, 1992.
Beck, U., and E. Beck-Gersheim. *Individualization*. London: Sage, 2002.
Blackshaw, T., and T. Crabbe. *New Perspectives on Sport and 'Deviance': Consumption, Performativity and Social Control*. London: Routledge, 2004.
Brown, A., T. Crabbe, K. O'Connor, and G. Mellor. *Football: An All Consuming Passion*. EA Sports Research. Manchester: Substance, 2006.
Butler, J. *Gender Trouble: Feminism and the Subversion of Identity*. London: Routledge, 1990.
Castells, M. *The Information Age, Volume 1: The Risk of the Network Society*. Oxford: Blackwell, 1996.
Conn, D. *The Football Business: Fair Game in the 90s?*, Edinburgh: Mainstream, 1997.
Crabbe, T. '"The Public Gets What the Public Wants": England Football Fans, "Truth" Claims and Mediated Realities'. *International Review for the Sociology of Sport* 38,4 (2003): 413–25.
———. 'Englandfans: A New Club for a New England? Social Inclusion, Authenticity and the Performance of Englishness at "Home" and "Away"'. *Leisure Studies* 23,1 (2004): 63–78.
Crabbe, T., and A. Brown. 'You're Not Welcome Anymore: The Football Crowd, Class and Social Exclusion'. In *British Football and Social Exclusion*, ed. S. Wagg, 26–46. London: Routledge, 2004.
Delanty, G. *Social Theory in a Changing World*. Cambridge: Polity Press, 1999.
———. *Community*. London: Routledge, 2003.
Garland, D. and R. Sparks. 'Criminology, Social Theory and the Challenge of Our Times'. In *Criminology and Social Theory*, ed. D. Garland and R. Sparks. Oxford: Oxford University Press, 2000.
Giddens, A. *Modernity and Self-Identity: Self and Society in the Late Modern Age*. Cambridge: Polity Press, 1991.
Giulianotti, R. *Football: A Sociology of the Global Game*. Cambridge: Polity Press, 1999.
———. 'Supporters, Followers, Fans and Flaneurs: A Taxonomy of Spectator Identities in Football'. *Journal of Sport and Social Issues* 26,1 (2002): 25–46.
King, A. *The End of the Terraces: The Transformation of English Football in the 1990s*. Leicester: Leicester University Press, 1998.
Lash, S. 'Reflexivity and its Doubles, Structures, Aesthetics, Community'. In *Reflexive Modernization: Politics, Tradition and Aesthetics in the Modern Social Order*, ed. U. Beck, A. Giddens, and S. Lash, 110–73. Cambridge: Polity Press, 1994.

Lash, S. *Critique of Information.* London: Sage, 2002.
Maffesoli, M. *The Time of the Tribes: The Decline of Individualism in Mass Society.* London: Sage, 1996.
Perryman, M. *Ingerland: Travels with a Football Nation.* London: Simon Schuster, 2006.
Presdee, M. *Cultural Criminology and the Carnival of Crime.* London: Routledge, 2000.
Redhead, S. *Post Fandom and Millennial Blues: The Transformation of Soccer Culture.* London: Routledge, 1997.
Robson, G. *'No One Likes Us, We Don't Care': The Myth and Reality of Millwall Fandom.* Oxford: Berg, 2000.
Slaughter, P. 'A Day Out with the "Old Boys"'. In *British Football and Social Exclusion,* ed. S. Wagg, 67–89. London: Routledge, 2004.
Sugden, J. *Scum Airways: Inside Football's Underground Economy.* Edinburgh: Mainstream, 2002.
Taylor, I. 'English Football in the 1990s: Taking Hillsborough Seriously?'. In *British Football and Social Change: Getting into Europe,* ed. J. Williams and S. Wagg, 3–24. London: Leicester University Press, 1992.
Tönnies, F. *Community and Association.* London: Routledge, 1974.
Weber, M. *The Protestant Ethic and the Spirit of Capitalism.* London: Unwin Hyman Ltd, 1930.
Williams, J., and S. Wagg, eds. *British Football and Social Change: Getting into Europe.* London: Leicester University Press, 1992.

Index

agents, Stevens inquiry into 11-12
Albirex Niigata 67-8, 70
Althusser, Louis 59
American youth soccer: club/high school comparison 117, 121-2; exclusionary practices 116-17; Massey's study 119-23; and the ODP 116; skill levels 115; social/ethnic balance 114-15; suburban domination 114-16, *see also* Richmond, CA
Amit, V. 29
Anderson, Benedict 25
Andrews, I. 3
Armstrong, G. 128
Asian financial crisis, impact on J.League 65
Ateek, Naim 104
Australia: Andrews' research 3, 4; typology of football 92; World Cup experience 97, 99
Australian Football League 3
Australian Rules football 92
Australian soccer: A-League teams and sponsorship 98-9; Bradley report 95; commercial interest in 99; Crawford report 97-8; de-ethnicization strategies 95-6; ethnic marginalization in 94; FIFA ban 94; history 93-4; importance of immigrant communities 93-4; match attendances 100; NSL establishment 95; repositioning and rebranding 95-9; Stewart inquiry 95-6; talent drain 97
Australian Soccer's Long Road to the Top (Cockerill) 97

Bar-On, T. 122
Bateson, Gregory 27
Batson, Brendan 110
Baudrillard, Jean 35, 40
Bauman, Zygmunt 6, 23, 28, 30-1, 33, 34-5, 39, 40, 48, 127, 133
BBC (British Broadcasting Corporation) 17
Beck, Ulrich 40, 127
Bellmare Hiratsuku 69

Ben-Porat, A. 105
Berlin, Isaiah 25
Blackburn Rovers 37, 39
Blackshaw, T. and Crabbe, T. 28
Blair, Tony 13, 14, 15
bonding 2-6, 5-6, 27, 32, 48, 49, 53, 60, 68, 79, 85, 134
boundary marking processes 26
Bourriad, Nicholas 38
Bradley report (Australia) 95
Brighton University, F4P participation 106, 107
British Council, F4P involvement 107
British Labour Party 12
Brown, A., Crabbe, T. and Mellor, G. 25, 26-7, 33, 34
BSkyB (British Sky Broadcasting) 17, 44
Burn, Gordon 33

carnivalization 33, 129, 133
Cashman, Richard 79
civil society, in Giddens' work 14-15
class: in American youth soccer 114, 115, 121, 124; and exclusion 24; in Indian football 76, 78-80, 93; and politics 12; and sense of identity 2, 24, 45, 132; and social change 127, 128; and tradition 30
Clinton, Bill 15
'cloakroom communities' 33, 133
club or country debate, India 86-7
Cockerill, Michael 97
Cohen, Anthony 5, 25, 26, 27-8, 52
Cole, Andy 39
collective memory experiences 33
commercialism 45, 99, 131
commercialization: and community disruption 3; impact on Israeli football 105; Japan 60; resistance to 52
communitas 5, 27
community: Cohen's theorization of 26-7; concept analysis 23-4, 25, 30-1; criticism of

Index

Bauman's theory of 34-5; orthodox sociological definition 25-6; reason for our obsession with 32
community building: bottom-up approach 68-70; top-down approach 63-8
community creation, and geography 47-8
community in football, contemporary theories of 25-6
community liquidity 31-4, 48-50
community policy, politics of 35-6
community work, typology of football clubs' 18-19
corporate model, of community building 59-62, 63-4
corporate social responsibility 14, 17-18
corporatism, in international tournaments 130
Cramer, Dettmar 61
Crawford report (Australia) 97-8
crime, tackling through sport 19
cultural politics, of fan expressions 52-4
culture, disposable nature of contemporary 33

Debord, G. 38
Delanty, G. 47, 54, 127
Derrida, Jacques 28
deterritorialization, of fan communities 29
Ding an sich 26
doxa 23
Dunning, Eric 130

East Bengal Club 84-5, 86
England: fan typology 132; FiTC (Football in the Community) programme 17; history of football and community in 2-4; impact of social change 4; market freedoms and social responsibility and 16-20; third way politics 13-16
English fans, World Cup 2006 experience 130-2
English football: calls for independent regulation 11-12; changing nature 126-7; and racism 4, 36-9; and social re-alignment 4, 126; Taylor report into 126, *see also* FC United; Manchester United; Premier League
English football clubs, community partnerships 19-20
ethnic marginalization, in Australian soccer 94
ethnic stereotyping, in anti-racism campaigns 38-9

Euro 96, impact on England's travelling support 129
European Union, employment law 17

F4P (Football for Peace): 2006 postponement 111-12; Brighton University's participation 106, 107; British Council's involvement 107; female inclusion 108-10; objectives 105-6, 108; project history and development 106-8; social and political context 103-4
FA Premier League *see* Premier League
fan communities: deterritorialization 29; fragility and conflict 46-7
fandom, imaginary togetherness of 134
Fawbert, J. 3
FC United of Manchester (FCUM) 35; community liquidity 48-50; face to face community creation 47-8; fan/player bonding 49; governance structure 51; importance of public houses 49; local focus 47-8; manifesto 51; match attendance 44, 46, 52; motto 46; online community 50-1; origins and background 44-6; self-policing 53; songs 53; and symbolic nostalgia 52-3; volunteering structure 50
female participation, in Israeli sport 105-6, 108-9
Field, Frank 19
FIFA: Australian ban 94; Middle East decisions 105; Oceania membership 99
FIFA World Cup *see* World Cup
Finlayson, A. 13
FiTC (Football in the Community) programme 17
football and community, history of 2-4
Football and its Communities (Football Foundation) 18
Football for Peace *see* F4P
football's communities, symbolic construction of 26-8
FoxSports cable network 94, 95, 99-100
free market 11
FURD (Football Unites Racism Divides) 37

Galatasaray 39
Gemeinschaft/Gesellschaft 2-3, 6, 32, 47, 48, 118, 129, 133
gender equality, promotion of in Israeli sport 106

geographical communities: disruption of traditional 3-4; distinction with supporter communities 3
Germany, as role model for J.League 61
Ghoti-Bangal conflict 83-4, 86
Giddens, Anthony 13, 14, 20, 25, 127
Gill, David 45
Giulianotti, Richard 2, 48, 127, 128
globalization: impact on community life 14; impact on Israeli football 105
grassroots development strategies, Australia 98

Halifax Town Football Club 12
Hegel, G.W.F. 30
Hill, David 96
Hillsborough disaster 126
Hindu Mela 76
history: Australian soccer 93-4; English football and community 2-4; Indian football 76-7; Japanese football communities 62-70
Hobsbawm, Eric 25
Holt, Richard 2, 47
hooliganism 4, 128-9
Hutton, Will 15

Ideological Soccer Apparatus (ISA), and Japanese football 59, 62, 70
illicit ticket trade, World Cup 131-2
imagined community, Anderson's idea 28-30
immigration, impact on Australian soccer 93-4
independent regulation, calls for 11-12
India: nationalism in colonial 77-9; partition 83
Indian football: beginnings 76-7; club or country debate 86-7; and the *Ghoti-Bangal* conflict 83-4, 86; host and migrant communities 83-6; Muslim representation 80-3; National League launched 86; suicides of supporters 85; violence in 83, 84-5
individualization 6, 32, 34, 127, 133
industrialization 47, 58
internationalism, of fans in World Cup tournament 132
Israel: creation of state of 103; politicization of sport 104-5; women's football 108-9
Israel-Palestine conflict, football in the peace process *see* F4P

Istanbul 39

Jameson, Fredric 27
Japan: bottom up approach to community building 68-70; bureaucratic approach to community building 65-8; corporate approach to community building 63-4; European football-community nexus comparison 57-8, 59; making of football communities in 62-70; social anomalies 58; stadia 65-6, 67; structure 68; World Cup hosting 65, 66; World Cup qualification 62-3, 65, *see also* J.League
Japanese football, and Ideological Soccer Apparatus (ISA) 59, 62, 70
JEF United 69
Jenkins, R. 27
J.League: and Chūetsu earthquake 68; clubs 60, 63-4, 66-7, 68-70; corporate community model 59-62; European influence 61; first-phase 63; impact of Asian financial crisis 65; industry investment 63-4; membership requirements 59; ownership model 66; second division launch 65
Johanneson, Albert 37

Kashima Antlers 63-4, 69
Kenyon, Peter 45
Kewell, Harry 96
King, Anthony 29-30, 47, 52, 127
Kozu, M. 67

Lash, Scott 6-7, 127, 128, 134
Latino community: American youth soccer and 114-25; Massey's study of American youth soccer participation 119-23; Richmond's 117-18
Leeds United, anti-racism campaign 36-9
liminality 5, 27, 38, 53
liquid modern community 31-4
liquid modernity 127, 134
liquidity, in FCUM fan community 48-50
Little Britain 36
Loftus, Christopher 39
Lowry, Frank 98

McKibbin, Ross 36
Maffesoli, Michel 7, 31, 128, 133, 134

Index

Manchester United 3, 35, 39; and the changing context of English football 44; fans' cultural-political position 45; Glazer takeover 44, 45; resistance to commercialization 52, *see also* FC United
Marginson, Karl 52
marketing, soccer's use as promotional tool 118-19
Martin, Bernice 38
Mason, Tony 2, 47
Massey, Douglas S. 119
merchandising, in J.League 61
Middle East *see* F4P; Israel
'The Mighty Zulu Nation', Elland Road performance 37-9
migrant communities, in Indian football 83-6
Mito Hollyhock 68, 69
mobile phones 31, 32
Mohammedan Sporting Club 80-3
Mohun Bagan 77, 77-8, 79, 80, 84-5, 86
moral tool, football as 76
Mulgan, Geoff 15

nation-states, and Anderson's 'imagined communities' 28-9
neo-tribes 31-2
networks 31
New Ambitions for Our Country (DSS, UK) 19
New Muslim Majlis 80
New Perspectives on Sport and 'Deviance' (Blackshaw/Crabbe) 134
Northern Ireland, sport in peace process 104
nostalgia 40, 45, 52-3, 58

Oceania, FIFA membership 99
ODP (Olympic Development Program) 116
Oita Trinita 66-7
Omiya Ardija 69
O'Neill, John 98
Otherness: in a colonial context 39; and football rivalries 24, 27; in Indian football 86
Our Towns and Cities (ODPM, UK) 18

Palestine-Israel conflict, football in the peace process *see* F4P
Palestinian Diaspora 103
Parsons, Talcott 25

peace process, use of football in Middle East *see* F4P
peace processes, sport's contributions 104
performativity 5, 9, 27, 35, 38, 53, 129, 131, 133-4
Perryman, Mark 129
Phillips, Adam 35
Phillips, Caryl 36-7
place, in Japanese communal life 58
political communities 54
politics: English third way 13-16; impact in Indian football clubs 82, 85; in Israeli sport 104-5
postmodernism, 2006 FIFA World Cup and 128-30
Premier League: creation of 16, 126; OFT action against 16-17; sale of television rights 17
Presdee, M. 133
Preston, Peter 36
The Protestant Ethic and the Spirit of Capitalism (Weber) 127

racism: in colonial Bengal 76-7; experiences of 36-7; FA's strategy development 105; Leeds United's campaign against 36-9; and neighbourhood/supporter community tension 4
Red Issue (fanzine) 45
Redhead, Steve 127
reflexive communities, in Lash's work 6-7
reports/inquiries: Australia 95-6, 97-8; Bradley 95; Crawford 97-8; Stevens 11-12; Taylor 126; UK 11-12, 126
Richmond, CA: Latino community 117-18; youth soccer in 118-23
rivalry 27, 45, 49, 80, 84-6, 89, 96, 123
Robson, G. 34, 127
Ross, Jonathan 36
rugby, Australian development 92
Russell, D. 47

Said, Edward 39, 103-4
Sandvoss, C. 29
self-identification 32
Sen, Amartya 34
Shankly, Bill 30
shared experience: in collective memory 33; intensity of 29

Shareholders United 44
Sheffield United 37
Sheilas, Wogs, and Poofters (Warren) 94
Shetland Isles, Cohen's research 26
Shimizu S-Pulse 69
Shonan Bellmare 69-70
Singer, Howard 33
Slaughter, Patrick 131
Smith, J. and Ingham, A. 5
social bonding, in Indian football 79
social bonds 32
social capital 15
social capitalism, limits of 35-6
social class *see* class
social exclusion, tackling through sport 18
social functions, of football clubs 3
social networks, soccer's use in strengthening 119
social programmes, typology of football clubs' 18-19
social responsibility: football clubs' attitude towards 20; market freedoms and 16-20
sociology, defining community in orthodox 25-6
South Africa, sport in peace process 104
Speight, Kevin 39
Spivak, G. 39
Sports Council (UK) 12
Stevens inquiry (UK) 11-12
Stewart inquiry (Australia) 95-6
suicides, of Indian football supporters 85
supporter communities, re-theorizing 4-7
symbolic communities, Cohen's notion 5, 52
symbolic construction, of football's communities 26-8
symbolic nostalgia, and FC United of Manchester 52-3

Taylor report (UK) 126
television 4, 16, 17, 24, 36, 43, 44, 46, 49, 52, 54, 65, 67, 95, 97, 99, 100, 110, 122
territory 25
Thespa Kusatsu 68, 69
'thin communities' 6

third way politics 13-16; term analysis 12
ticket pricing: and fan displacement 45; reduction campaigns 12
ticket trade, illicit 131-2
Tönnies, Ferdinand 2-3, 32, 133
travelling fans, commercial exploitation 131
tribes 128-9
'trust networks' 15
Tugay, Kerimoglu 39
Turner, Victor 5, 6, 27, 53

UEFA Cup, Istanbul final 39
UEFA (Union of European Football Associations) 17
Unsicherheit 31, 40
Urawa Reds 69, 70
urbanization, and the development of football 2
US (United States of America) *see* American youth soccer; Latino community; Richmond, CA

violence 39, 53, 75, 79, 83-5, 94, 96, 103

Warren, Johnny 94
Weber, Max 127
Williams, Raymond 30, 31
Wittgenstein, Ludwig 26, 40
women, in Israeli sport 105-6
women's football, in Israel 108-9
World Cup: Australian experience 97, 99; carnivalization 129; English fans in Cologne 130-2; fans' internationalism 132; illicit ticket trade 131-2; Japanese experience 62-3, 65, 66; and the postmodern community 128-30

Yokohama FC 68, 69
Yorke, Dwight 39
Young, I.M. 27

Zico 64
Zulu culture, and anti-racist activities 37-8